D0222996

Applied Linguistics and Language Study

General Editor: C. N. Candlin

Vocabulary and Language Teaching

Ronald Carter and Michael McCarthy

with contributions from
Joanna Channell
James Coady
A. P. Cowie
Paul Nation
James Nattinger
Antoinette Renouf
John Sinclair
Della Summers

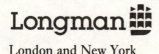

London and New York

Longman Group UK Limited
Longman House, Burnt Mill, Harlow,
Essex CM20 2JE, England
and Associated Companies throughout the world.

Published in the United States of America by
Longman Inc., New York

First published 1988
Reprinted 1988

BRITISH LIBRARY CATALOGUING IN PUBLICATION DATA
Carter, Ronald, *1947–*
   Vocabulary and language teaching. –
   (Applied linguistics and language study).
   1. Vocabulary – Study and teaching
   I. Title   II. McCarthy, Michael, *1947–*
   III. Series
   418   P53.9

LIBRARY OF CONGRESS CATALOGING IN PUBLICATION DATA
Carter, Ronald.
   Vocabulary and language teaching.
   (Applied linguistics and language study)
   Bibliography: p.
   Includes index.
   1. Language and languages – Study and teaching.
   2. Vocabulary – Study and teaching.   3. Second language
   acquisition.   I. McCarthy, Michael, 1947–
   II. Title.   III. Series.
   P53.9.C37   1988   41 8'.007   87-2733

Set in 10/12 pt Linotron 202 Erhardt
Produced by Longman Singapore Publishers (Pte) Ltd.
Printed in Singapore

ISBN 0-582-55382-2

Contents

Acknowledgements

The authors are grateful for permission to reproduce, in a re-shaped and re-edited form, material which first appeared in Carter, R. A. *Vocabulary: applied linguistic perspectives* published by George Allen and Unwin in 1987 and in an article 'Vocabulary and second/foreign language teaching', *Language Teaching* 20, 1 (1987) published by Cambridge University Press. A preliminary version of the article in section four of this book entitled 'Vocabulary cloze and discourse' was first given as a conference paper at a RELC seminar in Singapore (see Carter 1985). The author is grateful for comments of participants at that seminar and to RELC for allowing some of the material to be reproduced here.

The authors would also like to take this opportunity of thanking all the contributors to the book, the general editor Professor Chris Candlin, and Michael Johnson and Joy Marshall at Longman for their assistance at various stages in the completion of the book. We are also especially indebted to Margaret Berry, David Brazil, Mike Hoey, Walter Nash, Michael Stubbs and Jeanne McCarten for many invaluable discussions concerning the nature of lexis. The book is dedicated to Jane and Jeanne.

R.A.C.   M.J.M.

We are grateful to the following for permission to reproduce copyright material:

Associated Book Publishers (UK) Ltd for an extract from *Basic English and Its Uses* by I. A. Richards (pub Routledge & Kegan Paul plc, 1943); Newsweek Inc for an extract from an article in *Newsweek* 5/3/84 (c) 1984 Newsweek Inc. All rights reserved.

We have been unable to trace the Language Research Institute, Boston, the USA copyright holder in *Basic English and Its Uses* by I. A. Richards, and would appreciate any information that would enable us to do so.

Preface

One of the chief objectives of the *Applied Linguistics and Language Study* series is to offer books across the range of topics in language pedagogy, focusing research on issues which arise from educational practice. When one looks at the array of books presently available in the series it strikes one as surprising that we have not until now identified *vocabulary* as one such key topic. It is as if its subject-matter has been subsumed, as it were, within other fields, for example within the study of reading in a foreign language, or within writing, or as part of second-language acquisition more generally conceived. It has not had a separate identity. Why should this be so?

Partly perhaps because of the overwhelming concentration in linguistic theory, at least in United States research, on issues of syntactic structure. Partly because interlanguage research, following this focus, has very largely not treated lexical acquisition as a priority. Partly, too, because the emphasis within semantics on the study of paradigmatic structures and denotational meaning has seemed less central to current concerns with pragmatics and the analysis of discourse. Yet, as this book points out very clearly, the study of vocabulary is at the heart of language teaching and learning, in terms of the organization of syllabuses, the evaluation of learner performance, the provision of learning resources, and, most obviously, because it is how most learners see language and its learning difficulty. It is an apposite moment, then, to place *vocabulary* in a pedagogic spotlight, not to argue its relevance, but to indicate how its study offers insights into the process of acquisition, the organization of teaching and the social and linguistic structure of language.

Appropriately enough, the authors begin their account with a historical survey into vocabulary studies in a pedagogical context, showing not only that despite recent emphases on syntax, the groundwork of lexical description has a lengthy history, but also how research into vocabulary control was intimately connected to concerns with acquisition. This introductory chapter establishes the connection between language teaching, the organization and provision of vocabulary resources, and the structure of language which informs the whole volume.

Any discussion of acquisition necessarily raises questions of how learners come to master and exploit relationships and structure, in lexis no less than in syntax. In Chapter 2, therefore, the authors address the issue of the interdependence of the linguistic organization of vocabulary, its acquisition by learners, and its appropriate pedagogic structuring by teachers. They do so by focusing on the need to integrate paradigmatic and syntagmatic dimensions in lexical study as a way of providing organizational principles for pedagogy. The exploration of these dimensions is at the heart of the book, raising as it does the problems of not only the relationship of lexis to grammar but also of the independence of semantics from pragmatics. Problems of dictionary-making, of denotative and connotative meanings, of stable and dynamic interpretations reveal issues of theoretical model as well as those of the boundaries of linguistic analysis. It is here and in the more centrally pedagogic discussions of Chapter 3 that we see applied linguistics most characteristically at work: practical problems raising theoretical and descriptive questions for joint action by researchers and practitioners.

It is at this point in the book that its innovative structure is most valuable. The issues, both pedagogic and theoretical, have been displayed. What is now needed is that they should be taken up in detail. Ron Carter and Mike McCarthy have commissioned and edited six original contributions from researchers and practitioners directly involved in lexicology and lexicography, to which they have added two personal studies of their own. The range of topics matches the scope of the book: trends in vocabulary teaching; the nature of the learner's mental lexicon and the link between learning and teaching; the relationship between lexical study and reading research; the place of users' 'stable' locutions in lexicographic description; the relationship between user needs and styles of dictionary presentation; the use of large-scale computer corpora in lexicology and syllabus design; the implications for cloze testing of current research in lexicology; vocabulary patterns in discourse. Each of these papers by distinguished authors is followed by a set of points for further development, contributed by the editors. These are not to be seen as discussion topics only. They represent questions for action research, eminently appropriate for teachers to undertake as part of their practice with learners.

To this point, then, the book has set *vocabulary* in its pedagogic and research context and, incidentally, has placed it very necessarily

in its historical perspective. Links have been made between the prac-
tices of teaching, lexicography and syllabus design and the study of
linguistic structure, and connections between acquisition and organization emphasized. The importance of the final chapter, *Lexis and
discourse*, is not only to reaffirm the connection between research and
practice. Much more importantly it is to show how present studies
in lexical description, aided by quite massive advances in technical
capacity, can provide the data to underpin the integration of the
syntagmatic and paradigmatic axes in vocabulary study. Such readily
accessible data, however, would be impotent without an appropriate
theory of language, one which emphasizes lexical structure but which
does so in the context of the language user. It is this emphasis which
underlines the centrality of vocabulary study both to current issues
in linguistic theory and to present concerns of communicative practice.

Christopher N. Candlin   *Lancaster*
General Editor   *January 1987*

Introduction

This book is divided into five main chapters which are sequenced to provide an overall historical perspective on developments in vocabulary teaching in the past sixty years. Chapter 1 examines the important contribution of the vocabulary control movement and reviews some key issues in the learning of vocabulary. Research into vocabulary learning is both vital and in many respects necessarily antecedent to the teaching of vocabulary. A separate book would be required to present a proper psycholinguistic perspective on vocabulary learning, and we do not pretend to do more than acknowledge some highly relevant topics here. Also relevant to vocabulary teaching is a knowledge of the linguistic organization of vocabulary, and Chapter 2 attempts to provide a descriptive account of current research into the structure of the lexicon. Key topics in structural semantics and word meanings as well as studies of collocations and fixed expressions are examined here. Chapter 3 reviews advances in vocabulary teaching since 1945, and explores some interrelations between linguistic description of the lexicon, and discussion and design of vocabulary teaching materials during that period. A final section of this chapter reviews recent progress in pedagogical lexicography and computer-assisted lexicographic description. Chapter 4 brings us up to the present day and presents a selection of papers which we specially commissioned for this book, and in which the authors explore current issues in the teaching of vocabulary. Several of these papers draw on recent research into lexicology and lexicography. Topics covered include: vocabulary and reading, lexical syllabuses, pedagogical lexicography, lexis in spoken discourse, vocabulary discourse and cloze procedure, the mental lexicon and language teaching. The fifth and final chapter is possibly a little more programmatic and polemical. It is concerned with vocabulary in discourse. One of the main arguments which we advance here is that vocabulary teaching should pay greater attention to the role of vocabulary in naturally-occurring text, and in particular to the ways in which vocabulary is used to negotiate meanings across speaking turns and sentence boundaries. The chapter explores aspects of discourse analysis and communicative approaches to language pedagogy where they meet in the teaching of vocabulary.

This book does not claim to say all there is to say about vocabulary teaching, even though it may look as if we have tried to do so. Vocabulary teaching has a long history, and applied linguists and language teachers are only just beginning to turn their attention to it again after a couple of decades or so of relative neglect. There is much work still to be done and many approaches from many different perspectives to be considered. We hope that this book will contribute to developing discussion and debate.

Ronald Carter   *Nottingham and Birmingham*
Michael McCarthy   *1987*

1 Word lists and learning words: some foundations

Throughout this book we claim that vocabulary study has been neglected by linguists, applied linguists and language teachers. We believe that we are justified in claiming this. Although interest has grown quite rapidly during the 1980s, there is certainly not much evidence of interest in vocabulary in the last twenty-five years taken as a whole, and relative to investigation at other linguistic levels. This opening chapter gives us an opportunity for qualifying this claim, or, at least, placing it in some kind of historical perspective. For taken over the last sixty years, the picture is rather different, because the 1930s witnessed the beginnings of what has come to be called the 'vocabulary control movement'. There are a number of strands and offshoots to this movement both in Great Britain and in the United States, but we shall focus here on two particular developments: the work on *Basic English* of C. K. Ogden and I. A. Richards; and the work on definition vocabulary which led to the production by Michael West of *A General Service List*. A number of issues raised in this book, and a number of articles in Chapter 4, can be examined in relation to the aims and goals of these earlier pedagogically-inspired efforts at vocabulary control.

It may be useful, however, to begin this chapter by listing some questions which teachers and students have asked, usually quite persistently, about vocabulary and language study. The list is not exhaustive and answers will, in any case, not be forthcoming to all the questions, either in this chapter or after reading this book. But, we hope to try and lay some foundations from which answers might be found:

1. How many words provide a working vocabulary in a foreign language?
2. What are the best words to learn first?
3. In the early stages of learning a second or foreign language, are some words more useful to the learner than others?

4. Are some words more difficult to learn than others? Can words be graded for ease of learning?
5. What are the best means of retaining new words?
6. Is it most practical to learn words as single items in a list, in pairs (for example, as translation equivalents) or in context?
7. What about words which have different meanings? Should they be avoided? If not, should some meanings be isolated for learning first?
8. Are some words more likely to be encountered in spoken rather than written discourse? If so, do we know what they are?

1 Basic English: how basic is Basic?

The proposal for Basic English was first put forward in the early 1930s. Essentially, it was a project designed to provide a basic minimum vocabulary for the learning of English. The originators of the proposal were C. K. Ogden and I. A. Richards (Ogden 1930, 1968), though the latter author was responsible for numerous revisions, refinements and extensions to the scheme. Throughout the project had two main aims: 'the provision of a minimum secondary world language and the designing of an improved introductory course for foreign learners, leading into general English' (Richards 1943, p. 62). Its design has been outlined succinctly as follows by Richards (who, in fact, uses Basic English for the outline):

> Basic English is English made simple by limiting the number of words to 850 and by cutting down the rules for using them to the smallest number necessary for the clear statement of ideas. And this is done without change in the normal order and behaviour of these words in everyday English. It is limited in its words and its rules but it keeps to the regular forms of English. And though it is designed to give the learner as little trouble as possible, it is no more strange to the eyes of my readers than these lines which are, in fact, in Basic English
>
> (Richards 1943, p. 20)

In other words, for Ogden and Richards it is a basic principle that, although their scheme will not embrace full English, it will at least not be un-English. In Figure 1 (pp. 4–5) is the list of words selected by Ogden and Richards as their basis. And the fact that they can be conveniently listed on a single side of paper is seen as one of the advantages of the proposal.

At the basis of Ogden and Richards's *Basic English* is the notion of a communicative adequacy whereby, even if periphrastically, an adult's fundamental linguistic needs can be communicated. Even though more complex ideas may have to be paraphrased, it is claimed that the words supplied will both serve to express complex ideas and be in themselves easy and fast to learn. The learning burden on these words is likewise kept to a minimum because, instead of introducing a wide range of verbs which, in English, necessitates the additional learning of numerous and often irregular inflections, Ogden and Richards confine their list to no more than eighteen main verbs, or 'operations' as they prefer to term them. The verbs are *send, say, do, come, get, give, go, keep, let, make, put, seem, take, see*, plus the modal verbs *may* and *will* and the auxiliary words *be* and *have*. The only inflections to be learned (on verbs and nouns) are *-er, -ing* and *-ed*, and Basic English does not even permit the bound morpheme inflection *s* for verbs, so that *he make(s)* becomes 'ungrammatical'. An example of the kind of periphrasis made possible or, depending on your point of view, unnaturally enforced by the system, is the omission of the verbs *ask* and *want* from the list of operators for the simple reason that they can be paraphrased. That is:

    ask   ⟶   put a question;

    want ⟶   have a desire for.

The idea that many notions can be re-expressed using more basic language is central to the Basic English project. Other examples might be:

    smoke ⟶   have a smoke;

    walk ⟶   have a walk.

Closer scrutiny of the word list reveals further difficulties in the way of answers to some of the questions posed at the beginning of this chapter. Firstly, learning 850 word forms is not the same thing as learning 850 single senses. One calculation is that the 850 words of Basic English have 12,425 meanings (Nation 1983, p. 11). Which meanings should be learned first? Are there core meanings which are more easily retained or which are more important? Ogden and Richards seem to suggest that there are. For example, they have a category of 200 'pictured' words which, presumably, have defined physical or concrete properties. But even these items can be polysemous. Which 'picture' of the following items is the right one, and should it be learned first: *pipe, head, stamp, line*? Secondly, it is interesting to note just how many of the 850 words have more than one sense. This applies to both lexical and grammatical words as well as to words such as *round* or *right* or *past*, which can have either primarily lexical or grammatical functions. This raises an interesting psycholinguistic question of whether the senses of single word forms (however polysemous) are easier to retain than the same number of monosemous

BASIC ENGLISH WORD LIST

OPERATIONS 100

COME, GET, GIVE, GO, KEEP, LET, MAKE, PUT, SEEM, TAKE, BE, DO, HAVE, SAY, SEE, SEND, MAY, WILL, ABOUT, ACROSS, AFTER, AGAINST, AMONG, AT, BEFORE, BETWEEN, BY, DOWN, FROM, IN, OFF, ON, OVER, THROUGH, TO, UNDER, UP, WITH, AS, FOR, OF, TILL, THAN, A, THE, ALL, ANY, EVERY

THINGS

400 General

ACCOUNT	EDUCATION	METAL	SENSE
ACT	EFFECT	MIDDLE	SERVANT
ADDITION	END	MILK	SEX
ADJUSTMENT	ERROR	MIND	SHADE
ADVERTISEMENT	EVENT	MINE	SHAKE
AGREEMENT	EXAMPLE	MINUTE	SHAME
AIR	EXCHANGE	MIST	SHOCK
AMOUNT	EXISTENCE	MONEY	SIDE
AMUSEMENT	EXPANSION	MONTH	SIGN
ANIMAL	EXPERIENCE	MORNING	SILK
ANSWER	EXPERT	MOTHER	SILVER
APPARATUS	FACT	MOTION	SISTER
APPROVAL	FALL	MOVE	SIZE
ARGUMENT	FAMILY	MUSIC	SKY
ART	FATHER	NAME	SLEEP
ATTACK	FEAR	NATION	SLIP
ATTEMPT	FEELING	NEED	SLOPE
ATTENTION	FICTION	NEWS	SMASH
ATTRACTION	FIELD	NIGHT	SMELL
AUTHORITY	FIGHT	NOISE	SMILE
BACK	FIRE	NOTE	SMOKE
BALANCE	FLAME	NUMBER	SNEEZE
BASE	FLIGHT	OBSERVATION	SNOW
BEHAVIOUR	FLOWER	OFFER	SOAP
BELIEF	FOLD	OIL	SOCIETY
BIRTH	FOOD	OPERATION	SON
BIT	FORCE	OPINION	SONG
BITE	FORM	ORDER	SORT
BLOOD	FRIEND	ORGANIZATION	SOUND
BLOW	FRONT	OWNER	SOUP
BODY	FRUIT	PAGE	SPACE
BRASS	GLASS	PAIN	STAGE
BREAD	GOVERNMENT	PAINT	START
BREATH	GRAIN	PAPER	STATEMENT
BROTHER	GRASS	PART	STEAM
BUILDING	GRIP	PASTE	STEEL
BURN	GROUP	PAYMENT	STEP
BURST	GROWTH	PEACE	STITCH
BUSINESS	GUIDE	PERSON	STONE
BUTTER	HARBOR	PLACE	STORY
CANVAS	HARMONY	PLANT	STRETCH
CARE	HATE	PLAY	STRUCTURE
CAUSE	HEARING	PLEASURE	SUBSTANCE
CHALK	HEAT	POINT	SUGAR
CHANCE	HELP	POISON	SUGGESTION
CHANGE	HISTORY	POLISH	SUMMER
CLOTH	HOLE		SUPPORT
COAL			

200 Picturable

ANGLE	KNEE
ANT	KNIFE
APPLE	KNOT
ARCH	LEAF
ARM	LEG
ARMY	LIBRARY
BABY	LINE
BAG	LIP
BALL	LOCK
BAND	MAP
BASIN	MATCH
BASKET	MONKEY
BATH	MOON
BED	MOUTH
BEE	MUSCLE
BELL	NAIL
BERRY	NECK
BIRD	NEEDLE
BLADE	NERVE
BOARD	NET
BOAT	NOSE
BONE	NUT
BOOK	OFFICE
BOOT	ORANGE
BOTTLE	OVEN
BOX	PARCEL
BOY	PEN
BRAIN	PENCIL
BRAKE	PICTURE
BRANCH	PIG
BRICK	PIN
BRIDGE	PIPE
BRUSH	PLANE
BUCKET	PLATE
BULB	PLOUGH
BUTTON	POCKET
CAKE	POT
CAMERA	POTATO
CARD	PRISON
CART	PUMP
CARRIAGE	RAIL
CAT	RAT
CHAIN	RECEIPT
CHEESE	RING
CHEST	ROD
CHIN	ROOF
CHURCH	ROOT
CIRCLE	SAIL

QUALITIES

100 General

ABLE	
ACID	
ANGRY	
AUTOMATIC	
BEAUTIFUL	
BLACK	
BOILING	
BRIGHT	
BROKEN	
BROWN	
CHEAP	
CHEMICAL	
CHIEF	
CLEAN	
CLEAR	
COMMON	
COMPLEX	
CONSCIOUS	
CUT	
DEEP	
DEPENDENT	
EARLY	
ELASTIC	
ELECTRIC	
EQUAL	
FAT	
FERTILE	
FIRST	
FIXED	
FLAT	
FREE	
FREQUENT	
FULL	
GENERAL	
GOOD	
GREAT	
GREY	
HANGING	
HAPPY	
HARD	
HEALTHY	
HIGH	
HOLLOW	
IMPORTANT	
KIND	
LIKE	
LIVING	
LONG	

50 Opposites

AWAKE, BAD, BENT, BITTER, BLUE, CERTAIN, COLD, COMPLETE, CRUEL, DARK, DEAD, DEAR, DELICATE, DIFFERENT, DIRTY, DRY, FALSE, FEEBLE, FEMALE, FOOLISH, FUTURE, GREEN, ILL, LAST, LATE, LEFT, LOOSE, LOUD, LOW, MIXED, NARROW, OLD, OPPOSITE, PUBLIC, ROUGH, SAD, SAFE, SECRET, SHORT, SHUT, SIMPLE, SLOW, SMALL, SOFT, SOLID, SPECIAL, STRANGE, THIN

FIGURE 1 Basic English word list

(Richards 1943, *Basic English and its uses*)

								SUMMARY OF RULES
NO	COLOR	HOPE	PORTER	SURPRISE	CLOCK	SCHOOL	WHITE	
OTHER	COMFORT	HOUR	POSITION	SWIM	CLOUD	SCISSORS	WRONG	
SOME	COMMITTEE	HUMOR	POWDER	SYSTEM	COAT	SCREW		
SUCH	COMPANY	ICE	POWER	TALK	COLLAR	SEED	MALE	PLURALS IN 'S'
THAT	COMPARISON	IDEA	PRICE	TASTE	COMB	SHEEP	MARRIED	
THIS	COMPETITION	IMPULSE	PRINT	TAX	CORD	SHELF	MATERIAL	
HE	CONDITION	INCREASE	PROCESS	TEACHING	COW	SHIP	MEDICAL	DERIVATIVES
YOU	CONNECTION	INDUSTRY	PRODUCE	TENDENCY	CUP	SHIRT	MILITARY	IN 'ER', 'ING', 'ED'
WHO	CONTROL	INK	PROFIT	TEST	CURTAIN	SHOE	NATURAL	FROM 300 NOUNS.
AND	COOK	INSECT	PROPERTY	THEORY	CUSHION	SKIN	NECESSARY	
BECAUSE	COPPER	INSTRUMENT	PROSE	THING	DOG	SKIRT	NEW	
BUT	COPY	INSURANCE	PROTEST	THOUGHT	DOOR	SNAKE	NORMAL	ADVERBS
OR	CORK	INTEREST	PULL	THUNDER	DRAIN	SOCK	OPEN	IN 'LY'
IF	COTTON	INVENTION	PUNISHMENT	TIME	DRAWER	SPADE	PARALLEL	FROM
THOUGH	COUGH	IRON	PURPOSE	TIN	DRESS	SPONGE	PAST	QUALIFIERS
WHILE	COUNTRY	JELLY	PUSH	TOP	DROP	SPOON	PHYSICAL	
HOW	COVER	JOIN	QUALITY	TOUCH	EAR	SPRING	POLITICAL	
WHEN	CRACK	JOURNEY	QUESTION	TRADE	EGG	SQUARE	POOR	DEGREE
WHERE	CREDIT	JUDGE	RAIN	TRANSPORT	ENGINE	STAMP	POSSIBLE	WITH
WHY	CRIME	JUMP	RANGE	TRICK	EYE	STAR	PRESENT	'MORE' AND 'MOST'.
AGAIN	CRUSH	KICK	RATE	TROUBLE	FACE	STATION	PRIVATE	
EVER	CRY	KISS	RAY	TURN	FARM	STEM	PROBABLE	
FAR	CURRENT	KNOWLEDGE	REACTION	TWIST	FEATHER	STEM	QUICK	QUESTIONS
FORWARD	CURVE	LAND	READING	UNIT	FINGER	STOCKING	QUIET	BY INVERSION
HERE	DAMAGE	LANGUAGE	REASON	USE	FISH	STOMACH	READY	AND 'DO.'
NEAR	DANGER	LAUGH	RECORD	VALUE	FLAG	STORE	REGULAR	
NOW	DAUGHTER	LAW	REGRET	VERSE	FLOOR	STREET	RESPONSIBLE	
OUT	DAY	LEAD	RELATION	VESSEL	FLY	SUN	RIGHT	OPERATORS
STILL	DEATH	LEARNING	RELIGION	VIEW	FOOT	TABLE	ROUND	AND
THEN	DEBT	LEATHER	REPRESENTATIVE	VOICE	FORK	TAIL	SAME	PRONOUNS
THERE	DECISION	LETTER	REQUEST	WALK	FOWL	THREAD	SECOND	CONJUGATE
TOGETHER	DEGREE	LEVEL	RESPECT	WAR	FRAME	THROAT	SEPARATE	IN FULL.
WELL	DESIGN	LIFT	REST	WASH	GARDEN	THUMB	SERIOUS	
ALMOST	DESIRE	LIGHT	REWARD	WASTE	GIRL	TICKET	SHARP	
ENOUGH	DESTRUCTION	LIMIT	RHYTHM	WATER	GLOVE	TOE	SMOOTH	MEASUREMENT,
EVEN	DETAIL	LINEN	RICE	WAVE	GOAT	TONGUE	STICKY	NUMERALS,
LITTLE	DEVELOPMENT	LIQUID	RIVER	WAX	GUN	TOOTH	STIFF	CURRENCY,
MUCH	DIGESTION	LIST	ROAD	WAY	HAIR	TOWN	STRAIGHT	CALENDAR,
NOT	DIRECTION	LOOK	ROLL	WEATHER	HAMMER	TRAIN	STRONG	AND
ONLY	DISCOVERY	LOSS	ROOM	WEEK	HAND	TRAY	SUDDEN	INTERNATIONAL
QUITE	DISCUSSION	LOVE	RUB	WEIGHT	HAT	TREE	SWEET	TERMS
SO	DISEASE	MACHINE	RULE	WIND	HEAD	TROUSERS	TALL	IN ENGLISH
VERY	DISGUST	MAN	RUN	WINE	HEART	UMBRELLA	THICK	FORM.
TOMORROW	DISTANCE	MANAGER	SALT	WINTER	HOOK	WALL	THIN	
YESTERDAY	DISTRIBUTION	MARK	SAND	WOMAN	HORSE	WATCH	TIGHT	
NORTH	DIVISION	MARKET	SCALE	WOOD	HOSPITAL	WHEEL	TIRED	
SOUTH	DRINK	MASS	SCIENCE	WOOL	HOUSE	WHIP	TRUE	
EAST	DRIVING	MEAL	SEAT	WORD	ISLAND	WHISTLE	VIOLENT	
WEST	DUST	MEASURE	SECRETARY	WORK	JEWEL	WINDOW	WAITING	
PLEASE	EARTH	MEETING	SELECTION	WOUND	KETTLE	WIRE	WARM	
YES	EDGE	MEMORY	SELF	WRITING	KEY	WORM	WET	
				YEAR			WIDE	
							WISE	
							YELLOW	
							YOUNG	

words with different word forms. Ogden and Richards offer no guidance here (and do not seem particularly aware of the question), although, to be fair to them, this is still a problem today which requires more extensive exploration. Thirdly, there is little guidance given as to how Basic English might be extended, and thus how this list and any additions to it might be graded for relative difficulty or usefulness, or, indeed, how much further, if at all, a learner would need to go to have a 'working vocabulary'. Fourthly, the system is not designed to enhance social interaction through language. The object is one which bears not only on more specific features such as the fact that items such as *goodbye* or *thank you* or *Mr* and *Mrs* do not appear in Basic English, or that communication would be inevitably rather neutral or slightly formal stylistically (for example, *have a desire for*, *take a walk*), but also on the fact that the extent of periphrasis required can make communication a relatively clumsy affair. Additionally, there is the problem already noted that in the process of transfer to Standard English, a relatively large number of constructions which will have been created in the course of learning Basic English will have to be unlearned.

This is not to say that Basic English is not eminently 'usable' as an auxiliary language for general purposes of simplified international communication, and as a practical introduction to a more standardized form of English than can be found in many intranational contexts of English usage. It is also, as Ogden and Richards themselves have amply demonstrated, a useful system for producing clear and comprehensible *written* texts, particularly where high degrees of communicative expressivity are not required, such as in expository texts or material with high levels of information content. Although *Basic English* is not widely used or referred to today, the underlying impulse to provide systematically graded introductions to language, to specify lexical syllabuses and to construct core or nuclear Englishes for language learning purposes, is still an active one. (See, for example, Stein 1979; Quirk 1982; Stubbs 1986b; Carter 1982b, 1985, 1987a and b.)

2 Michael West and 'A General Service List'

Published in 1953, *A General Service List* (hereafter *GSL*) is the outcome of almost three decades of major work in English lexicometrics. The main figures associated with this work are Michael West himself, whose work in English as a foreign language was concentrated in Bengal in India, and Harold Palmer – one of the founding fathers of English language teaching – who was Director of the Institute of English Language Teaching in Tokyo from 1923–1936. The 'history' of their association and academic collaboration on the development of vocabulary and other teaching materials has been lucidly charted by Howatt (1983, Chapter 17). West is also known for his *New Method Readers* and his *New Method Dictionary*, which make use of controlled vocabulary for, respectively, graded reading in a second language and for a lexicographic definition vocabulary (see Nolte 1937).

West's General Service List grew organically from major studies in the 1930s on vocabulary selection for teaching purposes. These studies culminated in the Interim Report on Vocabulary Selection (1935) (known as the 'Carnegie Report') which in turn issued the first General Service List which was published in 1936. The revised *GSL* (1953) made particular use of word counts such as that of Thorndike and Lorge (1944) developed in the USA. It should also be noted that the *GSL* developed at the same time as and along not dissimilar lines to C. K. Ogden's *Basic English*, and that the two schemes ran in parallel and in competition for many years. West's *GSL* has had by far the most lasting influence, and the 1953 word list is widely used today forming the basis of the principles underlying the *Longman Structural Readers*. West's notion of a limited defining vocabulary is one of the main informing design principles of the *Longman Dictionary of Contemporary English* (1978). (See Chapter 3, pp. 52–4.)

The main criteria of West, Palmer and others for the selection of vocabulary for learning in the early stages of acquisition, are that:
a) the frequency of each word in written English should be indicated;
b) information should be provided about the relative prominences of the various meanings and uses of a word form.

Both these criteria, which were more extensively developed in the 1953 edition than in previous versions, provide particularly useful guidance for teachers deciding which words and which meanings should be taught first. The list consists of 2,000 words with semantic and frequency information drawn from a corpus of two to five million words. It is claimed that knowing these words gives access to about 80 per cent of the words in any written text, and thus stimulates motivation, since the words acquired can be seen by learners to have a demonstrably quick return. Other criteria adopted in the selection of words include their universality (words useful in all countries), their utility (enabling discussion on as wide a subject range as possible), and their usefulness in terms of definition value. The list can be seen to result from a mixture of subjective and objective selectional criteria.

A representative example of any entry for the General Service List, is that of the word *act* (*GSL*, p. 5). In the case of this word, 2184 here indicates the number of occurrences in five million words.

ACT, n.	2184	(1)	(*thing done*)	
			A noble act	
			The act of a madman	14%
		(2)	(*legal act*)	
			The bill became an act	22%
		(3)	(*part of a play*)	
			The third act of *Hamlet*	31%
act, v.		(1)	(*behave*)	
			Men are judged not by what they say but how they act	11%*
			Act for the headmaster; acting headmaster	7%
			My advice is not always acted upon	2%

*(This includes 'Acting strangely,' *etc.* = *behaving* -, U.S.A.).

		(2)	(*have an effect*)	
			The brake doesn't act	
			This acid acts on zinc	6%
		(3)	(*theatre*)	
			A well acted play	
			Act the part of	4%

The advantages for teachers of this kind of detailed breakdown are considerable. But there are some disadvantages, too. One is that the list is to some extent outdated. It contains words from counts made in the 1930s and even earlier. A number of common 1980s words do not appear; for example, there are no entries for *pilot*, *helicopter*, *television*, *astronaut*. Another is that the corpus on which the lists are based is a written corpus. As a result not only do a number of the words appear distinctly 'literary', but data about spoken usage are not available for contrastive purposes. This does reflect one of West's main aims, which was to provide a list for pre-reading or simplified reading materials. However, this main impulse to provide a practical research tool for basic literacy development conditions the 'usefulness' or 'utility' principles which, since they are mainly subjective, are in any case difficult to retrieve. Richards (1974, p. 71) has questioned the inclusion on this basis of certain items such as *mannerism*, *vessel*, *ornament*, *mere*, *stock*, *motion*, *urge*, which to him seem of limited utility, and has pointed to anomalies of exclusion from certain semantic fields. For example, *doctor*, *engineer*, *teacher*, *nurse* are included as occupations but *carpenter*, *plumber* and *mason* are excluded in favour of *footman*.

Also, *trader, merchant* and *dealer* are all included when under the principles of definition value any one could effectively replace the others.

More serious, though understandable given available concordancing procedures at the time, is the absence of information on collocations and collocational frequencies. Also, the notion of defining words which have 'coverage' because they are common or central enough in the lexicon to stand in for other words is insufficiently developed. The notion is more rigorously and extensively applied by West in his *New Method Dictionary* (1935) and *Minimum Adequate Vocabulary* (1960), which defines the meanings of 24,000 entries within a vocabulary of 1,490 words, but the relationship between these words and the *GSL* words is not particularly clear. Finally, West can be criticized for not giving adequate consideration to the notions of the 'availability' and 'familiarity' of words, though no current research was available to him at that time. (See Section 3 below.) The *GSL* is not without its disadvantages, but it was a considerable advance on any previous word lists, and remains one of the most innovative examples of foreign language pedagogy and lexicometric research this century.

3 Recent developments: problems and prospects

Although Michael West's *A General Service List* continues to be in active service, the issues raised by the production of pedagogic word lists continue to lead to further theoretical and practical outcomes. One of the most wide-ranging discussions of relevant issues is to be found in an article published in 1974 by J. C. Richards and entitled 'Word lists: problems and prospects'. In the article, Richards makes the following main points:

1. 'Objective' word counts, such as statistically-based frequency lists, do not necessarily produce lexical inventories which are of pedagogic relevance or utility. Richards draws on observations made by Bongers (1947) and Engels (1968) that frequent words are often low in information content. 'The relationship of frequency to information is an important factor in evaluating the role of word frequency in vocabulary selection' (p. 72). Even in the early stages of second-language learning, learners often need to be exposed to discourse with high information content. Also, high frequency words are not automatically those which the learner *needs*.

2. Frequency counts differ considerably. Obviously, much depends

on the nature of the corpora used. There are differences, too, between written and spoken contexts.

3. *Coverage* is important. The coverage of a word embraces the range of contexts in which a word is encountered. This can often be more significant than raw frequency. Here we are also referring to the capacity of some words to replace less useful ones. See particularly Mackey and Savard (1967). (Michael West's term for this is 'definition value', but his criteria for such words are never made explicit.)

4. Richards points to research by Michea (1953) who argues for the importance of *available* words. For example, concrete nouns are more readily recalled than non-concrete items, but this is a factor which exists independently of frequency of occurrence in discourse. 'Psychologically, a frequent word such as *come* and an infrequent word such as *pencil* are equally known but in different ways. Available words are known in the sense that they come to mind rapidly when the situation calls for them' (p. 76). They are often the most easy to teach.

5. Richards's own research reported in Richards (1970) also attempts to measure 'the subjective impression of words'. Richards's own term for this is *familiarity*, which 'has been shown to be a factor of the frequency of experiencing words, their meaningfulness and their concreteness'. In an appendix to the 'Word lists' article (1974), Richards lists the 300 most 'familiar' concrete nouns and compares these with frequency lists.

6. Richards argues that subjective and objective measures of vocabulary selection need to be combined if the validity and utility of such lists are to be improved.

The 1980s have witnessed a continuing concern with word lists. Among the most interesting and relevant for language teachers are Hindmarsh's *Cambridge English Lexicon* (Hindmarsh 1980), and McArthur's *Longman Lexicon of Contemporary English* (McArthur 1981). Although Hindmarsh's list is based on the largely subjective criteria of his own wide-ranging experience of English language teaching, it is especially useful and notable for its attempt to categorize words into seven main difficulty levels. McArthur's lexicon is characterized by (a) alphabetic indexization, (b) a thesaurus-like arrangement of words around particular topics, (c) largely as a result of (b), by indicating significant lexical and collocational relationships.

Useful reviews of current developments in word lists and lexicons can be found in Fox and Mahood (1982a and b) and Jeffries and Willis (1982). For further discussion of the notion of core vocabulary for pedagogic purposes, see Carter (1987a, Chapters 2 and 7), Carter (1987b), and for an especially innovative perspective, Sinclair and Renouf in this volume.

The previous three sections have only covered two main landmarks in the vocabulary control movement (for a fuller survey, see McArthur 1978). And the focus on minimum vocabularies should not obscure continuing vocabulary research with an etymological orientation which has considerably deeper roots. (See a recent advocacy by Ilson, 1983, of the role of etymological information in vocabulary development.) We shall now move on to review some key features in vocabulary acquisition research. We reiterate our earlier point, however, that vocabulary neglect is a fact even though it is only relatively true. The work in English lexicometrics started in the 1930s is a source of inspiration today, and many of the issues raised by such research are currently being investigated anew in the 1980s. And many of the issues involved have direct repercussions for pyscholinguistic description of the lexicon in relation to vocabulary acquisition and learning.

4 Vocabulary acquisition: some more basic questions

The main orientation of this book is towards vocabulary teaching and towards descriptions of the lexicon which seem to us best to facilitate successful vocabulary development, mainly with regard to second and foreign-language learners. Psycholinguistic accounts of the lexicon are not as fully represented as some would wish. This reflects the bias of our own interests towards lexis in discourse, and towards teaching methodologies which take account of the lexicological analysis of text and discourse. It should not be taken to mean that psycholinguistic accounts of the lexicon do not have much to offer.

It would be irresponsible, of course, to devote a book to vocabulary and language study and teaching without at least pointing to the inevitable connection with research into vocabulary learning. How words are taught has to take into account what we know about how words are learned. The aim in the final section of this chapter is to review some of the main questions raised by the examination of vocabulary acquisition and learning. The terms acquisition and learning are, however, used interchangeably, and issues of the sort raised by Krashen (1981) are not engaged delicately enough here for a distinction to be useful. Once again, the perspective sought will be a historical one, although, in contrast with research into vocabulary control, the main densities of activity here have been in the late 1960s and in the 1970s and 1980s.

The kinds of questions activated by lexical acquisition research can be roughly divided into the following main but still closely associated categories: *memorization*; *word difficulty*; *interlanguage*. The basic question which underlies most research in this area has, however, been clearly formulated by Meara (1982) and many studies have departed and will continue to depart from this basic question:

> What does a (second language) learner's mental lexicon look like and how is it different from the mental lexicon of a monolingual native speaker?
>
> (Meara 1982, p. 29)

4.1 Memorization

In the early stages of language learning, words are conventionally learned in lists of paired words or 'paired associates'. The lists contain a word from the target language, either a synonym in that target language, or a translation in the mother tongue, and these can be accompanied by a picture or some means of graphic or other mnemonic representation. Relevant research (e.g. Kellogg and Howe 1971; Crothers and Suppes 1967; see also Nation 1983, Chapter 9) has made claims for the efficacy of such learning procedures and has shown that large quantities of initial vocabulary can be learned efficiently and quickly by such means. In this connection, too, Atkinson and Raugh (1975, p. 126) have argued for the usefulness of the 'key-word' technique which involves an 'association' of the target second/foreign-language word with a native word. The association can be aural or imagistic and, preferably, incorporates both dimensions. For a more explicit account see Nation (1983, p. 101, 1980, 1982). The technique is not without its problems (see Meara 1980, pp. 224–6) but, linking as it does form, meaning and structure, and facilitating a combination of both productive and receptive word-attack skills, the techniques would appear to have advantages over an exclusive focus on straight translation or rote-learning. The principle of vocabulary learning which emerges is that the more words are analysed or are enriched by imagistic and other associations, the more likely it is that they will be retained.

But the question of retention is a complex one, too. As suggested in the previous sections, there is the problem of whether single word forms with extended meanings (polysemous items) can be retained more easily than the meanings of an equal number of separate word forms. At different stages in language learning do learners focus primarily on the forms or meanings of words or on a simultaneous combination of both? In terms of retention, there are also clearly differences to be drawn between short term and longer term memorization. And what are the connections between recall and the memorization procedures adopted, and between recall and whether the learning of the word has been predominantly productive or receptive? (But see Ostyn and Godin 1985, for an argument that 'productive' and 'receptive' are not as sharply divisible as is regularly assumed.) These questions are discussed in greater detail in Nation 1982; Meara 1980, 1983.

4.2 Word difficulty: what *is* a difficult word?

Learning vocabulary effectively is closely bound up with a teacher's understanding, and a learner's perception of, the *difficulties* of words. The difficulty of a word may result, *inter alia*, from the relations it can be seen to contract with other words, either in the native or target language, whether it is learned productively or receptively; as well as from its polysemy, the associations it creates, its pronounceability, whether it lends itself to key-word teaching techniques and, in the case of advanced learners, from the nature of the contexts in which it is encountered. The kinds of interplay between these and other complex factors cannot be adequately explored here. Instead, there will be an emphasis on early learning and on the kinds of 'language-internal' difficulties resulting from the *forms* of words and how these might be best presented. The emphasis on word-form is given because much research has highlighted this as a significant factor in learnability.

Consideration of form here follows appropriately from the preceding section because one important element in learning new words is the degree of effective *formal* linking learners can establish between a word in the target language and a cognate word in the mother tongue (and because issues of memorization and word difficulty are closely connected). According to research by Craik and Lockhart (1972), oral repetition is not necessarily an effective way of assimilating new words; recalling the *form* of a word is found to be more productive. As we saw in the previous section, the more opportunities that can be found for formal transfer between foreign and mother-tongue words, the better the chances of retention. But, concentration here on specifically *linguistic* form should not preclude the possibility or even necessity for other links and transfers to be made available to assist memorization.

Research reported in Nation (1982, pp. 18ff.) suggests that similarities in sound, morphology or etymology can assist word memorization. By such procedures the German word *Hund* (dog) may be more easily retained than the French *chien*, because of its etymological and sound similarity with the English *hound*. Another example would be the Malay word *buku* (book). More memorizable still would be words which are international 'loan' words such as *telephone, radio, television*, which have many close cognate forms in other languages. Significant related research here is that by Cohen and Aphek (1980). They found that students of Hebrew who tried a range of interlingual and language-internal mnemonic associations, generally retained new words with greater efficacy. (See also the paper by Channell in Chapter 4.) However, further research is needed before the requisite 'translations' between lexicons or within a single L1/L2 lexicon can be more precisely defined, and caution must be continually exercised to avoid the kinds of confusion and unlearning that can take place through misguided analysis of parts of words or through the establishment of false cognates. Examples of the former would be the German word *unbedingt* (definitely) which, if analysed morphologically, may misleadingly suggest from its prefix *un* that it is a negative. An example of the latter would be the word *Rezept* in German, which means 'medical prescription' as well as 'recipe'.

Reference to translation raises one further issue which should be dealt with at this stage: namely, the effect on the burden of learning of the *order* of presentation of equivalent word pairs. Here, research is limited and this issue itself is closely connected with whether the word is learned for productive use, or for purposes of comprehension only, but Nation (1982, p. 20) concludes that if vocabulary is needed for writing in the target language, then a learning sequence of mother-tongue word → foreign word, would be appropriate; a direction of foreign word → mother tongue may be more appropriate if only reading skills are required.

But concentration on learning words in pairs and from basic lists should not obscure the fact that as learners become more proficient so they have to learn to rely more on their own inferential skills by decoding words in *context*. That context may be spoken or written and the extent of decoding may stretch to several sentences before the word can be understood. Research here has quite deep roots and has been taken up again recently.

In an experiment conducted with Finnish learners of English, Pickering (1982) examined findings reported in Seibert (1930) (see also

Seibert 1945) that learning foreign-language words in context was inferior (that is, fewer words were learned) to learning words in pairs with native-language translations of the items concerned. Although most language teachers prefer to present words for more advanced learners in context, it has not been convincingly demonstrated that the information learners obtain from meeting words in a variety of contexts is more beneficial, either in terms of knowledge of forms or meanings of lexical items, than either translation or simply looking up the word in a dictionary. This may be especially the case when they have to recall a lexical item productively as opposed to decoding it receptively. Pickering's experiment enables him to conclude that the context condition was slightly more conducive to learning than paired associates, but his conclusions are heavily qualified and he points to the need for further research. The same general conclusions were reached by Cohen and Aphek in their work on the role of mnemonic associations in foreign-language word learning with reference to Hebrew and English (Cohen and Aphek 1980).

They concluded additionally that the recall of words in context is positively related to the proficiency level of the informants (measured by pre-tested knowledge of words in context and by reading comprehension). Thus, the more advanced the learners, the more likely they are to benefit from learning words in context. As yet, however, it is difficult to draw precise lines to suggest when a move from key-word techniques, or translation in pairs, or from using a monolingual or bilingual dictionary to context-based inferential strategies, is best instituted. The most realistic approach is probably to recognize that learning occurs along a cline or continuum with no clearly marked stages of transition, and that a mixture of approaches should be adopted.

4.3 Interlanguage: words between languages

Questions posed under this heading are numerous. They cannot also be disconnected from questions posed in the previous sections on memorization and word difficulty. Basic questions here include: How can we best understand the processes involved in integrating new L2 words into a learner's mental lexicon, and are there differences between monolingual and second-language learners in the way lexical knowledge is stored? Are an L1 and an L2 vocabulary stored separately, or is it appropriate to see them as an undifferentiated whole? Why is it that some words can be 'transferred' from one language to another with no apparent difficulty (even when there are no interlingual formal similarities)? What can be learned from the study of interlingual errors?

It is only possible to examine some of these questions cursorily here. More detailed treatments can be found in Carter (1987a, Chapter 7); Davies, Criper and Howatt (eds.) (1984); in reviews by Meara and Nation already cited, Meara (1980, 1983); Nation (1982); and in the paper in this volume by Channell.

Unless evidence is produced to the contrary, most researchers in second-language acquisition will continue to assume that an L2 user's mental lexicon *resembles* that of an L1 user and that learners make semantic, phonological and associational links between them. Examination of interlingual errors and associations will continue, therefore, to provide a secure foundation for study of both learning and teaching procedures. One piece of relevant research here is that into the relative 'transferability' of lexical items as perceived by learners themselves. In a series of papers (Kellerman 1977, 1983; Jordens and Kellerman 1981), Kellerman has argued that words which are 'psycholinguistically marked' – that is, 'perceived as infrequent, irregular, semantically or structurally opaque, or in any other way exceptional' (Kellerman 1983, p. 117) – will be transferable from one language to another in inverse proportion to their degree of markedness. Thus, when 'errors' occur it is valuable to investigate their connection with such notions as transferability, as well as to explore the extent to which the interlingual lexical store has produced different degrees of modelling based on L1 and (assumed) L2 structures. The more a second language develops, the more particular lexical instabilities occur. Projects such as *The Birkbeck Vocabulary Project* (directed by Dr Paul Meara at Birkbeck College, University of London) have attempted to explore these instabilities and have made use in the process of well-established research procedures such as association tests to measure interlingual associations in English learners of French (see Meara 1982). Subsequent research, reported in Meara (1984), also reinforces general assumptions that different languages produce different word-handling, storage and recognition problems. For example, for Spanish speakers, syllables may play a more important role in lexical manipulation, whereas for Chinese-speaking learners of English, there are difficulties with long words:

> They seem to pay more attention to the ends of words than native English speakers do, which suggests that they have to construct words out of their parts, instead of using sequential redundancies to enable them to read words as wholes.

> (Meara 1984, p. 234)

The above discussion, hopefully, reinforces our earlier position that issues in vocabulary learning cannot be divorced from the classroom teaching of vocabulary, any more than they can from theoretical and descriptive accounts of lexical structure and organization. Although the focus in subsequent chapters is not on vocabulary acquisition research, its importance is acknowledged, wherever possible, as well as explicitly in the papers of at least three contributors to Chapter 4.

If we now finally return to the eight questions asked at the beginning of this chapter, it will be clear that this review of both research into vocabulary learning and attempts at vocabulary control leads to yet more questions. Some guidance has been provided by the discussion. For example, there are possibilities available for grading lexical difficulty in general terms; frequency lists are useful, although raw frequency does not stand in a one-to-one relation with either learnability or usefulness; the creation of associations within and across languages can aid learnability; vocabulary 'control' can ensure that words are regularly encountered in the early stages and, appropriately designed, can lead to basic, if unnatural, communication. However, few positive answers are available concerning what kind of corpus constitutes a 'working vocabulary', distinctions between spoken and written vocabulary are thin on the ground, and further research is needed to assess the relative value of learning words in paired associates, in lists or in context. And, as we have seen in Section 3 of this chapter, learning words in another language cannot be easily divorced from motivational factors such as how important or useful lexical items are perceived to be by learners themselves.

Some of these issues are explored further in subsequent chapters, notably in Chapters 4 and 5, where questions of a lexical syllabus, learnability, and of the interfaces between written and spoken discourse are engaged. Of particular interest should be the papers in Chapter 4 by Cowie and Nattinger which question our assumptions about exactly what a word is. This may be, therefore, an appropriate point for us to go back to basics in another sense. That is, to what we know and need to know about the basic linguistic organization of the lexicon. This is the subject of our next chapter.

2 Lexis and structure

Introduction

One of the first questions which needs to be asked in considering ways and means of organizing vocabulary for teaching and in attempting an understanding of how vocabulary is learnt is: are the vocabularies of languages structured or organized internally or are they random, unordered lists of words? The answer to this question is not at all clear-cut and straightforward; there seem to be some principles of organization that can be applied to some areas of the vocabulary of a language like English, but it is by no means certain that these principles can be extended to the whole of the vast word store. To begin with, though, not least of the problems is the very notion of words.

1 Words and things

For our applied purposes, several assumptions will be made. We shall assume that a language like English has things called words, that words are composed of meaningful 'bits' of language (the word *mean/ing/ful* is itself composed of at least three such bits), and that words are freestanding: in the freestanding word *laughing*, we can see another potential word, *laugh*, but not a word *ing*. Much of how we recognize words is on this intuitive basis and we shall assume that this sort of intuition is a reliable basis for knowing what we mean when we talk of words. We should not, of course, deceive ourselves that recognizing words is always easy and foolproof. A typical group of native informants will be unable to agree on whether the post that supports street lights is a *lamppost*, a *lampost*, a *lamp-post* or a *lamp post*, and consequently whether it is one 'word' or two. Nor is the evidence for word boundaries always clear in spoken data. But words seem to have a strong psychological reality for all language users and learners everywhere, and so a degree of cautious assumption must be permitted in an applied linguistic consideration of words and meaning.

We shall finally assume that, when we talk of words, we are not excluding the fact that some multi-word units, such as compounds and idioms, behave largely like single words for the purposes of examining meaning-relations in the lexicon. The word *word* will therefore be used as a convenient shorthand for lexical items of varying kinds.

2 Does meaning organize the vocabulary?

If we can answer yes to the above question then it would suggest that teaching vocabulary through meaning and meaning relations in the ways discussed below should be the best way to give organized access to the lexicon. Chapter 3 will refer to several applied linguists who have suggested that this is so.

The massive word store of a language like English can be conceived of as composed around a number of meaning areas, some large, such as 'philosophy' or 'emotions', others smaller and more sharply delineated, such as 'kinship' or 'colour' or 'carpentry'. Viewing the totality of meaning in this compartmentalized way is the basis of **field theory**. The German linguist Trier, in the 1930s, wrote of meaning fields as 'living realities intermediate between individual words and the totality of the vocabulary' (quoted in Lyons 1977, p. 253). Field theory is presented in Lehrer (1974, p. 15) as the belief that 'the words of a language can be classified into sets which are related to conceptual fields and divide up the semantic space or the semantic domain in certain ways'. Trier saw vocabulary as 'an integrated system of lexemes interrelated in sense' (Lyons 1977, p. 252). The vocabulary of a language is in constant flux; old items drop out, new terms come in, and as the new replace and augment the old, so the internal relations of the whole set alter. A simple and familiar example of this is one corner of the personal address system in modern English. Twenty years ago, the 'semantic space' was divided up as in (1):

(1)	female	male
unmarried	Miss	
married	Mrs	} Mr
neutral	–	

The same semantic field has now reorganized itself as in (2):

(2)

	female	male
unmarried	Miss	
married	Mrs	} Mr
neutral	Ms	

At an earlier stage in the language *Master* (a term now reserved for addressing birthday-card envelopes to small boys) would have to be considered within the field in some way. So field theory attempts to capture features of the organization of vocabularies, how they have changed or are changing, how one language differs from another, and where each word has its place in the meaning-systems of languages. For instance, the mental processes referred to in English by the verbs *think* and *believe* are realized in an overlapping but distinct way in Swedish:

(3)   believe
        ─────────   tro
        think
                            tycka
                            tänka

Such representations do seem to capture some of the problems involved in learning a foreign language. We have to learn how the semantic space is carved up in the target language. In Trier's terms, the same conceptual field might be covered by different lexical fields in two different languages, or in the same language at two different points in its history. Colour terms are often quoted as being a semantic field which is divided up in different ways by different tongues. Other fields which often differ between languages that language teachers will be familiar with are such things as temperature terms (*hot/warm/cool/cold*, etc.) (see Prator 1963), divisions of the day (*morning/afternoon/evening/night*), kinship terms, parts of the body and names of common foods such as vegetables.

So far we may have suggested that dividing the vocabulary up into fields is a relatively simple matter, and that Trier's vision of fields joining together 'to form in turn fields of higher order, until finally the entire vocabulary is included' (quoted in Lehrer 1974, p. 17) is an unproblematic affair, but Lehrer raises a number of objections that are well-founded. For one thing, she suggests that Berlin and Kay's (1969) notion of 'focal points' might be a better way of describing how language users perceive lexical fields than the idea that there are clearly-defined boundaries between terms in a field. In other words, there may be a lot of agreement on what is typically *red* or *yellow* in the colour field, but far less agreement on the actual borders where *yellow* shades into *orange* or *green*, and these borders will remain fuzzy. Lehrer also notes that not all words (*even* and *only*, for example) are easily described in field terms: 'field theories are appropriate for analysing some sets of words – inappropriate for others' (1974, p. 17). Nor is it easy to define the precise relationship between lexical fields and the conceptual fields they refer to, since the conceptual fields can only be expressed in language (i.e. in the very words of the field), which leaves us with a worrying circularity. Lehrer's other main criticism of field theory is echoed by Lyons. Both remind us that field theory tends to view words paradigmatically only (e.g. the relation of each colour term to the other colour terms), whereas an important part of our knowledge of words is the syntagmatic aspect, i.e. how words combine with other words. Lehrer (1969) calls these 'syntagmatic presuppositions', while Lyons (1977, p. 261) recalls Porzig's illustrations of syntagmatic associations and their importance to meaning: we cannot explain the meaning of *bark* without reference to *dogs*, or *blonde* without reference to its exclusive collocation with *hair* and not with *car* or *jacket*. Lehrer's and Lyons's criticisms would therefore urge caution on the applied linguist over-keen to take field theory on board.

But Lehrer does develop some interesting examples of lexical fields and definable sets of lexical items found within them, for she feels there is sufficient agreement among informants to make the operation worthwhile. Her detailed descriptions of cooking terms and how they are related to one another in English and the discussions that accompany them are model applications of field theory. She shows how the more general words, such as *cook*, relate to more specific ones like *boil*, *fry* and *roast*, which in turn relate to highly specific terms like *poach* and *braise* (1974, p. 31), and also notes collocational restrictions (**stewed eggs*, **poached vegetables*). She similarly analyses words relating to different kinds of sound (*ibid.*, p. 35ff.). Lehrer does point out though that the sorts of charts produced by field analysis are of little use to someone who does not know that language; this suggests that the teacher or materials writer would need to be very explicit, giving full information on the relationship between each item in a given field. Nonetheless, field analyses do offer useable, visually-adaptable representations of groups of semantically related words.

The application of field theory is not limited to statements about the membership of sets and how the members are interrelated. Elsewhere in her work, Lehrer (1969, 1978) records some interesting features of the behaviour of sets as a whole, generalizing from the individual words. She observes relationships between field analysis and word formation regularities, for example the low likelihood of the occurrence of the suffix *-able* with all of the cooking verbs (1969), or how sets transfer in part or whole to other, figurative domains (1978). Thus taste words (*sweet*, *bitter*, *sour*, etc.) are also used to describe aspects of human behaviour (emotions, personality, humour, etc.). The tighter the relationship between items in the set, the more likely it is that the set will transfer *en bloc* to a figurative domain (e.g. the way *chop*, *cut* and *axe* can all be used to describe reductions of various sorts). Not that such principles should be applied without caution, however, in language teaching and learning; *warm*, *cool* and *cold* are equally useable to describe degrees of friendliness in a person, but we would not describe an extremely friendly person as *hot*.

Field theory, despite its problems and shortcomings, has certainly been influential in both theoretical and applied linguistics, the most notable application in English language teaching being the vocabulary materials of Rudzka *et al.* (1981, 1985) (see Chapter 3). The problem remains that a given field may contain dozens of words and we therefore need to ask whether there are further organizing principles within individual fields.

3 How are words in fields related to one another?

If we accept intuitively that fields exist and are realized in language through related sets of lexical items, then the next question is: how do items organize themselves within sets, and what are the types of relationships that can exist between items? Major work in semantics has been devoted to these areas, again by Lehrer (1974) but principally by Leech (1974) and Lyons (1977). (See also Nida 1975, and most recently Cruse 1986.)

Both Leech and Lyons suggest that there are basic or 'primitive' semantic relations between words, Leech starting with synonymy and antonymy, and Lyons concentrating principally on antonymy and hyponymy. Leech argues that the terms synonymy and antonymy are inadequate: to the question 'What is the antonym of woman?' the answer might be *girl* or *man*. Instead of antonymy, says Leech, we should think of *woman* as **incompatible** with *man*, *boy* and *girl* within its lexical field (1974, p. 92). When Lyons uses the term incompatibility, however, he uses it to refer to the relationship between items in many-membered sets such as the names of the days of the week, or names of flowers (1977, p. 288). This differing use of terms complicates matters somewhat, but Leech and Lyons are essentially interested in the same kinds of relationships: the internal organizing principles that create lexical sets. Both are concerned to point up the different kinds of oppositeness that exist between words.

Leech distinguishes between binary taxonomies, such as *alive/dead*, and multiple taxonomies, such as *iron/gold/copper/mercury*. One is either *alive* or *dead*; *gold* cannot be *copper* or *iron* at the same time (1974, p. 99). Lyons calls *alive/dead*, *male/female*, etc. **ungradable** antonyms, which are different from **gradable** antonyms, such as *hot/cold* or *big/small*, where there are terms in between the two extremes and even outside the two basic terms (*warm/cool*, *enormous/tiny*) (1977, p. 291). Leech in turn calls these gradable antonyms **polar oppositions**. Gradable or polar antonyms are relative in meaning and always imply comparison with a socially determined norm. To say 'our house is big' is to say 'big as houses go' (Lyons 1977, p. 274). The norm may be role-related: a 'good boss' is one who is good at that role as the norm dictates (Leech 1974, p. 102). Grading may be implicit, as in 'it's warm today', semi-explicit, as in 'it's warmer today', or fully explicit, as in 'it's warmer today than yesterday' (Lyons 1977, p. 274). The relativity of grading explains why the instructions on a food package which say 'keep warm in a cool oven' make perfect sense ('warm as food goes; cool as ovens go'), even if on the surface they may appear nonsensical.

Lyons indicates several interesting features of gradable antonyms (1977, p. 275–8). Firstly, many common gradables are morphologically unrelated (*big/small*, *dry/wet*, *good/bad*, etc.), while some are related (*friendly/unfriendly*, *formal/informal*), though the latter often also have unrelated antonyms, depending on context (*friendly/hostile, formal/casual*). Indeed, McCarthy will argue in Chapter 4 that there is no one 'true' antonym of a word; that it always depends on the discourse context. Also worthy of note is that, as mentioned above, terms such as *big/small*, *good/bad* will not necessarily be the absolute extremes of their scales, and will often have 'core' or 'focal' status in psychological terms (and in certain structural aspects; see Carter in this volume Chapter 4), so that they may be represented thus:

(4)   etc. ←— excellent GOOD average/fair BAD awful → etc.
      etc. ←— enormous BIG average/medium SMALL tiny → etc.

Informants may disagree over the precise relationship of the intermediate terms, but the core terms will be fairly consistently placed on the scale. Psychological 'coreness' might therefore be a more reliable criterion for deciding what should be presented as the antonym of what, rather than, say, morphology or the relativity and 'instability' of context (stability in meaning is the principle preoccupation of Cowie's paper in Chapter 4). Additionally, the gradables seem to be distinguished by their positive or negative polarity: *small* things lack size, *big* things do not lack smallness; *low* things lack height, *high* things do not lack lowness. This is another way of saying that gradable antonym pairs seem to have one item that is unmarked or neutral; if I want to know the size of your house I ask 'How big is it?', not 'How small is it?'; if I want to know the duration of a meeting I ask 'How long was it?', not 'How short was it?'. If I do ask 'How small is your house?' then it is presupposed that lack of size is at issue.

Gradable and ungradable antonymy are not the only kinds of oppositeness between words, as we have seen. Lyons distinguishes four principle kinds of oppositeness between pairs of terms (1977, p. 279). For him, **contrast** is a very general term which does not tell us how many words are being contrasted, **opposition** is reserved for binary contrasts only. Then come the four main types: (1) **antonymy**: this, says Lyons, is the most suitable name for gradable antonyms only. (2) **complementarity**: this will refer to ungradable antonyms (*alive/dead*). (3) **converseness**: this refers to a reversible relationship such as *parent/child*, *husband/wife*, where to say 'Martin is Anne's husband' is to say 'Anne is Martin's wife.' Lyons also includes pairs such as *buy/sell*, which involve greater grammatical change: 'Jim sold Linda a book' – 'Linda bought a book from Jim.' (4) **directionality**: pairs such as *up/down*, *arrive/depart*, *come/go*, where some sort of direction is involved. Leech subsumes these with the converses under a general heading of **relative oppositions** (1974, p. 102). Pairs such as *come/go* and *bring/take* involve deixis (a relative notion of orientation to where the speaker is, was, or will be) and are notoriously difficult to match one for one with their apparent equivalents in other languages (e.g. Spanish *venir/ir* and *traer/llevar*) and often present difficulties to language learners. *Lend/borrow* is an example of a pair in English not necessarily distinguished at all in other languages. Leech further notes the phenomenon of **inverse opposition**, where two terms can create synonymous sentences by the manipulation of negating particles: 'I was compelled to be a non-vegetarian.' = 'I was not allowed to be a vegetarian.'; 'Chris did not become a vegetarian.' = 'Chris stayed a non-vegetarian.' (1974, p. 107–8). Exploitation of such alternative realizations is a feature of native-speaker lexico-grammatical competence.

One final point worth noting about pairs of opposites is the way that they form a type of idiom or fixed phrase called **irreversible binomials** (see Malkiel 1959). These are such pairs as are found in '*hot and cold* water in all rooms', 'the road winds *in and out*', 'I searched *high and low*', etc., where the order of occurrence is never normally reversed. Other examples are: *back and forth, to and fro, up and down, ladies and gentlemen*, all of which have become culturally 'frozen'. Learners have to learn them as pairs. They are not the same in all languages: in German and Italian you go 'forth and back' (*hin und her, avanti e indietro*); in Malay you address 'gentlemen and ladies' (*tuan-tuan dan puan-puan*). Neither way is more logical than the other, and while some may see cultural pointers determining the order of the items, they are probably best seen simply as fixed, arbitrary strings that combine two opposing items from the same lexical field.

In considering sense relations, just as important as the general relationship of oppositeness between words is the relationship of inclusion, which Lyons calls **hyponymy** (1977, p. 291–5). Specific terms in the vocabulary are covered by more general terms. The words *rose/tulip/pansy* are all hyponyms of *flower*. *Flower* is the superordinate term. In semantics this relationship is described according to unilateral implication: if it is a *rose* then it is a *flower*, but not necessarily vice versa. If the implication is bilateral, then this is **synonymy** (if it is an *egg-plant* then it is an *aubergine*, and vice versa; therefore they are synonyms). Hyponymous sets include things like *hammer/saw/screwdriver*, etc., under the general word *tool*; *plaice/cod/herring*, etc., under *fish*. Hyponymy therefore is a relationship which creates taxonomies or tree-like configurations, with higher-order superordinates above the lower superordinates: a *cow* is a *mammal*, a *mammal* is an *animal*, therefore a *cow* is an *animal*. Again, hyponymy offers the possibility of clear, diagrammatical representations of meaning. It would seem conceivable that the whole of the vocabulary could be hierarchically organized in this way. However, there are problems. Cruse (1975) raises some significant objections to the notion of unilateral implication on which hyponymy is based. For example, in the following pairs of sentences, the direction of implication seems to be reversed:

(5) a) It is scarlet.
     b) It is red.
     implication from *scarlet* to *red*

(6) a) It is not scarlet.
     b) It is not red.
     implication from *red* to *scarlet*

If (5)(a) is true than (5)(b) is true; if (6)(b) is true then (6)(a) is true. Similarly, Cruse shows how statements such as 'a rose is a kind of flower' cannot be used of some cases where implication of the 'if it is an x then it is a y' kind applies. The sentence 'he is a waiter' implies 'he is a man', but 'a waiter is a kind of man' is an odd statement. For this reason Cruse prefers to separate true taxonomies such as *rose/tulip/pansy*: *flower* from other kinds of inclusive relationship. These other, more lax types of hyponymy ('pseudo-hyponymy') are, however, very important in language. The implication rules do not necessarily apply to them but they are a basic way of creating taxonomy-like relationships within fields that correspond to social or psychological concepts. They enable us to classify such things as *watches*, *ties* and *cameras* as *presents* in particular contexts and make possible statements such as 'watches, ties, cameras and other presents' without the permanent implication that if it is a *watch* then it must be a *present*. Cruse concludes that hyponymy as a logical relationship (the true taxonomies) 'has no special status in ordinary language' and that we should not confuse logic with the kinds of conventional arrangements found in natural languages.

Lyons, too, recognizes problems in the notion of hyponymy (1977, pp. 293–301). He observes that the relationship between a hyponym and its superordinate is rather like that between a modified headword and an unmodified one: we can explain *tyrant* as *despotic or cruel leader*, or *stroll* as *walk casually and slowly*, and these paraphrases can be used as definitions of meaning. But this does not always work. To say 'a cow is a bovine mammal' is likely to lead us to use our conventional knowledge of *cow* to understand *bovine* or *mammal*, rather than vice versa. Language teachers sometimes use such paraphrases, but their successful use depends on assuming the learner's knowledge of the superordinate to understand the hyponym, or the other way round. Lyons also reminds us that much of what is said about hyponymy applies to nouns only. When dealing with verbs, explanations such as 'strolling is a kind of walking' sound odd, and *way* has to replace *kind*. Sometimes there seems to be no item of the same grammatical class to act as superordinate: *round/square/oblong* is one such set; we have to use the noun *shape* as a pseudo-superordinate, just as *taste* acts for *bitter/sweet/sour*. This is **quasi-hyponymy**.

One might also finally note concerning hyponymy that users' working knowledge of the vocabulary may not include all terms in the taxonomy. Most people know what *cows*, *sheep* and *monkeys* are, but few might know (or need to know) what *mammals* are. Only people connected with farming need to know what *bullocks* and *heifers* are;

for the rest of us, a few terms such as *cow*, *bull* and *calf* will do. Similarly, groups of native informants will disagree on just what is included in a word like *vehicle* (*bicycles? caravans? mopeds?*) yet will have little trouble in sensibly interpreting a sign which says 'vehicles may not be left here'. We have to conclude that sets are 'fuzzy'. Once again, though, provided problems are not brushed aside, hyponymy, like antonymy, offers us another way in which vocabulary may be organized for language teaching (McCarthy 1984 and McCarthy *et al.* 1985 include practical applications).

4 Marked and unmarked terms: some words work harder than others

Another feature of the distribution of words within fields is how some words can cover 'gaps' in the language (see Lehrer 1974, pp. 95ff.); for instance the word *dog* is broadly useful in that it can cover any *dog*, *bitch* or *puppy*. Similarly, especially for city dwellers, *cows* is often used for all sorts of cattle, just as *ducks* does service for all duck-like creatures, including drakes. For most inexpert speakers, one term, often the male (but not always) will cover as an unmarked term for male, female and young in the animal kingdom; *fox*, *lion*, *tiger*, *pig* and *goose* all work this way. While it may look as if a comparable hyponymic relationship exists for *dog* and *sheep* in (7):

(7)
         dog   sheep
  dog ——┴—— bitch   ram ——┴—— ewe

the difference can be illustrated by the acceptability of (8) but not of (9):

(8) Is that a dog or a bitch?
(9) *Is that a sheep or a ewe?

                                     (Lyons 1977, p. 308)

Lyons also reminds us, however, that while many of these animal words often have an unmarked or neutral term, even where sex-marked terms for both sexes exist, the opposite also occurs, and words which are morphologically (and even semantically) unmarked become 'culturally' marked for sex:

(10) My cousin's a nurse
      (expectation that my cousin is a woman)
     My cousin's a male nurse
      (explicitly countering the expectation)

*My cousin's a female nurse
(unlikely to occur)

(Lyons 1977, p. 310)

Other such words are *secretary, prostitute, receptionist, burglar, crook, plumber* and many more that carry cultural marking (see McCarthy *et al.* 1985, p. 140). What this kind of marking shows, yet again, is that words in lexical fields are not equal partners, and a true field-model would be multi-dimensional, showing not only the flat-plane relationships of antonymy and hyponymy, but the other dimensions of markedness and usefulness, both of which necessarily bring in social and psychological features of usage.

5 Synonymy: are some words duplicated elsewhere in the lexicon?

So far, we have skipped over synonymy as a lexical relation, giving it only the status of a special kind of hyponymy with bilateral implication (see p. 25). This may seem surprising, since most language teachers confess to using the notion constantly in teaching; learners and teachers use it as a convenient way of talking about words which are, for many or most practical purposes, interchangeable. But, theoretically, it is not a watertight relationship. In English, *begin/start, furthermore/moreover, nearly/almost* and *despite/in spite of* would seem to be candidates for synonymy. Most linguists agree, though, that true synonymy (i.e. 100% interchangeability) is very rare. Ullmann (1962, p. 141) confines true synonymy to technical nomenclatures where alternative terms sometimes exist for the same phenomenon (e.g. some medical terminology). But Ullmann does admit that although synonyms may arise round, say, a new invention, they are 'eventually sorted out'; one of the words will drop out of use. Ullmann quotes Collinson's (1939) set of nine principles for distinguishing apparent synonyms:

1 One term is more general than another: *refuse – reject.*
2 One term is more intense than another: *repudiate – refuse.*
3 One term is more emotive than another: *reject – decline.*
4 One term may imply approbation or censure where another is neutral: *thrifty – economical.*
5 One term is more professional than another: *decease – death.*
6 One term is more literary than another: *passing – death.*
7 One term is more colloquial than another: *turn down – refuse.*
8 One term is more local or dialectal than another: Scots *flesher – butcher.*
9 One of the synonyms belongs to child-talk: *daddy – father.*

(Ullmann 1962, pp. 142–3)

What these show is that words are usually different from one another, whether on one dimension or several. Collinson might have added two further features. One is that apparent synonyms do not always collocate identically: we would say 'Sorry I'm late, I couldn't start the car', rather than '*begin the car'; we would say 'Before the world began, only God existed', rather than '*the world started'. Secondly, syntactic restrictions may mean that the frame within which one term appears may not be available to its apparent synonym (at least not without disturbance of meaning): we can say 'His second novel was not nearly as good as his first'; *almost* would drastically change the meaning here.

However, words certainly are frequently interchangeable in particular contexts, and this 'local' synonymy is an important feature of language use which will be raised again in this volume (see McCarthy's paper in Chapter 4). In general, true synonymy is a non-starter in language, and even if words are learnt by learners at an early stage as 'largely synonymous', sooner or later the task will be to discriminate them for accuracy at the advanced level. Methods of illustrating differences between apparent synonyms include those already discussed and, additionally, the 'antonym test': *profound* may be synonymous with *deep* when their antonym is *superficial* (as in talking of emotions, thought, etc.), but *profound* and *deep* are not synonyms when *deep* and *shallow* are antonyms in the description of water depth. This is another way of saying that the same word form may appear in different lexical fields (the phenomenon called polysemy): *deep* occurs in one field where it is related to water, perhaps another in relation to holes, valleys, etc. and yet another concerning thought and emotions. Whichever way we approach synonyms, the whole question is only resolved by looking at context. One must conclude that even if lexical fields seem to have words of almost identical semantic properties, on closer examination they are almost always seen to be different, if only subtly, and that differences may, in some contexts, be crucial.

6 Are words atoms or molecules? Componential analysis

In mentioning the semantic properties of words, we are assuming that words 'have' or 'hold' meaning rather as a container 'holds' water. Dictionaries proceed largely on the basis of this belief, and Summers's paper in Chapter 4 implicitly defends the view. Sinclair and Renouf's paper, however, suggests that the belief is not borne out by data. The discussion of synonymy concluded that each word in the lexicon was unique and special. What is more, while field theory sees all words as being in a constant tension or dialectic with one another, and all meaning as internally defined by relationships such as antonymy and hyponymy, there is still an underlying assumption that it is possible to take any word alone and talk about its meaning in terms of a set of features extrapolated from the properties of the field. This is the basis of **componential analysis** (hereafter CA).

Katz and Fodor (1963) outlined the 'components of a semantic theory', one of which was the dictionary of a language. They believed that sentences have meaning composed in part by the sum of the 'bits' of meaning of the morphemes within them. A dictionary entry for a word should consist of two parts: 'a grammatical section which provides the part-of-speech classification of the lexical item, and a semantic section which represents each of the distinct senses of the lexical item in its occurrences as a given part of speech'. The characterization of sense is done in terms of **semantic markers** and **distinguishers**. Using these we can 'decompose the meaning of one sense of a lexical item into its atomic concepts'. Katz and Fodor's example is:

(11)

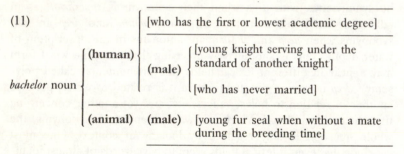

The markers (the basic properties) are in round brackets, the distinguishers (what uniquely separates the senses) in square brackets. With the markers we can denote that a word like *bachelor* has the attributes of **human** and **male**, when it means 'unmarried'. Features such as **human**, **male**, **animate**, etc. are primitive divisions of meaning, will be found (with their opposites) in the descriptions of hundreds of words in different lexical fields, and are held to be universals of human language.

Katz and Fodor's theory has not been without its critics; even shortly after it was published, Bolinger (1965) attacked the whole notion of 'atoms' of meaning which Katz and Fodor's decompositional theory presupposed. Much of language, Bolinger argued, works with 'wholes', which may consist of frozen, unanalysable strings of language (such as idioms, for example; see Cowie's paper in Chapter 4). Bolinger concludes that 'a semantic theory adjusted to natural language must somehow reconcile the way in which human beings operate with wholes and at the same time with forms – morphemes – that they have managed to decontextualise from the wholes'. Bolinger is sceptical of the value of decomposing words into bits or features of meaning in the way Katz and Fodor propose (see also Bolinger 1976).

Katz and Fodor's diagram for *bachelor* (example 11), is not the only way to represent the decomposition of the meaning of a word. CA has devised a notational language of its own, which Leech (1974, p. 94–5) calls 'signese'. Signese is neutral; it does not bear any cultural loading and tries to express primitive, universal features of meaning. A *man* can be described in signese as **+human +adult +male** by which we have distinguished *man* from *boy* (**−adult**), from *woman* (**+female** or **−male**) and from *horse* (**−human**). Thus CA can show that the phrase *male woman* is unacceptable in English (Leech 1967, p. 21). CA is economical. It can show how words in a field are related to one another using minimal notation; signese can indicate incompatibility, hyponymy, etc. Leech's example of *man/woman/boy/girl* is clear and simple and gives the necessary information for interpretation of the matrix:

(12)

	male	female
adult	man	woman
young	boy	girl
	human	

(Leech 1974, p. 89)

Leech is aware of the shortcomings and problems of CA, and he gives a good summary of the arguments for and against (1974, p. 117–9). Lyons, too, sees disadvantages in CA, not least that it has been applied to relatively few areas of few languages. Furthermore, it is possible to provide different analyses for the same words, and the pyschological reality of components for language users is questionable (1977, p. 333). We might agree with Lyons's criticisms; it is debatable whether CA would have much value as a language-teaching tool. It is too abstract and says too little about words. To talk about an 'adult male' would be for many speakers of English to talk about something different from a 'man'; signese captures nothing of the cultural values in words, their registerial characteristics or their creative potential. But then it does not claim to do so, nor is it designed for that purpose. Signese is thus restrictive in a way not dissimilar from the restrictiveness of Basic English (see Chapter 1). It is a highly abstract, theoretical construct which attempts to capture basic, stable, inherent characteristics of word meaning. It does not seem to have much psychological validity (see Cuyckens 1982) and for most language learners, their experience of words is probably like Sampson's, for whom words are not divisible and for whom 'the "semantic atoms" of our language are the same as the items listed in an ordinary dictionary' (1979).

7 Linguistic goings-on

It will be noticed that most of what has been said so far in this chapter concerns how words are related to one another on the vertical or *paradigmatic* dimension, that is to say, the relationship between any given word and what might have occurred in its place (e.g. a synonym, an opposite, a hyponym). This is only one way of looking at words; words also play a part in the left-to-right unfolding of language, the on-going nature of speech and text, the combinations that words enter into when discourse is produced: the *syntagmatic* dimension. Looking at lexis in this syntagmatic, on-going way has been the concern of a group of British linguists whose work in the 1960s and 1970s still inspires much of the vanguard lexicological work of the present years.

J. R. Firth is considered to be the father of this tendency; he was responsible for bringing the term **collocation** into prominence in lexical studies (although writers had used it occasionally in linguistic description since the 18th century). Firth believed in the separation of the study of lexis and semantics; these two, along with phonetics and grammar, played their roles in 'the complex of contextual relations' (1935/1957). Meaning operates at different levels; one type of meaning is collocation. Collocation is 'an abstraction at the syntagmatic level and is not directly concerned with the conceptual or idea approach to the meaning of words' (1951/1957). This is a departure from the 'container' or 'atomic' view of meaning; 'one of the meanings of *night* is its collocability with *dark*, and of *dark*, of course, collocation with *night*' (*ibid.*). Collocation, how words typically occur with one another, is therefore a central part of the meaning of a word in Firth's view. In a later paper (written round 1952–3 but not published until 1968) Firth notes that the verb *get* displays some thirty formal types of collocation which can be classified under ten general headings; these can be used as the basis for a dictionary entry for *get*. So what a word occurs *with* is just as important as any other kind of statement about its meaning. We recognized, as competent language users typical and untypical, or 'a-normal' (1951/1957), collocations. Studies of collocations can be used in the description of language change and in the stylistic analysis of literature. We would also argue that language teaching has much to gain from collocational studies.

Firth's notion of collocation was taken further by McIntosh (1961), who considered recurring *lexical* patterns to be just as important as regular *grammatical* ones. The lexical patterns he called **ranges**. An example of a range is the list of nouns which may be qualified by the adjective *molten* (*metal*, *iron*, *lava*, etc.). Our knowledge of this range and others such as the range of *postage* and *feather* enables us to dismiss 'the molten postage feather scored a weather' as unacceptable and uncontextualizable. According to McIntosh 'words have only a certain tolerance of compatability'. In selecting collocations we face a 'continual problem of decision'. However, when we meet a new or unusual collocation we do not immediately dismiss it; an important feature of language change is 'range-extension', how a word with a limited range might increase its range by attracting new partners, an example of which is *software* in computer parlance (an extension of the previously limited *hardware*). This may also be seen as an example of *correlativity* in lexis, where sense is defined in terms of such partnerships (Newmark 1967). One interesting point McIntosh raises, which never seems to have been fully researched, but which is probably relevant to how language learners process collocations and other multi-word units, is what happens when a native speaker encounters a new or unusual pair. If we find *constipated river*, or *transparent dog*, do we re-think our view of the meaning of the first item in the pair, the second, or the whole as a phrase? In the case of institutionalized compounds it is sometimes the whole phrase (e.g. speed-bumps on roads known as *sleeping policemen*), sometimes the first item (*slush-fund*) and sometimes the second (*user-friendly*). In raising these questions, McIntosh's paper makes the important point that there are matters in the on-going combinations of words that are independent of grammatical considerations and which require a lexical approach.

In 1966, in a volume of papers in memory of J. R. Firth, there appeared two seminal papers on the study of lexis, by M. A. K. Halliday and J. McH. Sinclair. Halliday's stated aim is a search for lexical patterns and a lexical theory 'complementary to, but not part of, grammatical theory'. Grammatical description leaves a lot unaccounted for, which can still be discussed *linguistically*, without the recourse to 'non-language' which semantics brings with it (Sinclair reiterates this). Halliday's central preoccupation is collocation and how collocation can be used to generate lexical *sets*. The word *set* has slipped into the discussion in earlier sections of this chapter as a working synonym for *lexical field*, but it is worth noting that in the Hallidayan view of lexis, *set* refers to a family of words whose membership is established purely on formal, statistical grounds, without recourse to meaning or to notions such as 'semantic fields'. If we take an example of the two words *strong* and *powerful*, we can describe their collocability in the following terms:

(13)

	argument	**tea**	**car**
strong	✓	✓	
powerful	✓		✓

This enables us to distinguish *strong* and *powerful* (which other methods of describing meaning might find difficult) as well as to illustrate their common ground. Their common occurrence with *argu(e/ment)* will qualify them for membership of the same set, yet each will also belong to a different set (one with *tea*, the other with *car*). The set therefore is a way of linking conceptually words which may not necessarily occur in the same text. Sinclair's illustration of this is the words *tome*, *paperback* and *cruelty*: the probability of any two of the three occurring together may be about equal; what brings *tome* and *paperback* together and casts *cruelty* to one side is the likelihood of their co-occurrence, when each occurs, with items like *edition* and *bookshop* and the far smaller likelihood that *cruelty* will co-occur with *edition* or *bookshop*.

Co-occurrence for Halliday and Sinclair does not just mean two words occurring as an adjacent pair in a fixed grammatical configuration. Co-occurrence has two important features. Firstly there may be a gap of several or many words between the two relevant items, or they may even occur over sentence boundaries, a point that Greenbaum (1970) resurrects in his example:

(14)   They *collect stamps*.
They *collect* foreign *stamps* only.
They *collect* many things, but chiefly *stamps*.
They *collect* many things, though their chief interest is in *collecting* coins. We, however, are only interested in *stamps*.

(Greenbaum 1970, p. 11)

A constant collocational relationship may be said to obtain between *collect* and *stamps*. Secondly, collocation seems to be independent of grammatical types. Thus we can have 'he *argued strongly*', 'the *strength* of his *argument*' and 'his *argument* was *strengthened*' (Halliday 1966), all of which again suggest a constant relationship between the two words. Sinclair (1966) is more explicit on this point: the primary consideration is co-occurrence, 'features such as preferred sequences, or habitual interventions, are secondary in structure'. It is interesting to compare Sinclair's stance now, twenty years later, with the benefit of the insights of the computer-based COBUILD project (see Sinclair and Renouf, Chapter 4), which represents a shift to an integrated approach. But in Sinclair's and Halliday's 1966 papers, co-occurrence is seen simply as a probabilistic matter of regular patterning between *lexical items* (i.e. that *strong*, *strength*, *strong* and *strengthened*, etc. are all word forms of the same *item*).

Neither Halliday nor Sinclair dismisses the importance of grammatical restrictions on co-occurrence; they simply wish to be able to make meaningful, separate statements about lexis. Halliday draws a clear parallel between the analysis of grammar and that of lexis: in grammar there are *structures* (syntagms) and *systems* (paradigms); in lexis there are *collocations* and *sets* respectively. But what is a set and how are sets established? Halliday offers an example: first take 2,000 occurrences of the word *sun*, then note what occurs with it for three words on either side of each occurrence. These 12,000 words (6 × 2,000) will likely show a high frequency of co-occurrence for *sun* with items like *bright/hot/shine/light/come out*, etc. Now do the same for 2,000 occurrences of *moon*; we will likely get *bright/full/new/light/shine*, etc. Cross compare these two lists and we see a provisional *set* of *bright/shine/light*, etc., which share a like privilege of co-occurrence with *sun* and *moon*. Continuing this process we can more and more sharply delineate the members of the set. Naturally, we will also get very frequent occurrences of words like *a* and *the* and *to*, but these will occur in virtually every set and can thus be 'filtered out' as non-set specific. These words are best described in terms of their grammatical properties; it is not that they have no lexical properties, 'there are no gaps where only grammar is to be found' (Sinclair), it is just that they collocate so 'weakly' that we cannot make useful statements about them in lexical terms, while we can make very precise prescriptions of their grammatical behaviour.

Once we have established the members of sets, we can also make statements about the thorny issues of polysemy and homonymy. Halliday suggests that two identical occurrences with different sets of collocates may be seen as homonyms, thus *bank*[1] collocates with *river/trees/steep*, etc., while *bank*[2] collocates with *money/deposit/cheque*, etc. Sinclair largely agrees, but leaves open the possibility of considering an occurrence as one polysemous item when the sets of collocates shade into one another. Also, identifying like sets of collocates may helpfully bring together non-cognates such as *town* and *urban* (Halliday). Perhaps even more usefully, occasions where collocability is 100 per cent predictable can be used to identify multi-word lexical items (*fro* never occurs without *to, kith* without *kin*, etc.) and the cline of predictability will continue through idioms, fixed phrases and 'restricted' collocations. Furthermore, strings such as idioms will display different sets of collocates to the collocates of their separate parts when these occur alone (Halliday's example is *nose, grindstone* and *nose to the grindstone*). Similarly, sets of collocates will enable us to distinguish between genuine lexical sets (such as *oak tree, beech tree* and *ash tree*) and lexical 'series' such as *inkstand, bandstand, hatstand* and *grandstand*, which will each have different collocates.

Halliday and Sinclair both recognize the size of the task of describing the lexicon of a language in terms of collocations and sets. Halliday reckons that a corpus of 20 million running words or $1\frac{1}{2}$–2,000 hours of conversation would be needed to get at any worth-while statistics. Sinclair recognized the size of the task, too, in 1966; he may be said to have grasped the nettle in his direction of the building of the COBUILD corpus at Birmingham University, which now more or less reaches Halliday's target of words.

The importance of a 'lexical level' in language teaching and learning has never been conclusively demonstrated, but the argument that collocation is a significant level of language choice is convincing, and can be seen to be active in Halliday's own attested examples, from foreign-learner texts, of deviant collocations: 'attired with culture', 'lying astray', 'merry admiration', 'funny art', 'light possibility', etc. These certainly seem to point to the need for an understanding of and a concern with collocation by teachers and learners alike. Finally, Sinclair stresses the relevance of collocation to the study of register: collocations such as 'vigorous depressions' and 'dull highlights' may seem odd out of context; placed in their register-specific habitats of meteorology and photography, they are normal. This, too, clearly has lessons for genre-analysis and the teaching and learning of languages for specific purposes.

The tradition established by Firth, McIntosh, Sinclair and Halliday was elaborated and modified by others. Greenbaum (1970) distinguishes between an 'item-orientated' approach to collocation (that is, one which works independently of syntax and semantics) and an integrated approach. The item-orientated approach has serious disadvantages; simply to state that *like* and *much* collocate ignores the acceptability of 15(a) and (c) but not of (b):

(15) a) I don't like him much.
      b) *I like him much.
      c) I like him very much.

(Greenbaum 1970, pp. 11–12)

Greenbaum concludes that an integrated approach, which concentrates on the collocative behaviour of a clearly delimited syntactic configuration (his choice is verb intensifiers), is likely to yield the best results. Mitchell (1971), in a thought-provoking article whose title is the inspiration for the somewhat cryptic heading of this section, makes points similar to Greenbaum's. Mitchell brings morphology and syntax back into the centre of lexical matters: *hard work* as a collocation seems to give a slightly different meaning to *hard* from its occurrence in the collocation *hard-working*, yet they differ only by the morpheme *-ing*. Similarly *on* and *going* collocate when we talk of the 'on-going' nature of language, but 'linguistic goings-on', while maintaining the collocation, suggests scandals or hanky-panky of a tantalizing order! Mitchell too, then, concludes that making grammatical generalizations (i.e. generalizations about typical inflexional or syntactic configurations) concerning collocations is the most valuable approach: the fact that there are many idioms in English of the type *verb + article + object* is significant (*kick the bucket, take the biscuit, see the light, hit the sack*, etc.). We would certainly agree with this view, combining as it does, lexical statements with useful grammatical generalizations, as an organizing principle for vocabulary learning and teaching. Elsewhere, Mitchell (1975) provides interesting illustrations of comparisons of collocability between English and French: English collocations such as 'the *height* of summer', 'the *depths* of winter', '*right/full/slap* in the stomach' are all covered by the single collocational frame *en plein* . . . (*été/hiver/ventre*) in French. Conversely, the English frame *heavy* . . . (*breathing/rain/drinker*, etc.) takes a variety of different forms in French. More work is needed on this aspect of usage from language to language.

To conclude this chapter, we might reflect that, while we claim in Chapter 1 that vocabulary is a neglected area of applied linguistics, there is no shortage of sources in descriptive linguistics for powerful models of lexical structure. We have seen how semanticists have elaborated the paradigmatic aspects of lexis in field theory, sense-relations and componential analysis, and how the Firthian tradition in Britain has vigorously pursued both the independent aspects of lexical structure and the integration of lexis and grammar. Language practitioners need not shy away from lexis as a boundless chaos; organizational principles are available and simply wait to be more fully exploited. Nonetheless, we have also argued for caution and against over-enthusiastic incorporation of semantic principles in vocabulary teaching without a full awareness of their complexity and limitations. Meanwhile, research does continue, and promises further clarification of the nature and functioning of the lexicon which applied linguistics will undoubtedly benefit from.

3 Developments in the teaching of vocabulary

Introduction

The old proverb 'what is new is not true and what is true is not new' is particularly relevant to the history of vocabulary teaching. Linguists, philosophers and pedagogues have been interested in the problems raised by words and the understanding of them for centuries. The philosopher, John Locke, writing in 1690 on 'Remedies of the Imperfection and Abuse of Words', urged that concrete words were best described by pictures ('little draughts and prints') rather than by paraphrase or definition (Locke 1690/1975, pp. 522–3), which might be seen as a precursor of modern learners' dictionaries or many present-day teaching materials. The Frenchman François Gouin, frustrated by his earlier failure to learn German vocabulary, in 1880 offered to the world a new system for the learning of vocabulary, that consisted of arranging words into sets corresponding to typical sequences of actions and processes, which strikes the reader as uncannily similar to present-day schema theory (Gouin 1880/1892). Many of us will remember our own school days and how the learning of vocabulary featured large in grammar-translation textbooks for learning foreign languages. In short, linguists and language-practitioners must beware of reinventing the wheel. Much of what is said nowadays on the teaching and learning of vocabulary has been around for a very long time; the history and development of vocabulary teaching is, therefore, not so much one of old insights leading to new; it is more a series of dominating ideologies or fashions that have succeeded one another and which sometimes come full circle. This is not to say there has been no progress; much refinement has taken place over the years and approaches to the teaching of vocabulary have drawn on advances in descriptive linguistics, psycholinguistics and, recently, computational linguistics. It is thus possible to see two principal strands emerging over the last forty years or so: the debates that have taken vocabulary in and out of fashion as an aspect of language teaching, and the developments that have nudged forward the methods, techniques and materials of vocabulary teaching. This chapter will trace the debates and developments, firstly in relation to vocabulary teaching in general, and secondly with regard to the developments in lexicography that have led to the creation of learners' dictionaries, and which are pushing the study of lexis into new territory.

1 Structural approaches

The fascinating work of the Vocabulary Control Movement and Ogden's *Basic English* in the 1930s has already been described in Chapter 1. Here we shall begin with the influential tendency, emanating from American linguistics, to push vocabulary into the background and to relegate its importance to a secondary level in the teaching of foreign languages. This view largely dominated the 1940s, 1950s and 1960s. It is epitomized in its early days by Fries's *Teaching and Learning English as a Foreign Language* (1945). Fries attributes language learners' concern with vocabulary to their naïve memories of their first language-learning experience; the fact is, says Fries, that in L1 acquisition the acquisition of syntax was so basic and fundamental that adults have forgotten the experience. The problem of learning a new language, Fries believed, was not, first and foremost, learning its vocabulary, but mastering its sound system and its grammatical structure; all the learner needs at first is enough basic vocabulary to practise the syntactic structures. In language there are four different kinds of words: function words, substitute words, words of negative/affirmative distribution and content words. The first three of these must be thoroughly mastered, with only a small number of content words needed (1945, p. 39). This small vocabulary should be taken from the immediate environment. After this initial, crucial stage of structural teaching, then, and only then, could the learner move on to the next three stages: the learning of vocabulary for *production*, the expansion of vocabulary for recognition and finally the learning of vocabulary for special areas of experience.

Such was Fries's view; it is one that held sway for a long period and can be seen to be alive even in recent coursebooks (see McCarthy 1984 for examples). Fries's views have to be seen against the background of American structural linguistics, with its emphasis on phonology and syntactic patterning. Parallel to this was a concern with contrastive analysis of languages: central to the problem of learning a new vocabulary was how much it resembled or differed from the learner's L1 (e.g. Lado 1955). Structuralism and contrastive analysis, along with behavioural psychology, gave rise to the audio-lingual method: echoing Fries's dicta, it is against the teaching of too much vocabulary and for the mastery of structure. There are several reasons for this view:

1. it is difficult to predict what vocabulary learners will need;
2. over-concern with vocabulary gives learners the impression that language learning is just the accumulation of words;
3. hesitancy of recall can result from excessive vocabulary teaching;
4. first-language acquisition proceeds with a small vocabulary until structural patterns are mastered (Rivers 1968, pp. 208–10; see also Rivers 1972/1983, p. 57).

There is no doubt at all of the overriding influence of this view on both sides of the Atlantic for many years. The shift to transformational linguistics in the 1960s under Chomsky's banner only served to reinforce the idea that lexis was somewhat peripheral, an irritating irregularity in an otherwise ordered grammar. In Britain, with its Firthian tradition, there was more attention paid to vocabulary, but Halliday *et al.*'s *The Linguistic Sciences and Language Teaching* (1964) simply continued the tradition of vocabulary control and devoted its attention mainly to the selection of vocabulary for teaching (frequency and availability) and did not tackle the issue of learners and their needs.

In summary, it can be said that the period 1945–1970 was a limbo for vocabulary as an aspect of language teaching in its own right, and that the arguments for teaching heavy doses of syntax, against the background of American linguistics, went largely unchallenged. Vocabulary was seen mainly as a problem of grading and selection, balanced by concerns of contrastive analysis and error prediction for target groups of learners. An article such as Higa (1965) is a notable exception (dealing as it does with the psycholinguistic concept of difficulty in vocabulary learning) in an otherwise unredeemed neglect.

2 Throwing down the gauntlet

It is in the 1970s that we begin to hear rumblings of discontent from both sides of the Atlantic against the prevailing view, though Bright and McGregor (1970, pp. 16–17) still seem keen not to raise vocabulary to a prominent level in teaching, despite devoting a number of pages to it. Among the first was Wilkins (1972), and this is perhaps not surprising given his later concern with the centrality of meaning in the notional/functional syllabus. Wilkins lamented the neglect of vocabulary in the audio-lingual years. The structuralist view is all very well if there is no pressing need to learn a language quickly and with palpable returns. While it is indeed true that to learn nothing but words and little or no structure would be useless to the learner, useless too would be to learn all the structure and no vocabulary: 'Without grammar very little can be conveyed, without vocabulary *nothing* can be conveyed' (1972, p. 111). However, Wilkins plays safe and concludes that delaying vocabulary expansion in courses with *long-term* aims can do no harm, and that in most situations the usual pattern of structure first, vocabulary later, is the wisest counsel (1972, p. 133). What Wilkins's work *is* significant for is his desire to bring to vocabulary teaching the insights of lexical semantics, which Chapter 2 of this book has dwelt upon at length, and which have become a major feeding ground for vocabulary practitioners in the 1970s and 1980s. Lexical semantics, says Wilkins, helps us to understand the process of translation, for one thing. Secondly, it enables us to organize the lexicon, which is necessary since words are not learnable as isolates. Thirdly, the study of sense-relations enables us to bring out the full meanings of words, and this is related to the complexity of the acquisition of meaning, so often travestied in the statement that someone has 'learnt' a word at a very early stage (1972, pp. 130–2). Wilkins's work therefore combines an engagement with the debate on the place of vocabulary with the belief that vocabulary teaching and learning can advance through the incorporation of insights from semantics.

Around the same time, Twaddell (1972 and 1973) was arguing strongly for the massive expansion of learners' vocabularies at intermediate level. Twaddell saw a fallacy in the view that vocabulary teaching was merely a question of selection of items on a criterion such as frequency. It is impossible to teach learners all the words they need to know, and so it is important to teach them guessing strategies that will enable them to tackle unknown words and lose their reliance on dictionaries (see also Bright and McGregor 1970, pp. 30–2). This is the beginning of viewing vocabulary learning as a language *skill*, of shifting the responsibility to the learner. The guessing skill is seen as central to reading comprehension by Nation and Coady in Chapter 4 of this book, and this reflects a growing move away from seeing vocabulary learning in terms of word lists and how to absorb them, a trend in which Twaddell's was an early voice. The mid 1970s saw further concern with the relationship between vocabulary and the learning task. It was generally accepted that reading (extensively) played an important part in vocabulary expansion (e.g. Connolly 1973); Donley (1974), however, argued that extensive reading was not enough. Nor did the addition of intensive reading passages for vocabulary expansion solve the problem either: lexis in small, intensive doses is restrictive. Donley held that the learner must be encouraged to confront the internal structure of the lexicon, something that structuralism, but not transformational linguistics or contrastive analysis, could contribute to. The structure of the lexicon should be turned to teachers' and learners' advantages: paradigmatic associations not only of meaning but of sound too (e.g. *wine/whine*) should be exploited; words should be learnt in 'context' and in 'contrast'.

The challenge to reinstate vocabulary teaching was issued again by Lord (1974). Vocabulary should no longer be the 'Cinderella' of language teaching; not only had vocabulary been an outcast at the hands of transformationalists but it had too long been seen in terms of a 'static' lexicon. Lord takes Vygotsky's view that the relationship between thought and words is a *dynamic* one: it is a *process*, not a *thing*. If we cling to the view that words are *items* to be acquired in certain quantities at certain rates, vocabulary teaching will not progress; we need to study first-language acquisition to understand the processes of second-language lexical acquisition. First-language acquisition shows that vocabulary expansion proceeds against a background of fuzziness of reference, the development of conceptual notions for words, and instability of meaning. Lord's arguments represent a further shift from the 'vocabulary-control' approach to one more concerned with the acquisition of meaning.

Around this time too, more articles were appearing in which engagement with the semantic structure of the lexicon was seen as a central part of the challenge of reviving vocabulary teaching. Brown (1974) brought collocation to the forefront, and offered it as a way of sensitizing learners to contextual redundancy; she also gave practical useable exercises. Anthony (1975), in a theoretical article on structural clustering in the lexicon, discussed the implications of such lexical theory for language pedagogy, and Nilsen (1976) followed with a strong view of the role of semantics in vocabulary teaching. For Nilsen, the development of the 'paradigmatic' approach (examining vocabulary out of context and in contrastive systems) is 'a prerequisite to the syntagmatic approach' (vocabulary in context). Nilsen proposed organizational principles for ordering vocabulary to be taught (e.g. hierarchies, matrices, series, cycles, etc.).

By the mid 1970s, then, we have a picture of a growing concern with vocabulary teaching and learning which, on the one hand, is concerned to redeem what had become a neglected area and, on the other hand, to incorporate the insights of lexical semantics. What is more, we have the beginnings of the view of vocabulary as a skill in which the learner is actively involved, and a concern with what and how the learner might learn. The question of selection did not go away (see Richards 1974) nor is it ever likely to; it was simply supplemented by other preoccupations.

3 Bring on the learner

The move away from seeing vocabulary as lists of items to be learnt and towards the learner raises the question of precisely what it means to 'learn' vocabulary. Richards (1976) tries to tackle this issue, considering 'some of the knowledge that is assumed by lexical competence'. It is necessary to examine the question as a basis for formulating objectives in vocabulary teaching and for the assessment of teaching techniques. Richards brings the characterization of lexical competence down to eight broad assumptions:

1. Native speakers continue to expand their vocabulary in adulthood. Little is known about the average language-user's vocabulary but anything from 20,000–100,000 words could be within a person's receptive vocabulary.
2. Knowing a word means knowing the degree of probability of encountering it and the sorts of words most likely to be found associated with it (frequency and collocability).
3. Knowing a word means knowing its limitations of use according to function and situation (temporal, social, geographical; field, mode, etc.).
4. Knowing a word means knowing its syntactic behaviour (e.g. transitivity patterns, cases).
5. Knowing a word means knowing its underlying forms and derivations.
6. Knowing a word means knowing its place in a network of associations with other words in the language.
7. Knowing a word means knowing its semantic value (its composition).
8. Knowing a word means knowing its different meanings (polysemy).

Richards then refers to published materials which attempt to come to grips with these eight assumptions. We should, Richards concludes, prepare materials beginning with a 'rich concept of vocabulary', and goals must be related to techniques. Richards's article is important because it tries to relate different ways of teaching and practising diverse aspects of vocabulary to the separate features of learner lexical competence, and acknowledges the complex nature of the vocabulary teaching/learning processes.

4 Consolidation: the lexicon meets the learner

The last years of the 1970s saw a combined interest in further studies of the lexicon itself, and a more detailed look at the various needs of learners. It must be remembered that, in applied linguistics in general, these years were abuzz with mottos such as *notional/functional*, *communicative* and *specific purposes*, heralding a new wave of course-books and other materials. Vocabulary teaching did not escape this frenzy, even if it felt the breeze only indirectly. Interest in the lexicon became more and more attuned to learners' needs: Martin (1976), reporting on materials developed at Stanford University in the first half of the 1970s, isolated a common-core academic vocabulary for college students' needs (see also Cowan 1974) and hints at a discourse approach with headings such as 'The Research Process', 'The Vocabulary of Analysis' and 'The Vocabulary of Evaluation'. Identifying *useful* generalizable vocabulary as a strategic resource for target groups of learners in this way is a trend that has continued into the 1980s (see below).

In 1978, Judd published an article that reasserted the call to give vocabulary the status of a skill in its own right; not only should it not be seen as subservient to syntax, but it should not be seen as an appendage to reading and listening comprehension either. Judd is in favour of massive vocabulary instruction as early as possible, and stresses the importance of presenting vocabulary 'in a natural linguistic context'; words taught in isolation are generally not retained; the full meaning of words (which includes their *sociolinguistic* contexts) can only come from encountering them in a rich linguistic environment. Crucially, words should be meaningful *to the learner*; words should be reviewed and revised constantly, for without this the learner cannot come to know their polysemic and registerial characteristics. The learner must be allowed to be vague about meaning at first; precision will come later (Judd 1978). These remarks of Judd's combine the desire to give vocabulary a proper status and the need to give the learner the breadth of resource that the lexicon can offer. Meaningfulness and communicativeness are the two poles of receptive and productive language use in the communicative ideology, and these aspirations began more and more to influence applied vocabulary studies. The lexicon was beginning to be seen as a resource for communication: as important as what it *was* (its structures and networks) was what can be *done* with it. This led to an interest in lexical strategies. Blum and Levenston (1978a and b) looked at lexical simplification and saw universal strategies at work. Just as simplified readers alter original stories by using superordinates, approximations, synonyms, circumlocutions and paraphrases, so do native speakers when they talk to non-natives they sense have difficulty in comprehending; so too do language learners, who also use avoidance strategies (avoiding morphological difficulties, for example) and who overgeneralize use (e.g. simplistic use of antonyms). Bialystok and Fröhlich (1980) also studied learner strategies during moments of lexical difficulty. Brown (1979), citing examples of native-speaker lexical strategies, concluded that students 'must learn how to be imprecise', to learn to make use of general words, to develop the skill of 'talking around a word'. Brown suggests techniques for motivating learners to achieve effective communication although using general and imprecise lexis. On the receptive side, the learner must use guessing and inferring strategies (see Alderson and Alvarez 1979). Towards the end of the 1970s, too, in the USA, the development of the 'Natural Approach' stressed the motivational benefits of an early stage of receptive vocabulary growth encouraged by 'comprehensible input' from the teacher. This meant simplification on the teacher's part: the use of high frequency vocabulary, less slang, few idioms, a high incidence of 'names' instead of proforms (Terrell 1982).

By the end of the 1970s, vocabulary teaching was coming of age. Its place within language teaching had been reasserted, insights from lexical semantics had been brought to bear in the incorporation of notions such as sense-relations and collocation into teaching materials (e.g. Cowie 1978), the learner had been brought centre stage, and the lexicon was beginning to be seen as a resource for the needs of the learner and for strategic use in the gaining of communicative objectives.

5 The present and the future

That vocabulary teaching has come of age in the last decade is attested by the publication of several works entirely devoted to the subject. First of these, reflecting a continuous interest on its part in matters lexical, was the publication by the Regional English Language

Centre (RELC) in Singapore of a collection of papers under the title
Guidelines for Vocabulary Teaching in 1980. The collection commences
with a paper by Dorothy Brown (pp. 1–17), in which she outlines
'eight Cs and a G' of vocabulary teaching. These are: (1) collocation,
(2) clines (e.g. scales such as *cold/warm/hot* expressed diagrammatically), (3) clusters (something akin to the Hallidayan notion of
sets – see Chapter 2), (4) cloze procedures, which reinforce clusters
and collocations, (5) context (using features within the text such as
definition, word analysis, inference), (6) consultation (using dictionaries and thesauri), (7) cards: students should keep a card index of
new vocabulary, (8) creativity: students should be given free rein to
describe pictures, etc. and (9) guessing: students should learn this
skill. In Brown's heterogenous list we see the diverse preoccupations
that have accumulated in the 1970s fused into a set of principles for
vocabulary teaching. Also in the *Guidelines* volume we find Madden
(pp. 111–17) taking the question of guessing further and making a
distinction between important vocabulary that should be pre-taught
because it cannot be guessed from the text, vocabulary which *can* be
guessed in context, and vocabulary which can be ignored and studied
after using the text. The British Council Teachers' contribution to
the volume (pp. 80–94) makes some similar points, as does Chandra-
segaran (pp. 61–8), who gives examples of inference processes, and
Nation (pp. 18–23), who presents a step-by-step guessing strategy
(see also Chapter 4). Sarawit's contribution to the collection
(pp. 73–5) shows the influence of role-play and group-work methodologies on vocabulary teaching.

   Equally important as evidence of coming of age is Meara's (1980)
survey of vocabulary acquisition (many of the issues of which have
been discussed in the latter part of Chapter 1) and Nation's (1982)
survey of research into vocabulary learning, which raises questions
concerning the usefulness of word-list learning and learning from
context. 1983 then saw the culmination of Meara's bibliographic work
in the CILT publication of his comprehensive annotated bibliography
of vocabulary teaching, an indispensable source for all interested
language practitioners. 1982 and 1983 saw three other significant
publications: Wallace (1982), Allen (1983) and Rivers (1983).
Wallace asserts that 'if we have the vocabulary we need it is usually
possible to communicate, after a fashion' (p. 9). He then proceeds to
analyse the symptoms of bad vocabulary teaching and learning: an
inability to retrieve taught vocabulary, inappropriate use of vocabulary, using the wrong level of formality, using vocabulary unidiomati-
cally, and so on (pp. 9–13). The task, says Wallace, is to know a

word so that it may be recognized, recalled at will, related to an object or a concept, correctly used, pronounced and spelt, appropriately collocated, used at the right level of formality and with awareness of its connotations and associations (p. 27). Overall Wallace emphasizes as a remedy meaningful presentation of vocabulary in situations and contexts, the encouragement of inferencing, the use of realia, pictures and mime in presentation, the focusing of attention by the teacher and the activation of the learner's background knowledge (pp. 28–46). Once again the many directions taken by vocabulary studies are brought together in a set of general principles. Wallace furthermore encourages learners to find meaningfulness for themselves in words and in relationships between words they encounter in texts (p. 50). This view corresponds to the trend towards individualization and self-management in language learning. Allen (1983) echoes this development, talking of the importance of 'creating a sense of need for a word' (p. 9) (note the shift to the active engagement of the learner) and the importance of going from meaning to words (p. 13), a century-old echo of Gouin's self-discovery (1880/1892, pp. x and 44). Allen also stresses the introduction of a social and cultural dimension to vocabulary teaching: the learner needs to know that, in Britain, for instance, the *kitchen* is a pleasant, family room, not a place for servants, etc. (p. 75). Rivers (1983) illustrates admirably how the tide has rolled back to the shore again; now we find her advocating vocabulary with all her might, recognizing the place of the learner and the discrepancy between frequency lists and individuals' needs; learners 'must eventually develop their own vocabularies' (p. 118). Rivers sees Halliday's idea of 'meaning potential' as all-important: the task of vocabulary teaching is to give learners the means to mean, to help learners to 'analyse their own meanings, in relation to the linguistic and cultural ideas of their native background, as they select from the options the new language provides' (p. 124). Retention of vocabulary is directly related to purposes and goals: 'students have very personal semantic networks into which they process what they find to be useful. Consequently, vocabulary cannot be taught' (p. 127). By this last remark Rivers means that vocabulary can be presented and explained but ultimately it is the individual who learns: 'students must learn how to learn vocabulary' (p. 130) and find their own ways of expanding and organizing their word stores.

Wallace, Allen and Rivers hint at developments that will undoubtedly fuel approaches to vocabulary expansion and the spate of lexically-oriented materials which are due to follow in the wake of the revived interest of the 1970s and early 1980s. Gairns and Redman

(1986) a recent, excellent, handbook for the teaching of vocabulary, lays great emphasis on learner engagement, on the need for new words coming from students themselves, and suggests a variety of practical techniques for achieving this self-motivation (e.g. peer-teaching, group-work with 'interest groups', students attempting their own categorizations of randomly collected items in word lists, etc.) All in all, the recent trend, and the one likely to continue, has been to assist the learner to learn, to engage the learner with the task of making sense of the apparent chaos of the lexicon, and to personalize vocabulary expansion according to needs, purposes and goals.

Parallel with these significant pedagogical trends in the last half-dozen years have gone further advances in the applications of lexical semantics and lexicology in general to language teaching. Interest in the syntagmatic aspects of the lexicon has led Nattinger (1980 and Chapter 4) to propose that vocabulary teaching should shift its ground from words alone to a variety of multi-word lexical phenomena that are a central part of the fabric of everyday communication, and which are neglected since they seem to fit into neither traditional notions of grammar nor of vocabulary. Yorio (1980) also takes up the question of these conventionalized syntagms. Aisenstadt (1981) describes types of restricted collocations that occur in English and which are also a significant part of the lexicon. These can be grouped for teaching purposes under word-class headings (e.g. *verb + noun*, *verb + adverb*, etc.). Similarly, research in the Netherlands into vocabulary learning has recently emphasized the importance of collocations and 'conventional syntagms' (see Schouten-van Parreren 1985).

Paradigmatic aspects of lexis have also found direct applications. Channell (1981) confronts the problem of what to do after a basic vocabulary has been mastered, and suggests ways of incorporating semantic insights from field theory and componential analysis (see Chapter 2). Fields and components can be adapted into grids and scales both to illustrate the semantic *features* of items and their collocability. What the learner needs to know about a word is how it relates to words of similar meaning and which other words it can be used with, which correspond to the two basic axes (the paradigmatic and syntagmatic) upon which lexicological investigation proceeds. Channell's work bore fruit in the two volumes of Rudzka *et al.*'s *The Words You Need* (1981 and 1985), where we find grids and matrices used to present word relations. This one illustrates the overlapping but distinct collocability of *distant* and *remote*:

distant	remote	
+		view of the tower
+		cousin of ours
+		future
+	+	past
	+	possibility
	+	little town

(Rudzka *et al.* 1981, p. 30)

Ramsey (1981) also offers an interesting diagrammatic representation of lexical relations in the form of the 'lexigram' for presenting associated terms. Continued interest in paradigmatic relations can be seen in Martin (1984), where the problem of synonyms is addressed, and in Crow and Quigley (1985), where a semantic-field approach to vocabulary teaching is claimed to be not only effective but popular with learners, too.

Interest continues, also, in the investigation of a strategic and generalizable vocabulary, for general and for academic purposes. Such work includes Carter's on core vocabulary (see Chapter 4) and research within ESP by Hutchinson and Waters (1981). Hutchinson and Waters challenge the assumption that technical terminology is the most useful input material for students of ESP: what such students require is 'not a corpus of technical language but the ability to mobilize the resources of general English in the solving of technical problems'. The 'procedural' or more general vocabulary helps the learner to get at the specific, technical vocabulary. Widdowson (1983, pp. 92–4) further investigates the nature of this general or procedural vocabulary that structures and supports the specific, field-related vocabularies in texts: procedural vocabulary is not 'schematically bound'; it is independent of any particular schema or specific mental construct of an event or process; it is the vocabulary of definition, of paraphrase. A verb such as *do* compared with the verb *dote* illustrates the argument: *do* can be used to structure virtually any chain of events or processes, *dote* is highly schema-specific. The general, procedural vocabulary is a strategic resource. Current research at the University of Birmingham into vocabulary use, by Robinson, is leading to conclusions that the type of lexical competence aimed at in vocabulary teaching which uses matrices and grids (e.g. Rudzka *et al.*, 1981 and 1985) gives only a 'knowledge base' which needs to be supplemented by a procedural vocabulary as 'a strategic resource for extending this "meaning bank" to suit unlikely or unforseen occasions of use' (Robinson 1986). Robinson sees grids and matrices as 'the product of analysis, while the user's procedural orientation to establishing word meaning is a continuing process' (*ibid*).

Concern with general or procedural and 'sub-technical' vocabularies is an aspect of a wider, growing interest in the way some words contribute to structuring others in the creation of text and discourse. This research is commented on in detail in Chapter 5; it is undoubtedly a research direction which will filter through to vocabulary materials, and which promises to enrich the field of vocabulary teaching in general (see McCarthy 1984).

The other main research impetus which holds great promise is that of computers, not only the massive corpus-assembly of a project such as the Collins/Birmingham University COBUILD enterprise (see below, this chapter), but more modest, personal-computer-based activities too. COBUILD is certainly producing data and results that will influence dictionary design and teaching materials (see Sinclair and Renouf's paper in Chapter 4). Smaller-scale research has also shown the advantages of computerized data: McKay (1980a and b) shows how differing characteristic patterns of use of verbs can be revealed as a way of helping learners distinguish items in the same field; Johns at the University of Birmingham has demonstrated how even modest micro-computers can produce vocabulary concordances which engage learners actively in problem-solving activities related to meaning and usage of items (see Johns 1986). Such work is largely in its infancy and will doubtless progress in the years to come, alongside anticipated advances in machinery and programming.

To conclude, it may be said that vocabulary teaching and learning, despite a few loops and U-turns, has come a long way since François Gouin bemoaned his inability to learn German words. Although it suffered neglect for a long time, vocabulary pedagogy has benefited in the last fifteen years or so from theoretical advances in the linguistic study of the lexicon, from psycholinguistic investigations into the mental lexicon (see Chapter 1), from the communicative trend in teaching, which has brought the learner into focus, and from developments in computers. What is perhaps missing in all this is more knowledge about what happens in classrooms when vocabulary crops up, especially given the recent interest in the classroom as a learning environment and interaction in the classroom in language teaching in general. Brutten (1981) has offered positive evidence of teachers' ability to predict vocabulary difficulties and how classroom 'glossing' can help, and Taylor (1986) offers some evidence for the way teachers can assist (or hinder) vocabulary learning in interaction with learners, but much more research is needed. Such research will probably be done sooner or later, and when it is it will further enrich vocabulary teaching and learning.

The other principal area which impinges upon the success or otherwise that learners have in tackling foreign vocabulary is their use of, and the effectiveness of, dictionaries. It is, therefore, to lexicography and learners' dictionaries that the rest of this chapter is devoted.

6 Lexicography and language learning: users and uses

Dictionaries have a good image. Almost every learner or user of English as a second or foreign language owns one; and it is probably one of the few books which are retained after following a language course. The last fifteen years have seen rapid developments in lexicography directed at improving the image of dictionaries within the language teaching profession. And this is reflected in recent academic work; see papers in Cowie (1981), and Ilson (ed.) (1985). Two dictionaries, in particular, the *Oxford Advanced Learners Dictionary of Current English* (*OALDCE*) (1974) and, more recently, the *Longman Dictionary of Contemporary English* (*LDOCE*) (1978/1987), have contributed considerably to the development and design of dictionaries for non-native learners of English. Their appearance and widespread adoption serves to highlight the differences which exist between *bilingual* and *monolingual* dictionaries, and between dictionaries for the native speaker and for the second or foreign-language learner.

Bilingual dictionaries are more generally employed in the initial stages of learning a language. As proficiency develops, greater use is made of a monolingual dictionary; in fact, Baxter (1980) concludes that prolonged dependency on bilingual dictionaries probably tends to retard the development of second-language proficiency, even though such dictionaries are usually retained for use when definitions given in a monolingual dictionary are insufficiently understood. Major distinctions between monolingual dictionaries for native and for non-native speakers lie in the kinds of information supplied. For the non-native user, a main aim is to supply encoding information which will allow for productive *use* of the language. In particular, guidance is given concerning the *syntactic behaviour* of individual items. For example, the monolingual *Concise Oxford Dictionary* (*COD*), gives one piece of grammatical information about the noun *luck* (i.e. luck n.) – whereas the *OALDCE* marks it as an uncountable noun (u) thus preventing the production by learners of:

It was a bad luck.

Such mistakes could be produced because the *COD* is not designed to provide encoding information. Learners' monolingual dictionaries also often provide more detailed guidance both on matters of syntax (see particularly the coding of verb 'patterns' in *OALDCE* originating in Hornby 1948), and pronunciation (see Gimson 1981), and on cultural and stylistic restrictions (see Hartman 1981a, 1981b, 1983; and Carter 1983).

Another marked distinction is in the different *definitions* of words which are supplied. Particularly notable here is the use of either restricted defining vocabularies or, at least, a concerted effort to write clear and unambiguous definitions. In the case of *LDOCE* the use of a defining vocabulary is explained by Procter (1978) as follows:

All the definitions and examples in the dictionary are written in a controlled vocabulary of approximately 2,000 words ... particular reference having been made to *A General Service List of English Words* (1953) by Michael West ... This very important feature marks this dictionary out from any but the smallest of its predecessors as a tool for the learner and student of language ... the result of using the vocabulary is the fulfilment of one of the most basic lexicographic principles – that is, that the definitions are always written using more simple terms than the words they describe, something that cannot be achieved without a definite policy of this kind.

(Procter 1978, pp. viii–ix)

Defining or restricted vocabularies are not without problems, however. First, even though the words used in *LDOCE* are supplied in a list at the back of the dictionary, the learner may first have to learn a number of them; there is no guarantee that they will be known by the learner. And not all the words are particularly common. For example, the Longman defining vocabulary contains the following items; *account*, *bacteria*, *arch*, *bitter*, *conscience*, *determine*, *empire*, *grey*, *character*. Second, defining vocabularies can achieve simplicity at the expense of accuracy. When more words are needed, the result can also sometimes be clumsy or unnaturally circumlocutory. Compare the *LDOCE* definition of *totalitarian* with that in *OALDCE* which seeks to avoid difficult words, but which is not restricted by a list of defining words.

(1) ... of, being, or related to a political system in which a single person or political party controls all thought and action and does not allow opposition parties to exist: a *totalitarian government*
(*LDOCE 1978*)

(2) ... of a system in which only one political party and no rival loyalties are permitted: *a totalitarian state*, e.g. Germany under Hitler
(*OALDCE 1974*)

Third, as Michael West has himself acknowledged (West 1935, p. 12) defining vocabularies work rather better in the explanation of concrete rather than abstract terms. Learners themselves, however, report that they *prefer* a restricted vocabulary (see research by MacFarquhar and Richards 1983) although the relationship between the perceived intelligibility of a definition and the actual learning of lexical items has yet to be investigated. Searching examinations, too, of definitions in learner dictionaries reveal that advantages clearly outweigh disadvantages, (see Jain 1979, 1981; Bauer 1980). For discussion of the use of synonyms in definitions and of the problematic distinction in learner dictionaries between whether entries should *define* or *explain*, see Hanks (1979).

In spite of many recent innovations and continuing development in foreign and second-language lexicography, it is important not to lose sight of what learners use dictionaries for. In this regard studies reveal that users are predominantly conservative in attitude and practice, and that there can be potentially dangerous gaps between the sophistication of some features of dictionary design and the user's often rudimentary reference skills. Bejoint (1979, 1981) reports that students tend to use EFL dictionaries rather as they would general monolingual dictionaries, that is, for looking for meanings and synonyms (especially low frequency specialist terms), for checking spellings and for decoding activities in the written medium such as translation and reading. The image of the dictionary as a source of encyclopedic and factual information is one which dies hard. (See also Quirk 1973.)

7 Fixed expressions and the dictionary

In the design of a monolingual EFL dictionary it is clear that a balance must be preserved between a portrait of the vocabulary of the language and an adequate description of the use of words in the productive mode. Obviously, the expectations of learners that they will be supplied with explanations of the rarer senses of words has to be met; at the same time too much attention to the complex syntactic relations which 'core', high-frequency items often enter can be impractical. In this respect the nature of the syntactic information supplied by the lexicographer will be crucial.

For example, in the case of a relatively frequent item such as the verb *spread*, it is not adequate for the EFL learner to be told, as occurs in the general monolingual *Oxford English Dictionary* (*OED*), that the verb is normally transitive and that it takes a range of collocating objects, including [rumours, fears, reports, etc.]. Learners of English need to have detailed information about the range of possible colligations contracted by this verb. For example, information about the prepositions taken by the verb are crucial. For example:

> He spread jam *on* the bread/the bread *with* jam.
> She spread rumours *about* his guilt.
> They spread fear *in* many people.

Additionally, learners would need to know that certain collocations allow an intransitive form of the verb, for example, 'Rumours *spread* quickly'; and that certain collocations are formed using the present participle form of the verb, for example, a *spreading* yew. Another apparently 'simple' verb such as *live* also lends itself to the production of errors with prepositions. Second-language learners should be familiar with at least the following main patterns: live *on* fruit; *with* a boyfriend; *in* Paris; *at* No. 73, High Street, York; *on* his name; *for* socialism; *in* luxury; *by* his wits; *through* the war; and so on. For further discussion of grammar in relation to the EFL dictionary, see Cowie (1983a and b).

The relationship between grammar and the dictionary is certainly a complex one, and considerable care is needed in order to specify accurately and as unambiguously as possible, the role of items in a syntactic framework. Syntactic patterns do, however, generally exhibit stability, and have been codified extensively. Learners, too, are anxious to achieve grammatical acceptability in their use of language. But more complex questions of *lexical* acceptability also require solutions; it is immediately noticeable here that some of the units we are dealing with are less stable, have not been extensively codified, and the particular problems they present for inclusion in learner dictionaries extend beyond economy of entry. As we have seen, such units are generally referred to as 'fixed expressions'. The existence of these lexical relations and the attempts to represent them highlights the need for greater refinement in lexicological theory.

One of the most significant of recent developments in lexicographic description of fixed expressions is the *Oxford Dictionary of Current Idiomatic English* (*ODCIE*); Volume 1, edited by Cowie and Mackin

(1975); Volume II by Cowie, Mackin and McCaig (1983). The presentation of entries in these volumes represents in particular some imaginative solutions to the complex problem of the clines of fixedness in lexical units, and certainly points the way to future developments.

In its present form, *ODCIE* has advanced the principled lexicographic treatment of fixed expressions and is particularly strong in its presentation of idiomaticity. For the authors, there is no real advantage in drawing strict lines between idioms and non-idioms, or in treating collocations separately from idioms; instead, it makes more sense to try to illustrate the different degrees of variability of fixed expressions. In this, Cowie *et al.* in *ODCIE* have made great strides, particularly in the specification of relevant formal properties. But considerable problems remain.

Firstly, students require information concerning the relative frequencies and currency of particular patterns. Secondly, style levels are notoriously variable, too, in the area of conventionalized language. The differences in formality level between, for example, *pick an apple*, *pick a team*, *pick a scrap*, *pick your nose/nails*, *pick a bone with*; or, *pick up speed/passengers/girls/profits/computer programming*, need to be specified. Connected with this would also be fuller descriptions of particular connotations or associations, which attach to some of the expressions. Thirdly, it will be clear that the greatest problems arise at the points in the cline where patterns and collocations are neither clearly fixed nor not fixed, but rather 'familiar' or 'semi-restricted'. Alexander (1984) illustrates the problem with respect to the complex collocability relations contracted by ostensibly synonymic items such as *small* and *little*. And the freer the possible collocations of such synonyms, the more complex the learning becomes. Lexical errors of this type are frequently made by advanced learners, but it is difficult to illustrate distinctions unless dictionary entries are synonymically, rather than alphabetically, arranged. Fourthly, there are groups of idiom-prone items such as *go*, *give*, *break*, *hit*, *take*, *come*, *read*, which have very extensive, but not completely open, collocations. The problem to be resolved by lexicographers here, is whether the idiom-proneness, and thus polysemy attributed to them is, as Ruhl (1979) argues, due more to contextualized and inferential meanings when, in fact, the single inherent general sense conveyed by the item remains constant. From the example:

> Read a book
> a novel
> a timetable
> a clock

a hieroglyph
a meaning
German (as a degree subject)
German (as a language)
an action
someone's mind/intentions

it could be argued that the meaning of these phrases cannot be easily separated from their meaningfulness to individuals who bring different kinds of knowledge to the process of interpretation. The question is whether numerous separate sub-entries are required, or whether the basic sense of *read* should be explained with some clear indication that users can generate a wide range of possible meanings according to context, (see Moon 1987; Stock 1984). Finally, lexicographers and compilers of separate dictionaries of fixed expressions need to resolve how far the *complete range* of fixed expressions is to be represented. The growth of interest in the implications to language teaching of conventionalized language, the fact that pre-patterned chunks of language are extensively used as exponents of particular communicative functions, has led to proposals to include more fixed expressions in language coursebooks and related materials (see particularly, Yorio 1980; Nattinger 1980, this volume; Pawley and Syder 1983). Among the problems here might be the ephemeral nature of allusions and catchphrases, the domain-restrictedness of certain stylistic formulae, and the fact that explanations of 'stereotypes', conversational 'gambits' and 'social formulae' would need to be sufficiently detailed to allow appropriate use in the right context, but not so detailed that they became descriptions of the contexts themselves. Consider, in the case of the following examples, the complexities involved in explaining the appropriate use of 'stereotypes' such as *That's more like it; It's not what you're thinking; I thought you'd never ask; You don't say!; No sooner said than done; if you must know.* (For example, explanation of *It's not what you're thinking* would have to include reference to a context in which the speaker has been caught in a compromising fashion, and is seeking to allay suspicions.)

The emphasis on problems may in itself be dangerous, since it concedes to idiomaticity and fixed expression a problematic status, and thus ignores arguments concerning the naturalness and pervasive normality of such 'universal' relations in language (see Makkai 1978). Neither should an emphasis on problems conceal the developments already undertaken, nor the possibilities revealed by increasing access to extensive computer-based corpora of naturally occurring written and spoken texts.

8 The COBUILD project

The COBUILD project is an ambitious lexicographic research programme which is designed initially to lead to publication of a monolingual foreign learner's dictionary of English. The project is based in the Department of English Language and Literature at the University of Birmingham, under the general direction and editorship of Professor John Sinclair, and in association with William Collins, Publishers. The project manager is Patrick Hanks (who was general editor of Collins English Dictionary 1979), and he is assisted by a large team of lexicographers.

From the beginning, the project aimed to create a dictionary for foreign learners which was based on extensive naturally-occurring data, and which, therefore, clearly differentiated itself from other recently published dictionaries such as *LDOCE* and *OALDCE*. The deployment and utilization of naturally-occurring data in this dictionary is made possible by significant innovations in computational methods. The principal contribution here is the availability in machine-readable form of a concordance based on 7.3 million words from *The Birmingham Collection of English Text* (*BCOET*), which is itself one of the largest collections of contemporary English data in Great Britain. The corpus is following, and the dictionary will have access to about 20 million words.

The main corpus exists in two separate forms: a spoken corpus and a written corpus. These can be accessed separately, but the dictionary data-base is an amalgam of both corpora (for a fuller description of sources and selection criteria for the *BCOET*, see Renouf 1983).

The main advantages claimed for the foreign learners' dictionary (Sinclair (ed.) 1987), are that:

1. Citations are not made-up examples. They are based on actual usage and are attestable by reference to a major corpus of text, (for discussion of lexicographic evidence see Sinclair 1985).
2. Concordancing procedures making the text available for lexicographic purposes allow citation which illustrates predominant collocational and colligational patterns in the co-text. This aids the clear presentation of syntactic information; and the most *frequent* partnerships contracted by particular lexical items can be used in examples. (See Sinclair 1985 who discusses the presentation of information about the item *decline*).
3. Differences in spoken and written usage can be marked.
4. Information about the operation of lexical items in their normal discourse environments is made available. This is invaluable in the case of proposition- and content-less grammatical words and discourse markers (very much a neglected area in previously published dictionaries) which can be illustrated in so far as they

function for a range of pragmatic purposes. Most importantly, the more frequent grammatical words are accorded detailed treatment.
5. The provision of a unique extra column on each page of the dictionary allows more detailed coding of grammatical information. There are no complicated numerical codes which require reference to other parts of the dictionary. And for purposes of vocabulary enlargement, synonyms and antonyms of many words are given in the same column.

Thus, as the article in this volume by Sinclair and Renouf shows, it is the *database* for the Collins COBUILD English Language Dictionary which allows more detailed lexicographic treatment than hitherto of the most frequent words in the language. Above all, the examples and weighting for frequency can be *trusted* because information is drawn from *real* texts with true-to-life rather than the more usually made-up examples.

With such a data-base considerable potential exists for innovative diversification into areas such as: the construction of lexically-graded syllabuses appropriate to textbooks for foreign-language learners; frequency counts for language-learning purposes, especially for the design of more 'lexically authentic' materials; dictionaries of collocations; lexicons with field-specific semantic groupings; fuller specification of style levels: all in all, a movement towards the kind of 'associative lexicon' advocated by Makkai (1980) and all of which would, together with the dictionary, contribute substantially to the teaching and learning of English.

As a whole, vocabulary teaching and learning now has an increasingly broad base of research to draw upon in a variety of fields. The present chapter has tried to trace the development of vocabulary teaching over the last decades and the further expansion of lexicography in the field of language learning. Chapter 4 offers a selection of papers by authors representing those varied fields of interest as a continuing and forward-looking contribution to research in the subject.

4 New directions in vocabulary studies

In this chapter of the book we bring together a number of specially commissioned papers. We invited contributors who have made important contributions to vocabulary study and teaching to address what they see as key issues in the field and, where relevant, to report on relevant research.

In the first paper James Nattinger performs the valuable service of linking with Chapter 3 by reviewing key current trends in the area of vocabulary teaching. Nattinger then proceeds to develop his own 'lexical-phrase' approach to vocabulary teaching (first outlined in Nattinger 1980) offering in the process helpful distinguishing categories for the teacher, as well as particular pedagogical methods which are designed to routinize such phrases with reference to specific social and discourse contexts. Professor Nattinger's discussion also provides a necessary North American perspective on aspects of vocabulary teaching and learning.

In the next paper Joanna Channell focuses on the mental lexicon and on what aspects of research into vocabulary learning can tell us for developing approaches to vocabulary teaching. As co-author of two major instructional textbooks on vocabulary use, Dr Channell is well placed to isolate and evaluate relevant domains. Of particular interest here is her exploration of the boundaries of first- (L1) and second-language (L2) vocabulary acquisition in order to probe the extent of overlap in the storing processes in the brain of the lexical inventories of two or more languages.

Paul Nation's work on vocabulary teaching, previously widely recognized in Australasia, has now gained international recognition. In this paper (written with James Coady, an American linguist and ESL researcher with considerable experience and expertise) the authors examine research into reading which has a lexicological orientation. Nation and Coady develop Nation's own approach to strategies for guessing lexical items in context – described in Clarke and Nation (1980) and elsewhere – but do so within the framework of a critical survey of trends in reading in relation to first- and second-language learning. Nation and Coady's paper balances others in this chapter concerned with spoken discourse and links interestingly with Carter's proposals for a more discourse-based use of cloze procedure.

Tony Cowie's work as director of the Lexical Research Unit at the University of Leeds has led to much-praised innovations in lexicological and lexicographic description. His experience in this field is considerable and he has been involved for several years in the development of learner dictionaries, and has acted as co-author of both volumes of the *Oxford Dictionary of Current Idiomatic English* (*ODCIE*). In this paper he examines a dimension to vocabulary organization which has been relatively neglected in the encouragement to more creative, individual-centred language learning: that is, the fact that users rely on a vast store of fixed phrases and pre-patterned locutions by which they routinely manage aspects of interaction. Cowie offers descriptions of such 'stable' aspects of language use, and assesses their relevance to vocabulary teaching in particular and language teaching in general. His paper contrasts interestingly with the paper by McCarthy in this chapter, where the negotiation of lexical meanings is under scrutiny, and compares well with Nattinger's account of 'lexical phrases' and their teaching.

Della Summers is a leading member of LINGLEX – a lexicographic and reference research group founded by Longman Group. Longman have been in the forefront of several vocabulary research and publishing projects during the past fifty years and their *Longman Dictionary of Contemporary English* (*LDOCE*) has been especially influential. In this paper Della Summers focuses on research into the needs of the user of learner dictionaries in decoding different styles of presentation for lexical entries.

The sixth paper emanates from a major lexical research project stimulated by the needs of user-orientated lexicographic research. Professor John Sinclair was one of the pioneers of lexical research in the 1960s (see Chapter 2), and in this paper he engages with questions which he had formulated in the 1960s and which now, thanks to considerable advances in computing technology, he is in a more secure position to answer. For this innovative paper into the principles and practice of designing a lexical syllabus for language learning he is joined by a co-researcher from COBUILD, Antoinette Renouf, who has herself many years experience both of lexical research and of EFL teaching. Their paper complements other reference to lexicographic work in this chapter, but also provides interesting links with the more discourse-based approach to lexis advocated by the two authors of the book in their contributions to this section, and in the next and final chapter.

Some current trends in vocabulary teaching

James Nattinger

Introduction: comprehension and production

Any discussion of vocabulary acquisition and of language performance in general needs to draw a clear distinction between comprehension and production, for these seem to be different skills that require different methods in the classroom. Comprehension of vocabulary relies on strategies that permit one to *understand* words and *store* them, to commit them to memory, that is, while production concerns strategies that activate one's storage by *retrieving* these words from memory, and by *using* them in appropriate situations. The priority this distinction assigns to comprehension is one of many reasons why a growing number of researchers believe that comprehension should precede production in language teaching (Asher 1969; Postovsky 1974). The object of a vocabulary lesson is one of enhancing the different strategies for comprehension and production.

1 Comprehension

1.1 Enhance understanding

The first task is helping students understand what unfamiliar words mean. It would be well at the beginning to assure them that they do not have to know all the words of a passage before they can understand its meaning, that, usually, a single mysterious word – or two or three – will not prevent comprehension, and that, as will be discussed below, it is this understanding of the text that will be their greatest aid in deciphering these difficult words. We must also assure them that they need not know *all* the meanings of any particular word, but that they can be content knowing only a general meaning for it. After all, native speakers usually settle for a hazier definition: also, it is only after experiencing a word in its many contexts that one approaches a complete understanding of its meaning. Finally, we need to convince students that instead of looking up every word in a dictionary, they should rely on the kinds of techniques discussed below for discovering meaning. The dictionary means security for many, of course, so this cannot be a prohibition, only an encouragement; but we should advise that the dictionary be used only as a last resort.

Context clues

Guessing vocabulary from context is the most frequent way we discover the meaning of new words, and to do it, we have learned to look for a number of clues. First of all, our guesses are guided by the topic, which in conversation is obvious from the type of social interaction involved, and which in reading may be signalled by an abstract or outline of what we are about to read. Even a title provides an effective source of clues for guessing (Dooling and Lachman 1971). Secondly, we are guided by the other words in the discourse to help us guess. Discourse is full of redundancy, anaphora and parallelism, and each offers clues for understanding new vocabulary. Finally, grammatical structure, as well as intonation in speech and punctuation in writing, contain further clues.

Clarke and Silberstein present exercises that work with these three kinds of context clues and help sharpen students' ability to discover meaning through context alone. The following examples 'emphasize the redundancy of language by demonstrating the types of contexts which can provide the meaning of an unfamiliar word' (Clarke and Silberstein 1977, p. 145):

synonym in apposition: Our uncle was a *nomad*, an incurable wanderer who never could stay in one place.
antonym: While the aunt loved Marty deeply, she absolutely *despised* his twin brother Smarty.
cause and effect: By surrounding the protesters with armed policemen, and by arresting the leaders of the movement, the rebellion was effectively *quashed*.
association between an object and its purpose or use: The scientist removed the *treatise* from the shelf and began to read.
description: Tom received a new *roadster* for his birthday. It is a sports model, red with white interior and bucket seats, capable of reaching speeds of more than 150 mph.
example: Mary can be quite *gauche*; yesterday she blew her nose on the new linen tablecloth.

Word morphology

Morphology also offers clues for determining word meaning. It has long been popular in vocabulary lessons to introduce lists of stems and affixes with their meanings for students to memorize, a practice which is as popular for first-language texts as it is for second. Some texts present students with unfamiliar words for them to interpret by using the meanings of the affixes they have memorized; others *invent* nonsense words for the student to unravel this way, as well. The usefulness of word morphology will be further explored below.

1.2 Enhance storage in memory

The second task in teaching comprehension is helping students remember words or, more precisely, helping them store words in memory. Before discussing various strategies that aid storage, it will be useful to review some characteristics of the relationship between vocabulary and memory.

  As regards memory and comprehension, the most effective distinction among vocabulary items may not be between content and function words, but may lie among the different types of content words. Function words can be committed to memory rather quickly, simply because there are few of them and because they reoccur frequently, just as there should be little problem in storing concrete nouns, since these words carry with them a definite image. Most problems will occur with those content words that are not so easily pictured, i.e. those nouns, verbs, adjectives and adverbs that stand for abstract concepts. Those words cannot be ignored for they carry sufficient content to be necessary for proper understanding of a text, but they are too abstract and occur too infrequently to be easily remembered. Most vocabulary problems will centre around these (Burling 1982, p. 107).[1]

A second fact about vocabulary and memory is that *form* may be more important than meaning in remembering a vocabulary item. We rely on the form of a word to lead us to its meaning, for we see or hear a particular 'shape' and try then to remember what that shape means. Therefore, in teaching comprehension, we need to teach strategies that take form as the principal path to meaning. For production, on the other hand, it is the meaning that guides us to an appropriate form for a particular situation.

Research in memory suggests that words are stored and remembered in a network of associations (Stevick 1976, p. 18). These associations can be of many types and be linked in a number of ways. Words in our mental lexicon, for example, are tied to each other not only by meaning, form and sound, but also by sight – we link similar shapes in our mind's eye – and by other parts of the contexts in which we have learned or experienced them. To know the meaning of a word becomes the task of knowing its associations with other words: therefore, to teach it most effectively, we must present it in this network of associations.

Research also shows that mental activity has a powerful effect on memory, that there is a tight relationship between 'cognitive depth' and retention (Craik and Lockhart 1972). What this means is that the more we actively work out a solution to a problem (the more commitment we make to the task of learning something that is), then the more likely we are of storing this information permanently.

Finally, one of the earliest findings from memory research was that short term memory holds a fairly constant number of units (Miller 1956), units which later research has shown likely to be 'chunks' of information, composed of several rather than single items. Even though these chunks may be larger and contain more information than discrete items, their number still remains fairly constant in memory (Simon 1974), and their size increases as we become more familiar with remembered material, permitting us to store and recall more information. Since a great part of the learner's task is to chunk unfamiliar material in meaningful ways, the teacher who makes this chunking easier increases the number of items the learners retain.

Mnemonic devices

One way we can enhance storage is by encouraging students to use memory techniques that will aid them in committing words to memory. Although there is a great deal of resistance in many countries towards introducing mnemonic techniques in the classroom, just as there is towards requiring any sort of memorization at all, students everywhere seem to use these techniques and find them very helpful.[2]

Loci

Loci are the world's oldest and best-known memory device, described in every self-help book on improving memory (Neisser 1976). **Loci** are based on the fact that we operate by 'cognitive maps', which are familiar sequences of visual images that can be recalled easily. These images (the **loci**) are usually situated along a well-travelled path, but can also be objects in a familiar room, events in a well-known story or any other such familiar sequence. To memorize an item, one forms a visual image of it and places it at one of the loci in one's imagined scene. Retrieval of these items then comes about effortlessly when the entire scene is brought back to mind.

Paired associates

Just as loci aid memorization of certain sequences of words, there are other memory techniques that help one remember by using other sorts of associative bonding, and many of these have long been an integral part of classroom procedure. The familiar Direct Method, for example, often attempts to associate a visual image with a new word. In teaching the word *hard*, the teacher might hold up a rock so that 'hard' would be stored not as an isolated item but as one paired with the image of a rock, and therefore easier to recall.

Apart from such visual associations, researchers are also beginning to explore associations of meanings and sounds. A memory device called **paired associates**, which links two words of similar sounds and meanings, has also proved effective. Curran calls such associates 'security words' and advocates their use for acquiring vocabulary. He suggests, for example, that for associating the meaning 'black' with the German word *schwarz*, one might associate the word *swarthy*, 'which has the meaning of "dark, black"' (Curran 1976, p. 77).

Key words

A rather strange extension of paired associates is the **key-word** technique. This technique is, on the face of it, slightly ridiculous, for it seems to go against what theories of language acquisition tell us is reasonable, and for that reason its success is all the more astonishing.

The student learns a word in the target language by associating it with its translation in the native language in a special way. For example, in learning that the Spanish word *perro* means 'dog', one might notice that the first syllable of the new word sounds like 'pear' and would then visualize a large pear-shaped dog waddling down the street. Later on, when faced with differentiating *perro* from the word *pero*, 'but', one might visualize the dog 'grrring' with lots of 'r's to remember which word had two 'r's. Empirical testing of the technique has produced encouraging results. Groups using **key words** demonstrate immediate and delayed recall of vocabulary words that is superior to control groups (Atkinson 1975; Merry 1980).

Characteristics of this technique are that concrete words which one can easily form an image of seem to work best, bizarre images make the most effective associations, key words can be invented by the student, or they can be provided by the teacher without reducing the effectiveness of their recall, the techniques for forming key words can themselves be taught, the key-word method may actually facilitate rather than interfere with pronunciation, and finally, the technique is valuable for students at both advanced and beginning levels of ability.

1.3 Perception and action

Perception and **action** are basic processes that affect language acquisition. The subject's interaction with the environment is a major factor in language acquisition, for this relationship provides the associations and requires the mental activity necessary for language learning. Forging interactional associations among the words we teach, then, seems a likely way to increase the potential of their acquisition. Even the recognition of isolated words may depend on re-establishing the particular mental context present at the time of learning them (Tulving and Thomson 1973).

Total physical response

One technique that makes use of such interaction is Asher's **total physical response** (Asher 1969; Asher, Kusudo and de la Torre 1974). Here the foreign language is introduced as a series of imperatives which link the language with various kinds of overt action that the student can perform in the classroom. These associations of vocabulary with physical actions have a dramatic effect on memory because students must commit themselves to the learning task by performing appropriate actions. This commitment may be a rather shallow one on the depth scale (Stevick 1976, p. 37), but it still results in students' remembering much more than when they are simply passive learners.

Craik's cognitive depth

Craik and Lockhart gave students a list of words, and for each word they asked one of the following five questions, each requiring different degrees of cognitive depth to process (Craik and Lockhart 1972, p. 49). The first question requires almost none, whereas the fifth requires a great deal:
1. 'Is there a word present?'
2. 'Is the word printed in capitals, or in lower-case letters?'
3. 'Does it rhyme with . . .?'
4. 'Is it a member of . . . category?'
5. 'Does it fit into the following sentence?'

What they found was that the deeper the decisions a task forces upon a learner, the superior the retention and recall. Stevick believes that the reason vocabulary is easier to learn in context than in isolated word lists is that such meaningful contexts permit this more complex and deeper processing (Stevick 1976, p. 30).

Curran feels that people learn best from language in which they have a strong personal stake or 'investment'. The method known as **community language learning** has the students discuss subjects of personal interest which they themselves initiate, while teachers provide information only when the students request it (Curran 1976). Lozanov, the leading proponent of Suggestopaedia, also wants to evoke the students' personal commitment in the learning task. He concentrates on their psyche, and attempts to get around their 'anti-suggestive barriers', leading them to a state of 'infantilization' in which he feels they are able to store hundreds of vocabulary words in a short amount of time (Lozanov 1979).

Formal groupings

As suggested above, it is by the *form* of vocabulary items that we usually try to remember a word. Therefore, exercises to enhance storage and recall should most often be centred on these forms; and since associations of forms help us remember the forms themselves, we should gather words together so that these associations can be seen and give each other mutual support.

For learning vocabulary, the study of morphological features is not a desirable end in itself, but knowledge of basic affixes helps learners decode words and for that reason has long been a part of vocabulary teaching texts. Generally, students are taught to recognize basic forms of words and how they combine with certain commonly occurring affixes.

These affixes have been taught in a variety of ways, most frequently, but not necessarily most effectively, as lists of affixes and their general meanings. Such lists might be memorized more effectively with loci, or with one of the other mnemonic devices mentioned above.

Familiarity with more esoteric affixes is necessary for certain specialized registers, also. Since Latin and Greek affixes often occur as compound words with bound bases, they are handled differently from roots with derivational affixes. Most lessons divide these words into two groups, those commonly occurring in general vocabulary, such as *telephone*, *photograph* and *thermometer* which are constructed out of a relatively small number of morphemes, and a second group of those whose use is almost entirely restricted to specialists, such as *hysography*, *schizogenesis* and *electroencephalograph* (Francis 1963, p. 271). The first group is usually taught by list definitions – *tele*, 'far, distant'; *phone*, 'sound'; *photo*, 'light'; *graph*, 'write, mark'; *thermo*, 'heat'; *meter*, 'measure' – and the second, since it consists of rarely occurring words immediately recognizable in the scientific literature, is usually not taught at all.

Word families

Presenting vocabulary in word 'families' is an extension of the above. Here, many words built about a particular root are gathered so that the associations among them can be seen. Even though the meanings of these words may be slightly different, clustering them will aid students in remembering their general meaning. There are several ways to do this. One is simply to list such a family (along with the definitions for each word); *part, partition, partly, partner, participant, particular, particle.* Burling (1982) suggests isolating the word families that occur in a particular passage and pointing them out to students. This would provide a more natural context than the simple listing above, and would give students the chance of tracing words through a discourse and seeing how forms change in accordance with function, for example:

> It is no good to *experiment* with that sort of thing. An *experiment* is valid only insofar as the *experimenter*. . .
>
> (Burling 1982, p. 112)

Historical, orthographical similarities

Making formal groupings on the basis of historical and orthographical similarities is another possibility, but one that will be most useful when students are learning a cognate language. Certainly, a knowledge of the sound changes separating the two languages will be of help, not only for understanding the vocabulary of classical languages, but for contemporary ones as well. English students of German find a knowledge of the second sound shift quite useful for guessing the meaning of unfamiliar words. Likewise, a knowledge of spelling conventions is useful, since many of these obscure what would otherwise be obvious cognate relationships. English students of French, for example, are aided greatly by recognizing the relationship of French <ê> to English <es>.

Collocations

Whether defined broadly or narrowly, collocation entails two of the characteristics important for comprehension that were mentioned above. One is that the meaning of a word has a great deal to do with the words with which it commonly associates. Not only do these associations assist the learner in committing these words to memory, they also aid in defining the semantic area of a word, for 'every useful collocation is another step towards understanding the concept of a word' (Brown 1974, p. 3), and in helping the student infer meaning from context. A second characteristic is that collocations permit people to know what kinds of words they can expect to find together. We have certain expectations about what sorts of information can follow from what has preceded, and so often are able to guess the meaning after hearing only the first part of familiar collocations. This is another demonstration of the fact that we understand in 'chunks'.

There are many types of exercises that deal with collocation, and they range from the simple and manipulative to ones that allow the students more flexibility and deal with larger collocations. For example, of the latter, Brown offers the following exercise:

> Choose the items that collocate most usefully with each verb. The number of lines left after each verb is a guide to the number of useful collocations possible.
>
> 1. to appeal ....   the slow student
>   ....   against the judge's decision
>   ....   to my friend for help
>   ....   him to learn from his
> 2. to encourage ....   mistakes
>   ....   etc.

(Brown 1974, p. 9)

The whole notion of collocations is extremely important for acquiring vocabulary and has yet to be exploited to its full potential. I will have more to say about its effectiveness in language production below, and particularly in the final section of this paper concerning lexical phrases.

2 Production

2.1 Vocabulary use

It is more important for students to use the newly stored language as effortlessly and quickly as possible than it is for them to wait for control of precise vocabulary (or perfect grammar), even though what they produce may stray far from the standard. Being able to participate in conversations with some degree of fluency leads to the self-confidence necessary to take more chances with the language.

Pidginization

One way to promote fluency is by encouraging 'pidginization', urging students to put language together the best they can and avoid the self-monitoring that would inhibit its use. Content words will be much more useful in a rudimentary pidgin than function words; for example, concrete nouns and verbs are more useful than abstract ones. Certainly we should never insist that a precise or a rare word be used when a general, common one would get much of the same meaning across. There is no reason to insist on inflectional affixes at first, for beginning second-language pidgins operate quite effectively with invariable noun and verb shapes.

Finally, we should teach students the knack of circumlocution. One kind of circumlocution makes use of the ways we have of coining words to fill lexical gaps in the language, such devices as derivation, compounding, blending, imitation and back-formation. Teaching the most productive of these to students may help ease them to greater fluency by giving them ways of filling these gaps. Derivation, in which we take a root and add affixes to it, is the most common method for creating new words, for it allows us to expand vocabulary without memorizing new words and thus aids fluency. Students who know their affixes and do not know the word 'inability', for example, could easily create the word 'unableness', and go on their way.

Another common way of forming new words is by compounding. The semantic relationships between members of the compounds are varied (consider *salesman*, *table top*, *pocketbook*, *bird cage*, *whitewash*) and comparative linguistic studies of this phenomenon are slim, to say the least, so it is difficult to suggest systematic ways for teaching the rules of compounding. Current research may soon change that, however. In her comparative study of Hebrew and English, Clark finds evidence that the rules for compounding may be quite different from one language to another. Lexicalized agent compounds like *milkman*, which are numerous in English, are rare in Hebrew, a language which also seems restricted to noun-noun and adjective-noun combinations, and which does not allow adjective-verb compounds, such as English *whitewash* (Clark and Berman 1984). More systematic information of this sort will provide useful information for language teachers.

2.2 Vocabulary retrieval

The storage of information does not guarantee its retrieval. We therefore need ways to increase the probability that retrieval cues will be effective, just as we need techniques that will permit the recall of words that are appropriate for the situation. Techniques that enhance production will have to be centred on the meanings of words rather than on their forms, because, except for restricted uses of language that search for a form first (looking for a proper rhyme, perhaps, or an item to fit into an acrostic), most of our production has to do with searching for an appropriate *meaning* to fit the particular occasion. The most effective associative bonds for production, therefore, connect the word and its meaning. The following are techniques that gather words in such a way.

Situational sets

Situational sets are cohesive chains of lexical relationships in discourse. They are groups of words that are associated because of the subject of the text, its purpose or its construction; they are words related to a particular situation. Conversation about a department store, for example, would most likely contain vocabulary such as *price, floor, sales, charge, clothes*; that about school would involve *teacher, student, class, textbook, lesson*. A situation defined rhetorically, as that in an argumentative essay, might contain the logical connectives *therefore, nevertheless, consequently, notwithstanding*. This is all highly familiar, and is a frequent organizing device for vocabulary lessons entitled 'At the Post Office', 'In the Classroom', 'Meeting a Friend', and so on.

Semantic sets

Semantic sets contain words linked by other sorts of inferential relationships, and so describe the chains of associations into which we must tap to bring words to mind. Semantic sets, like situational sets, are ways of bringing words together so that these inferential associations are more obvious. Words can be grouped as: **synonyms** (*sofa, couch*), a category which itself can be subdivided into more socially realistic ones, such as formal and informal synonyms (*child, kid*), poetic and non-poetic synonyms (*bough, branch*), positive and negative synonyms (*thrifty, stingy*), core and intensifier words (*mad, furious*): **antonyms** (*wide, narrow*): **cordinates** (*oak, elm*): **superordinates** (*skunk, animal*): and **subordinates** (*fruit, pear*), all of which can be further subdivided along the lines suggested for synonyms. Another kind of semantic set has to do with **stimulus–response** pairs, such as *accident, car*, and *baby, mother*. There seems to be a great uniformity in people's responses to certain stimulus words (Richards 1976), which ought to be exploited to help students form more effective associations.[3]

A typical exercise treating synonyms is provided by Martin (1976). For teaching academic vocabulary, she groups several verbs of analysis along with a sentence context:

consists of – the proposal consists of several parts
be composed of – the report is composed of four sections
contain – the solution contains many inert compounds
be made up of – water is made up of two elements

(Martin 1976, p. 94)

Such groups help form associative bonds, while at the same time they 'illustrate how semantically similar verbs can have different syntactic, semantic, and pragmatic restrictions' (McKay 1980b, p. 19).

McCarthy, who is also concerned with these paradigmatic bonds of associations, tries to exploit the discourse potential of lexical repetition by having students practise the communicative effects of such relations across discourse boundaries. One of his exercises for practising production of semantically related items is the following:

A. Agree, with synonym
   a. He was very strange.
   b. Yes, very odd.
B. Agree, with antonym
   a. Joe didn't stick to the subject.
   b. He wandered off too much.
C. Agree, with a more general word (a superordinate)
   a. The cat is great company.
   b. All pets are.
D. Agree, with a more specific word (a subordinate)
   a. Books are badly printed nowadays.
   b. Especially paperbacks.

(McCarthy 1984, p. 19)

Metaphor sets

Lakoff and Johnson (1980) believe that the conceptual system which structures how we perceive and what we remember is largely metaphorical. These metaphors, which permit us to understand something that often is abstract or mysterious in terms of something that is more concrete or familiar, exert a powerful influence on the ways we think and the actions we take. As an example of such a metaphor, they give *argument is war*, and list some of the ways we express it:

Your claims are *indefensible*.
He *attacked every weak point* in my argument.
His criticisms were *right on target*.
I've never *won* an argument with him.
You disagree? Okay, *shoot!*
If you use that *strategy*, he'll *wipe you out*.
He *shot down* all of my arguments.

(Lakoff and Johnson 1980, p. 4)

Lakoff and Johnson go on to say that because of this metaphorical connection, we have a tendency to think of arguments as being war-like and prepare to *attack, conquer, demolish* or *concede* accordingly. They say:

> We can actually win or lose arguments. We see the person we are arguing with as an opponent. We attack his positions and we defend our own. We gain and lose ground. We plan and use strategies. If we find a position indefensible, we can abandon it and take a new line of attack.

Whether one yields to this larger argument or not, it is clear that metaphor is a pervasive organizing principle for words and phrases in a language, and might well be taken advantage of for vocabulary acquisition. Certainly these metaphorical frames provide for associative bonding. Words like *waste, spend, cost, invest, spare, worth, borrow, profit*, though possible to organize as a situational set, are easily associated in terms of the metaphor *time is money*:

> You're *wasting* my time.
> How do you *spend* your time?
> That flat tire *cost* me an hour.
> I've *invested* a lot of time in her.
> I don't *have enough* time *to spare*.
> Is that *worth your while*?
> He's living on *borrowed* time.
> You don't use your time *profitably*.

(Lakoff and Johnson 1980)

The vexing problems of teaching prepositions and two-part verbs might also be alleviated somewhat by a different kind of metaphorical set. Lakoff and Johnson introduce metaphors which they claim have arisen from the relationship of our bodies with physical surroundings. One of these, of a kind they call 'orientational metaphors', is *'more' is up; 'less' is down*, arising from the fact that if one adds more of a substance to a container or pile, the level goes up. This metaphor can be expressed with the following prepositions and two-part verbs:

> The number keeps going *up*.
> Turn *up* the heat.
> Turn *down* the radio.

Another orientational metaphor is *'having control' is up; 'being subject to control or force' is down*, whose basis is that 'physical size typically correlates with physical strength, and the victor in a fight is typically on top' (Lakoff and Johnson 1980, p. 15). Some of the uses of prepositions linked by this metaphor would be:

I have control *over* her.
I am *on top of* the situation.
He ranks *above* me in strength.
He is *under* my control.
He is *below* me on the administration.

Collocations

Collocations are as useful for teaching production as they are for teaching comprehension. First of all, by memorizing collocational groups, students will already be somewhat aware of certain lexical restrictions. By being familiar with collocations like *a convenient situation* and *a convenient time* but not with ones like *a convenient person* or *a convenient cat*, they will realize, however subconsciously, that the adjective *convenient* is only used with inanimate nouns. For the same reasons, they will be less likely to make mistakes in register, such as *never did she go for Shakespeare*.

Most important, however, is the fact that collocations teach students expectations about which sorts of language can follow from what has preceded. Students will not have to go about reconstructing the language each time they want to say something but instead can use these collocations as pre-packaged building blocks.

3 Lexical phrases

3.1 Prefabricated speech

Many theories of language performance suggest that vocabulary is stored redundantly, not only as individual morphemes, but also as parts of phrases, or even as longer memorized chunks of speech, and that it is oftentimes retrieved from memory as these preassembled chunks (Bolinger 1975). This prefabricated speech has both the advantage of more efficient retrieval, and of permitting speakers to direct attention to the larger structure of the discourse, rather than keeping it focused narrowly on individual words as they are produced.

Prefabricated speech in ESL

Vocabulary teachers have always recognized the need to include more than single words in their lessons. Two- and three-part verbs (*put up*, *put up with*), and noun compounds (*elevator operator*, *card player*) and idioms such as *keep tabs on* are usually treated no differently from other vocabulary. Many teachers thus see language as a dichotomy opposing 'vocabulary' which is any stretch of language in some way single and frozen, against the rest of language, which is multiple and generated from 'scratch'.

Krashen and Scarcella, summarizing previous research, describe a third, intermediate category – language that is not completely fixed but is at the same time limited in the shapes it can take (Krashen and Scarcella 1978). They refer to phrases such as *a little while ago* or *down with the king*, which permit some variation (*a year ago, a month ago, a short time ago, down with feudalism, up with people, away with all pedants*) yet still are relatively fixed in shape. These they call 'semi-fixed patterns', which have alternatively, and more helpfully, been described as 'formulaic frames with analyzed slots' (Wong-Fillmore 1979). Peters (1983) summarizes research that takes the idea further, and claims that ordinary conversation consists almost entirely of 'institutionalized clauses', which, unlike idioms, can be analysed by the normal rules of syntax, yet because of their usefulness or frequency in conversation, are stored and produced as single units. If we broaden the definition to include such stretches of language, Peters feels, then, any sharp distinction between vocabulary and syntax collapses into a dynamic and fluid continuum, ranging from the completely fixed to the completely original.

One attempt to describe these conventional structures for teaching purposes was work based on research in natural language processing (Nattinger 1980). This research sees language use as basically a 'compositional' process, one of 'stitching together' preassembled phrases into discourse, and describes the following six types of 'lexical phrases' in terms of functional and structural characteristics:

1. Polywords: short, fixed phrases, whose meaning is often not analysable by the regular rules of syntax. They can substitute for single words, so are often treated like regular vocabulary in ESL lessons: idioms (*kick the bucket*), euphemisms (*powder room*), slang (*better half*), two- and three-part verbs (*put up, put up with*).
2. Phrasal constraints: short, relatively fixed phrases with slots that permit some variation, many being non-canonical forms (*a year ago, by pure coincidence, down with the king*): greetings (*how do you do*), partings (*see you later*), exclamations (*you can't be serious!*), insults (*you creep*).
3. Deictic locutions: short to medium length phrases of low varia-bility, consisting of clauses or entire utterances. They are essen-tially monitoring devices, whose purpose is:
   a) to direct the flow of conversation by marking attitudes, expec-tations, concessions, challenges, defences, supports, retreats (*as*

far as I know, don't you think, if I were you, for that matter,
frankly, I mean to say, further to my letter of);
  b) to exercise social control (*hey, wait a minute, now look, see here,
  shut up, and then what*).
4. Sentence builders: phrases up to sentence length, highly variable,
containing slots for parameters or arguments. These provide a
skeleton for the expression of the entire idea. They are often non-
canonical and discontinuous, and are used in a wide variety of
social contexts (*not only X but also Y, if I X, then I Y, the . . . er
X, the . . . Y*).
5. Situational utterances: usually complete sentences, amenable to the
regular rules of syntax and highly dependent on the social context.
They provide the framework for particular social interactions –
greetings (*how are you today*), partings (*I'll see you next week*),
politeness routines (*thanks very much for . . .*), questions (*could you
tell me . . .*) – and much of the language of social maintenance
(*what's new? cold enough for you? I won't tell another living soul, how
have you been getting along with . . .?*).
6. Verbatim texts: entire texts of different length with extremely low
variability. Used for quotation, allusion, or frequently, as in the
case of institutionalized chunks, direct use. These are memorized
sequences (numbers, the alphabet, the days of the week), aphor-
isms (*the public seldom forgives twice*), proverbs (*a rolling stone gathers
no moss*), and all of those chunks that a speaker has found efficient
to store as units. Some of these may be general units, used by
everyone in the speech community, while others may be more idio-
syncratic, phrases that an individual has stored because they have
been found an efficient and pleasing way of getting an idea across.

3.2 Reasons for teaching lexical phrases

The theoretical justifications for teaching lexical phrases are encouraging, but perhaps the most immediate reasons for teaching them are
practical ones, some of which have already been cited as reasons for
teaching collocations. First, these phrases provide raw material for
later analysis and segmentation. Such phrases will likewise enable
students not to violate certain lexical restrictions, nor produce as
many incongruities of register. Perhaps most importantly, these
phrases will lead to fluency in speaking and writing, for they relieve
the learner of concentrating on each individual word as it is used by
allowing them to focus attention on the larger structure of the
discourse and on the social aspects of the interaction.

3.3 Methods of teaching lexical phrases

One method of teaching lexical phrases is to get students to make use of them the same way that first-language learners do, that is, by starting with a few basic fixed phrases, which they then analyse as smaller, increasingly variable pieces, finally breaking them apart into individual words, and thus finding their own way to the regular rules of syntax. More specifically, such a method might be put to work as follows. Pattern practice drills could first provide a way of gaining fluency with certain basic fixed phrases (Peters 1983). The challenge for the teacher would be to use such drills to allow confidence and fluency, yet not overdo them to the point that they became mindless exercises, as has often been the unfortunate result in strict audio-lingualism. The next step would be to introduce the students to controlled variation in these basic phrases with the help of simple substitution drills, which would demonstrate that the phrases learned previously were not invariable patterns but were instead frames with open slots. The range of variation would then be increased, allowing students to analyse the patterns further.

But there must be more. We not only have to ask *how* learners go about learning language, we need also to ask *why* they learn it; and from research in first-language acquisition, as from that in the memory research cited earlier, it seems clear that the answer has to do with social motivation: children learn language as part of a social inter-action in which they have something they want to say. To recall Stevick's words: language is best learned when it connects 'with our plans, with our most important memories and with our needs' (Stevick 1976, p. 36). This sociolinguistic dimension provides the cognitive depth that is crucial to successful acquisition of lexical phrases.

What follows is an attempt to group routines in a way that will be pedagogically useful for language teaching based on such views. These groups are not traditional grammar or semantic categories, but are to some extent, based on Wilkins's notional-functional categories, where emphasis is on the lexicon needed to perform specific speech 'functions' (Wilkins 1976). I have called these groups **social inter-actions**, **necessary topics**, and **discourse devices**, and list some examples of each below:

Social interactions

greetings/closings:	*hello, good morning, goodbye, see you later*
politeness/routines:	*please, if you don't mind*
question/answer:	*do you . . ., are there . . ., of course, yes, there . . .*

requesting: *of course, sure thing*
refusing: *of course not, no way*
etc.
Although this category, as well as the two that follow, contains all six types of lexical phrases mentioned earlier, it is characterized mostly by phrasal constraints, situational utterances and polywords.

Necessary topics
language: *do you speak . . ., how do you say . . .*
shopping: *too expensive, department store*
autobiography: *my name is . . ., I'm from . . .*
quantity: *how much is . . ., a great deal*
time: *what time . . ., for a long time*
location: *where is . . ., what part of the . . .*
etc.
These are characterized mostly by situational utterances and sentence builders.

Discourse devices
fluency devices: *you know, it's never been said that . . .*
conjunctions: *which means, less likely that*
subordinators: *in other words, not only . . . but also . . .*
logical connectors: *as a result, in spite of*
temporal connectors: *the day after . . ., yesterday*
reinforcers: *O.K., and then what happened*
probability/certainty
a) modals :   *might, may have*
b) sensory predicates: *it seems to me, I think that . . .,*
    etc.

These are often characterized by deictic locutions and sentence builders.
   Social interactions and **discourse devices** provide lexical phrases for the *framework* of the discourse, whereas **necessary topics** provide them for the *subject* at hand. Most linguistic encounters are composed of a patchwork of routines from all three of these categories.

4 Further research

As promising as a lexical phrase approach appears to be, there are many questions about it that have to be answered. Just what sorts of routinized language are used in particular encounters needs to be explored and then assigned to appropriate categories. The categories themselves must be evaluated, not only pedagogically but also empirically and theoretically. It is quite possible that the distinction among **social interactions, necessary topics,** and **discourse devices** obscures rather than clarifies, and more realistic ways of grouping are possible. There are also many questions about the method for introducing these phrases to students. It is clear that the best time to introduce controlled variation should come after students have automatic control of basic patterns, but before these patterns have become fossilized and resistant to change. Just when such an optimum segmentation period occurs, though, needs to be investigated.

In spite of the uncertainties with method and description, a lexical phrase approach offers a promising new direction for vocabulary acquisition, and for language learning in general.

Notes

1. This is an excellent and curiously unrecognized source of practical advice for vocabulary teachers and for language teachers in general. This paper owes a great deal to the innovative methods Burling describes.
2. Burling suggests that this resistance is the result of a theoretical (anti-behavioural) bias and, in countries such as the United States, a cultural bias as well (Burling 1982, p. 114).
3. Rivers has an excellent discussion of such stimulus-response pairs (Rivers 1983, p. 128).
4. Among the many labels suggested have been the following: *idioms* (Fraser 1970); *holophrases* (Corder 1973); *praxons* (Bateson 1975); *preassembled speech* (Bolinger 1975); *routines* (Krashen and Scarcella 1978); *frames* (Wong-Fillmore 1979); and *conventionalized forms* (Yorio 1980).

Points for further development

1. Nattinger suggests that vocabulary teaching for comprehension should have a range of techniques of its own, as should teaching for production. The aim of the vocabulary lesson should be to enhance strategies for comprehension and production. Compare this use of terms with Ostyn's (1986) (see point 2 in the discussion following Channell, p. 95).

2. In comprehension we work from forms to meanings; in production vice versa. Comprehension embraces understanding, storing and committing to memory. Production involves retrieval and use. What implications does this have for the relative weighting given to form and meaning in vocabulary teaching?

3. Learners should be encouraged to view understanding at different levels; it need not always be complete or perfect, but often needs to be no more than hazy. Generally, we do not need to know all the meaning of a word. Guessing is very important in comprehension: guessing from context, from the text itself and a variety of other clues. One problem here might be that learners will be unhappy with only a 'vague' understanding of a word; learners frequently expect that all meaning should be precise, and clearly defined by teachers and/or dictionaries. How can we overcome this psychological barrier?

4. Nattinger argues that, for the purposes of word storage, the distinction concrete/abstract may be a more significant predictor of learner difficulty than function- versus content-words, that word form may be as crucial as word meaning, that words seem to be stored in a 'network' of associations, and that effective storage is relative to 'cognitive depth' in the learning task. Compare the concrete/abstract, function/content distinctions with the types of vocabulary discussed in Chapter 5 Section 2. Do 'text-structuring' words present their own kind of difficulties for storage? What sort of cognitive depth is likely to be involved in processing them?

5. Techniques for memorization and storage which might be developed further include mnemonics, perception and action techniques, manipulating cognitive depth and concentrating on formal aspects of lexis (derivation, collocation, etc.). References to practical suggestions along these lines can be found in Chapter 3; also Meara (1980) gives a wide-ranging survey and evaluation of research into different techniques.

6. Nattinger says that, for production, the learner should be encouraged to use newly-confronted vocabulary and should not have to wait till knowledge of it is perfect. How does this fit in with Sinclair and Renouf's idea of how elementary-level learners using a 'lexical' syllabus should be encouraged to produce?

7. Pidginization and circumlocution should be encouraged even if they generate incorrect forms; do you agree?

8. Techniques to encourage production ought to concentrate more on meaning than form, and teaching should utilize insights from lexical theory as ways of activating the organized lexicon. Can learners at elementary and lower levels be expected to grapple with notions like collocation and hyponymy? McCarthy (1984) seems to think it is feasible; what types of exercises and activities can be devised that will not frighten learners off?

9. Perhaps Nattinger's most important argument is that lexical phrases are a feature of language use which should be brought more into the centre of vocabulary teaching and learning. They provide raw material for subsequent analysis, they offer the learner the opportunity of fluent production with less likelihood of producing deviant language, and they can be organized on notional-functional lines to correspond to learners' needs. Nattinger (1980) is worth a close reading; it gives further detailed discussion of lexical phrases and many examples.

Psycholinguistic considerations in the study of L2 vocabulary acquisition[1]

Joanna Channell

Vocabulary has rapidly changed in status from 'a neglected aspect of language learning' (Meara 1980) to an area of growing research and publication, as exemplified by this collection of papers. There are now theories of L2 vocabulary acquisition, a wide (and growing) range of teaching techniques available, and a greatly increased awareness on the part of most teachers (and learners) of the importance of vocabulary development. At the same time, understanding of the psychological aspects of L2 vocabulary acquisition and vocabulary use is still rather limited. There is a considerable history of research on memory which has provided many valuable insights, and also useful experimental work on short and medium term retention of L2 vocabulary (for references see McDonagh 1981, Chapter 5; Meara 1982; Nation 1982; Cohen and Hosenfield 1981). Equally there is a large literature on psycholinguistic research into the mental lexicon of bilinguals (for references see Albert and Obler 1978), but this work generally focuses on balanced bilinguals, not L2 acquirers. Hence a key question for L2 theory to which we still need an answer is: what is the nature of the representations of L2 words in a learner's long-term memory, or to put this another way, what does the L2 mental dictionary look like? For L1, research on the nature of the mental lexicon is reasonably well developed, with research findings and resultant models available. This paper describes some relevant theoretical and descriptive work in the psycholinguistics of L1, and discusses its possible applications to L2 acquisition (for a similar approach, see studies by Meara 1982; Ingle and Meara forthcoming; James 1984). The psycholinguistic work concerns the analysis of one type of speech error made by native speakers, and a model of the mental lexicon which has been proposed by Fay and Cutler to account for such errors (Fay and Cutler 1977; Hurford 1981; Cutler and Fay 1982).

Readers of this volume, whom I visualize to be teachers and applied linguists, rather than psycholinguists, need to be clear that Fay and Cutler are psycholinguists whose interest lies in investigating the nature of the L1 mental lexicon. They have not applied their research to L2 acquisition. I am attempting to have a foot in both camps and to present psycholinguistic research evidence in a form accessible to people working in another field: L2 teaching. It is important also to point out that the psycholinguist's notion of a speech error is very different from the concept of 'errors' found in the error analysis literature in applied linguistics. Psycholinguists mean 'unconscious slips of the tongue, resulting from wrong mental processing', while applied linguists mean 'observable systematic deviations from the standard norm of the target language, from which we can analyse which bits of the target language the learner does not yet know, or half knows'. Hence L1 errors are taken to be evidence of what L1 speakers know, whereas L2 errors are taken (mainly) to be evidence of what L2 speakers do *not* know (for some similar points, relevant to phonological errors, see James 1984, p. 501).

I shall now consider some methodological and terminological preliminaries, after which follows a summary of the research findings and a discussion of their implications for the teaching and learning of L2 vocabulary.

The first preliminary concerns acquisition and learning. It is not appropriate here to become involved in the continuing debate inspired chiefly by Krashen (see, for example, 1981) but definitions are in order. I regard an L2 word as having been acquired by a learner when a) its meaning can be recognized and understood (rather than guessed at), both in and out of context and b) it can be used naturally and appropriately to situation (for a characterization of what acquisition involves, see Broughton 1978; Channell 1981). Learning then covers the conscious strategies employed to lead to acquisition. Learning is the process, acquisition is the end result.

This point has to be considered alongside the distinction between *productive* and *receptive* use of vocabulary. It is generally assumed (and observed) that learners gain receptive control of new words before active control. Here I wish to talk about acquisition. What happens in the classroom may be quite different. We often require learners to *say* words whose meaning they are not really yet sure of (especially where new vocabulary is introduced by reading). But teacher-initiated saying of a word does not represent in any way evidence of acquisition. Taking the definition of acquisition of vocabulary given above, receptive acquisition precedes productive acquisition. It is true also, both for L1 and L2 acquirers, that many vocabulary items never become part of productive capacity, but remain part of receptive competence. So acquisition of individual vocabulary items consists first of comprehension, then (for some items only) of comprehension plus production.

As a second preliminary, we need a working hypothesis or model of how speech processing might take place. Fay and Cutler propose that a device for speech production might create a grammatical frame for an intended meaning, marked with the syntactic categories of words, which are then found in the mental lexicon and placed in the grammatical frame for onward processing. A comprehension device, conversely, decodes sounds into word length segments and searches its mental dictionary for meanings to pair with them. Such a view would imply that for both the L1 and the L2 user of a language, the two distinct processes of production (whether speaking or writing) and comprehension (whether listening or reading), make differential use of the store of words in the mind. Part of the production process must consist of selection of appropriate words according to the meaning to be conveyed. The word form is then converted into a phonological shape for onward processing into speech. Thus the direction of mapping is meaning → sound. In comprehension, the direction of mapping is sound → meaning. (This summary is based on that given by Fay and Cutler 1977.) These differences might suggest that for the mental word store the optimal arrangement for production will be according to meaning, while the optimal arrangement for comprehension will be according to sound. This has led to the speculation that there could be two listings (stores) of words in the mind, one for each process. To substantiate this there is some experimental and clinical neurological evidence that the linguistic processes of perception and production are partially independent of each other (see Albert and Obler 1978, pp. 220–2; Dirven and Oakeshott-Taylor 1985 for a review of evidence). We shall return to this question below.

The third preliminary remark involves three related questions concerning the relationships between mental lexicons in different speakers and within the same speaker who has more than one language. The first question is how much the mental lexicon of any L2 might or might not resemble the mental lexicon of any L1 within the same individual. This is part of the wider question of the general organization of language in the mind of a person who speaks more than one language. There exists a considerable literature on neuro-logical and psychological aspects of bilingualism, much of which remains equivocal on the issue of lexical organization. Some studies seem to point to separate listings for the two languages, while others argue that there is a single lexical store. Most studies seem to show that there is interaction between the lexicons of the two languages in one user (e.g. word association tests with and without switching from language to language; for references see Albert and Obler 1978; Meara 1982). Summarizing the research evidence, Albert and Obler conclude:

> It is clear that words in one language, and their translation equivalents in the other (when such exist), are related in the brain in a nonrandom way, much as a word and its synonym in the same language may be connected in an associational network.
>
> (Albert and Obler 1978, p. 246)

A second, related question is whether the bilingual's linguistic mental organization is similar to the monolingual's or qualitatively different – that is, is bilingualism more of the same, or something different? Again, we do not really know. Albert and Obler, summarizing their review of research, state that differences of perceptual strategies can be substantiated, but then are forced to say guardedly that, 'It is possible that the differences in perceptual strategy relate to differences in cerebral organization for language' (p. 248). If the second language is more of the same, then psychological models developed for monolinguals are applicable; if it is different, they may be less useful. Thirdly, what (if any) is the resemblance between the L2 learner's lexicon of a language, and the mental lexicon of monolingual native speakers of that language? Here also there is still an absence of the right kind of research. There is some fairly clear evidence that the lexical associations of the two groups are quite radically different (see Meara 1982) in the sense that the relative stability of responses to many word association stimuli recorded for monolinguals is not found in L2 learners. In the absence of definite research evidence either way, it makes sense for L2 theorists to draw on L1 models, and hence to test their validity for L2 theory, until there is definite evidence that they should not do so.

Native speaker speech errors are slips of the tongue occurring in ordinary conversation. They are often self-corrected by speakers. Data for speech error studies is assembled over a long period by experimenters who note, from ordinary conversation, slips which they hear, together with the version the speaker actually intended. Errors in English have been extensively studied and analysed into types (Fromkin 1973, 1980, provide a useful survey). The type we shall be concerned with here are lexical errors involving substitution of a whole word (**error**) for an intended word (**target**). These are of two kinds. **Semantic errors** are those where error and target are related in meaning, e.g. (E → T):

(1) This room is too damn hot ———→ cold
(2) The two contemporary er sorry adjacent buildings

(Fromkin 1973, p. 236)

Related kinds of semantic errors are **blends**. These are nonexistent words which seem to consist of a mixture of sounds from two words which are close together in meaning, and which could both be appropriate in the given context. Examples are:

(3) sleast ———→ slightest/least
    minal ———→ minor/trivial
    dentars ———→ dentals/velars

(Fromkin 1980)

In contrast to these semantic errors, **malapropisms** are those where error and target are related in pronunciation but *not* in meaning, e.g.:

(4) tambourines ———→ trampolines
(5) apartment ———→ appointment
(6) miraculous ———→ spectacular

(Fay and Cutler 1977)

It should be noted that most work on L1 speech errors has discussed single words and has assumed the word to be a salient item in processing, mainly because the errors observed involve individual words rather than multi-word units. While I recognize that the notion 'word' is not unproblematical I shall not pursue that line in this paper. (See especially Chapter 2 and papers by Cowie, and Sinclair and Renouf in this chapter.)

Considering the two classes of speech errors introduced above, we can see that the occurrence of semantic errors is predicted by the hypothetical process model previously outlined. If words are arranged to be looked up according to meaning, then a mistaken path in look-up might well result in an error with related meaning. However, such a model cannot account for the occurrence of malapropism errors (those related by pronunciation similarities, like examples (4) to (6)). Consideration of how to account for the different types of speech errors leads to several conclusions about the probable nature of the mental lexicon.

Firstly, on the question of one mental lexicon (for a single given language), versus two (or more), Fay and Cutler claim that the existence of malapropisms argues strongly for a single listing. Malapropisms could not occur if the lexicon used for production was arranged according to meaning, since words with similar pronunciation would not have any access channels in common. Hence they posit a phonological arrangement (according to sound). However this would not explain semantic errors. Therefore, they argue, there must be a single mental lexicon, phonologically arranged, and accessed by two different networks, one phonological and one semantic. This model will account for the fact that both semantically and phonologically based errors occur in production.

A key observation on malapropisms is the correspondence of syllable structure and stress between errors and targets. In Fay and Cutler's corpus, 87 per cent of malapropisms had the same number of syllables as their targets, and 98 per cent had the same stress pattern, as in the following examples:

    lawn ⟶ line (one syllable)
    easy ⟶ early (two syllables)
    accident ⟶ appetite (three syllables)

and so on. This leads them to argue that words are organized first by syllable structure and/or stress pattern, and only then into exact sounds. They note that this arrangement is likely to be optimal for comprehension, since the comprehension device has to segment incoming speech into words, and will use syllables and stress to do so. A further important observation (clarified by Hurford in his 1981 reply to Fay and Cutler) is that malapropisms and targets resemble each other, not only at their beginnings, but at all points in the two words (so there are errors such as *provocation* → *indication, miraculous* → *spectacular*. This tends to show that the arrangement of the mental dictionary is not on a left to right basis (i.e. like a written dictionary) since this will not relate pairs like the above two.

While the model propounded by Fay and Cutler is in some senses purely speculative, it arises directly from consideration of their data, which have been painstakingly assembled and subjected to careful statistical analysis. Hence both data and model merit our attention for the light they may throw on L2 vocabulary acquisition, to which I now turn.

One of the questions raised earlier concerned the likely resemblance between the native speaker's lexicon and the L2 learner's lexicon of a particular language. One resemblance in what we might term lexical behaviour concerns the nature of lexical errors for the two groups. Lexical errors from native speakers are hardly ever totally random – there is always some link to the target, semantic, phonological or pragmatic (Cutler and Fay 1982, p. 111). The same appears to be true of the errors made by L2 learners (although we must remember that the concept of error is different for the two groups).

Some are linked semantically to their targets (see Channell 1981), e.g.:

(7) *a voyage by train (——— journey by train)

others are pragmatically appropriate but not idiomatic, e.g.:

(8) ?He closed the door with the key (——— locked the door)

Yet others are phonologically linked, as shown for example by the studies of Meara (1982) and Ingle and Meara (to appear). Meara describes inappropriate word associations between L1/L2 which are phonological in nature, for example (French/English):

(9) stimulus: *béton* (='concrete'), response: *animal*, source of confusion: French *bête* (='animal')
(10) stimulus: *traire* (='to milk'), response: *essayer* (='to try'), source of confusion: English *try*

A second similarity is that L2 learners experience the tip of the tongue phenomenon in the same way as L1 speakers. In a well-known experiment (Brown and McNeill 1966) L1 speakers were asked for words to fit with definitions. Those who could not find any particular word, but had it 'on the tip of their tongue' were often able to supply correct information about such characteristics of the target word as first sound, number of syllables, and suffix. Teachers and learners will be aware of this in L2 production. These data, though far from conclusive, are indicative in two ways. Firstly they show that at some level L1 and L2 lexicons are similar in that they produce similar behaviour. Secondly they are consistent with the model of the mental lexicon hypothesized by Fay and Cutler.

I turn next to a consideration of L2 comprehension. What are the demands on the learner's mental lexicon of the process of comprehension? According to the model sketched above, a learner must divide the incoming stream of speech into processable units. The model proposed by Fay and Cutler is consistent with the view that syllable recognition and stress recognition play important roles in decoding what has been said, and thence in accessing meanings in the lexicon. This would be true for English, and for all other languages where words have individual stress patterns. Hence to optimize comprehension of such languages, methods used to present new vocabulary to learners should lead them to internalize accurately (a) pronunciation of individual sounds, (b) number of syllables, and (c) stress. Logically then, as a first consequence, reading would appear *not* to be a good way to present a new item, since it gives either a poor guide, or no guide at all, on each of these three characteristics. This is unfortunate, since reading is frequently the method of presentation of new vocabulary, especially in coursebooks, once learners are beyond beginner level. On syllable structure and word stress, it is generally true that neither of these has had the attention they deserve in the L2 learner's programme (with certain notable exceptions, e.g. Mandarin L2 materials). Stress has traditionally been regarded as the icing on the cake, to be sorted out when the learner has got some basic things, like individual sounds, right. This would appear somewhat misguided when we consider Fay and Cutler's model of the way that comprehension takes place.

Tarone (1974) too, in her model of speech perception of L2, suggests the importance of both word and sentence stress. She proposes that in the early stages of learning to comprehend, learners rely on selective processing (because they cannot cope with everything) and that one unconscious strategy is to use stress to help select what is important. Hence, for comprehension, learners need to know both the citation form stress of a word, and also the permissable permutations of stress placement that a word can undergo in continuous speech. Therefore it is important that at least the citation stress pattern be attached to the mental representation of a word as it is acquired. (Notice that this specifically *excludes* the question of whether the learner uses the right stress pattern in production, since that is a separate issue). We must here face the uncomfortable fact that many non-native teachers use non-standard word stress both for citations forms and in continuous speech, and hence pass on misleading input about stress patterns to their students. Such learners are then unable to comprehend native speaker speech or the speech of non-natives from other parts of the world because it 'sounds wrong' to them.

Turning now to production, it is obvious that the demands it makes on the L2 mental lexicon are different, according to the sketch of speech processing previously given. To optimize production, learners need accurately programmed lexical associations, enabling them to make choices which faithfully reflect intended meaning. We know that on the production side, access is via meanings, and there is psycholinguistic evidence in favour of a psychological model in which words with like meanings are 'close together' in accessing terms. This has led to the now quite widely propounded idea that vocabulary teaching should make overt associations between semantically related words (for discussion and theoretical background see Channell 1981). The most large-scale explicit application of this method is in the two books by Rudzka *et al.* (1981, 1985) which use semantic fields and componential analysis to present new vocabulary, as in the following example:

Reducing to small pieces

chop	dice	cube	shred	slice	mince	grate	
+							cut through
+							with a blow or blows from a sharp-edged instrument
							or
+	+	+	+	+			cut
							or
		+					tear
				+			reduce to small pieces
					+		by forcing under pressure through small holes
						+	rub against a surface containing small sharp-edged holes
+							into small pieces
	+						into small cubes
		+					into cubes
			+			+	into small irregular strips or long narrow pieces
				+			into flat pieces

Chop, dice, shred and *slice* may occur with *up.Chop* may also occur with *down.*
EXAMPLES
Could you *chop* the onions *up?*
We had to *chop down* the oak tree because it was rotten.
He carefully *shredded up* the documents so that they could not be reconstructed.
Chop is often used in colloquial speech as a synonym of *cut.*
EXAMPLES
What a pity you have *chopped off* all your beautiful hair.
This article is far too long and will have to be *chopped.*

(Rudzka et al. 1985, p. 187)

Further examples can be found in articles by Stieglitz (1983) and Harvey (1983). The method has been empirically tested by Mansouri (1985) who demonstrated positive gains in vocabulary competence for students taught with semantic grids over a control group taught by other methods.[2]

A related finding on L1 speech errors which has ramifications in our consideration of the L2 lexicon is the importance of syntactic category. In Fay and Cutler's corpus, 99 per cent of malapropism errors were in the same syntactic category as the target word, which shows that, at some level in processing, syntax is a powerful and reliable organizer of the mental lexicon. Errors which show this are, for example:

> borrow ———→ bother (verbs)
> musician ———→ magician (nouns)
> genuine ———→ general (adjectives)

Hence when we are attempting to help learners to programme their lexical associations, paradigmatic associations between related words in the same syntactic category are equally as important to mental lexical organization as syntagmatic associations. This means that *crucial* as a new item needs to be consciously related, by the learner, to *important, vital*, as well as to *discussions, factors*, etc.; or *soak* to *wash, rinse*, as well as to *clothes* or *stains*. Evidence that the high level organization of the mental lexicon depends on syntactic category comes also from word association studies of bilinguals who respond to nouns with nouns and adjectives with adjectives, even across languages, more frequently than they make syntagmatic associations (i.e. the *wash/clothes* type) (cf. Albert and Obler 1978, p. 223).

Considering now the conscious strategies learners use to try to memorize vocabulary, it is interesting to relate the Fay and Cutler model of the mental lexicon to the findings reported by Cohen and Hosenfeld (1981) and Cohen and Aphek (1980). Briefly, Cohen and Aphek invited L2 learners of Hebrew to introspect about any association device they thought they had used to try to learn a new word. Firstly they found that students who tried to generate associations for new words were able to retain them better over time and secondly that the nature of the associations were:

a) phonological together with semantic between L1 and L2, e.g. Hebrew *benatayim* (= 'meanwhile') associated with English *been a time;*

b) phonological within L2, e.g. *tsava* (= 'army') with *tsena* (= 'leave');

c) phonological together with semantic in L2, e.g. *lifney* (= 'before') with *lifamin* (= 'sometimes').

Associations of type a) fit in with data about mental links between the L1 and L2 lexicons. The fact that associations of type b) aid retention is to be expected, if mental lexicons are organized on a phonological basis, such that *tsava* and *tsena* will be very close together. Type c) associations are predicted as even more helpful because they make use of two network associations between items.

Summary and conclusions

In this chapter I have looked in particular at one kind of psycho-linguistic evidence bearing on the organization of the mental lexicon, and in brief at several other kinds of evidence and argument. From this the following theoretical conclusions are proposed:

1. For L1 there is one mental lexicon, phonologically arranged, with word stress, syllable structure and syntax acting as high level organizers. This lexicon is accessed by distinct but interlinked networks for production and perception.
2. L1 and L2 lexicons within the *same* speaker are clearly linked, phonologically, semantically and associationally. Speakers can make conscious links between them.
3. Evidence that the L2 user's mental lexicon of a given language resembles the L1 user's mental lexicon is sparse. There are both similarities and differences in lexical behaviour.

The discussion in this chapter, and the conclusions reached, point directly to two areas for further research. The first arises from conclusion 3. We urgently need a wide-ranging study of naturally occurring speech errors in L2, to parallel the many studies of L1 speech errors and to enable comparisons (on the lines of the study of phonological errors made by James 1984). Such a study should provide a clearer understanding of the nature of the L2 mental lexicon. The second arises from conclusion 2, and is an expansion of the work of Cohen and his two associates which has been referred to. The prediction that associations which are both semantic *and* phonological in nature are most helpful in aiding recall of vocabulary invites empirical testing.

Finally there are obvious implications for the ways vocabulary is taught in the classroom, and teachers will be in a position to relate the theoretical discussion to their own observations of the processes of learning and remembering used by their students. The following seem to me to be the main implications for classroom practice:

1. Since the lexicon appears to be an independent entity in processing, there is justification for teaching approaches which make vocabulary work a separate learning activity. It is not essential always to integrate vocabulary with general communication.
2. Presentation of vocabulary should pay specific attention to pronunciation, in particular word stress. So visual presentation and reading may not be the best ways to introduce new vocabulary.
3. Learners should be encouraged to make their own lexical associations when they are actively learning new vocabulary. (However, at present we do not know which kind of associations are the most useful in aiding retention.)
4. Semantic links play an important role in production. This suggests the use of semantic field based presentation methods on the lines of that exemplified.

Notes

1. I gave a paper on this topic at a conference on *Theories of Meaning and Lexicography* held at the University of Lodz 19–21 June, 1985 (see reference with this title for related papers (Channell, in preparation)). I am grateful to participants for their comments which have helped to shape this paper. In addition I should like to thank the following people who have provided detailed suggestions: Walter Grauberg, Patrick Griffiths, Paul Meara, Paul Ostyn, Brygida Rudzka. The guidance of the editors has also been most helpful. Any remaining inadequacies are my responsibility.
2. In Mansouri's research, five groups of Iraqi secondary learners of English used the same materials for three months, with two of the five groups learning vocabulary using componential and collocational grids. The two experimental groups achieved higher scores (at a statistically significant level) on a post test than did the control groups.

Points for further development

1. A useful and widely drawn distinction is between productive and receptive vocabulary. Channell points out that words are normally 'known passively' before being actively used. An interesting question here is whether *active* and *passive* are automatic polarities. For example, is it the case that a word can be used without a user fully comprehending all its senses? Does production, in the context of creatively playing out or testing meanings, sometimes precede comprehension? Should this process be given greater encouragement by teachers?

2. Ostyn and Godin (1985) argue that the term 'receptive lexical knowledge' – with *receptive* being used 'in its strongest sense' – should be used in place of 'active' or 'passive'. The implications of this are that knowing a word can mean not just working out its meaning from contexts but also recognizing it instantaneously without reliance on context.

3. Current psycholinguistic research allows us to assume one mental lexicon each for L1 and L2 with learners making 'associations' between the two languages. Channell points out that semantic and phonological links, in particular, should be encouraged. What are the implications of this for the presentaton of words to learners in the early stages of language learning? Many textbooks teach paired associates with one item usually a translation of the other. What kinds of modification to this practice can we experiment with?

4. In the light of Channell's discussion should the somewhat derided practice of learning words in lists be dismissed without fuller examination?

5. Much current language-teaching theory emphasizes the importance of learning how to decode meanings from context, especially in reading materials. But can vocabulary ever be fully acquired without considerable decontextualized attention being given to the phonological shape and characteristic stress patterns of a word? What are the implications here for classroom teaching of reading and writing?

6. In addition to grids and charts indicating the semantic associations between words, what other ways can be exploited for teaching the semantic arrangement of words? Re-read here Chapter 2 (Sections 2 and 3).

7. If words are to be taught in semantic networks, which meanings do we teach first in the case of polysemous words?

8. One possible objection to Channell's rich suggestions for teaching words is that, viewed as a whole, they may lead to a neglect of the syntagmatic axis in the organization of vocabulary. (The tendency in much psycholinguistic research is to focus on paradigmatic associations.) How can the simultaneous learning of, say, collocational expectancies be fostered? Given the shifting nature of many collocational partnerships, are the two processes compatible? And what about multi-word units, idioms, the 'stable' chunks of language (of which individual 'words' are only a component)? See here particularly Cowie's and Nattinger's papers.

9. Another objection to teaching words in their semantic networks is that it can encourage a rather static view of the lexicon. Learners tend to acquire knowledge *about* words rather than of words. Knowledge *of* words may be dependent on developing strategies for not delimiting the boundaries of word meaning and learning instead to take creative risks with words, leaving a certain 'fuzziness' intact. This sense creation depends on learning contexts such as role play where meanings become more negotiable. Clearly, a balanced approach between sense delineation and sense creation is an important prerequisite for successful vocabulary teaching. Cowie also argues for such a balance in teaching.

10. Channell's paper offers some valuable insights into the storage of words. It is also worth considering the extent to which words are stored at different levels of comprehension, according, for example, to perceived usefulness, their availability or 'familiarity' as words (see Chapter 1, p. 13), or indeed the mode of study adopted for learning them (see Nattinger's comments on 'cognitive depth', p. 67).

Vocabulary and reading

Paul Nation and James Coady

The purpose of this paper is to discuss the relationship of vocabulary to reading with an emphasis on reviewing the relevant research relating to guessing as well as learning vocabulary in context. The effect of vocabulary on readability is also discussed. Although the focus is on learners of English as a foreign language, research with native speakers provides the main source of information.

The paper begins by looking at the effects of vocabulary knowledge on reading and then looks at how reading increases vocabulary knowledge. A strategy for teaching the guessing skill is proposed and the steps are elaborated with reference to research.

Vocabulary and text readability

In measures of readability of a text, vocabulary difficulty has consistently been found to be the most significant predictor of overall readability (Chall 1958; Klare 1974). Moreover, 'once a vocabulary measure is included in a prediction formula, sentence structure does not add very much to the prediction' (Chall 1958, p. 157). Vocabulary difficulty is estimated in various ways; the most usual are word frequency and/or familiarity and word length. That is, sentences are more readable if they contain words that are of high frequency in occurrence and that are shorter rather than longer. Other measures are the degree to which a word calls up other words quickly – association value – and concrete versus abstractness. Klare (1963) points out that 'The characteristic of words most often measured in readability studies is, directly or indirectly, that of frequency' (p. 167).

However, it must be kept very clearly in mind that readability formulae or predictors are an index or measure of text difficulty, not a causal analysis of why a given text is difficult. That is to say, there are a number of factors in a text which contribute to its ease or difficulty for a given reader, but we can most accurately predict that fact by measuring one variable, vocabulary, and extrapolating from it to the overall case.

Davis (1968, 1972) did extensive investigation into the question of whether there are identifiable subskills within the overall ability to read. He did empirical correlational studies and factor analysis arriving at four clear factors:
1. recalling word meaning
2. determining meaning from context
3. finding answers to explicit questions
4. drawing inferences

Of all the factors, vocabulary was the most important and had the strongest effect. In subsequent studies by Spearritt (1972) and Thorndike (1973) remembering word meanings was the only consistent subskill which persisted across the various analyses.

Thus, vocabulary knowledge would seem to be the most clearly identifiable subcomponent of the ability to read, at least when one uses current experimental and statistical methodology as the tool of investigation. Yap (1979) concludes that 'causal links probably do exist between vocabulary and comprehension and that vocabulary is likely to be the predominant causal factor' (p. 58).

The effect of low frequency vocabulary

While research indicates that the presence of low frequency vocabulary in a text has a negative effect on comprehension (Marks, Doctorow and Wittrock 1974; Kameenui, Carnine and Freschi 1982; Freebody and Anderson 1983), the answers to the following questions have been difficult to find.

1. *What is the optimal ratio of unknown to known words in a text?*
Marks *et al.* (1974) found that replacing 15 per cent of the words in a reading text with low frequency words led to a significant decrease in comprehension. Freebody and Anderson (1983), however, have called Marks *et al.*'s criteria for high and low frequency words into question. Freebody and Anderson compared two low frequency word ratios – one low frequency word in three content words, and one low frequency word in six content words. Counting both function and content words, these translate into ratios of roughly 1 in 6 (17 per cent) and 1 in 12 (8 per cent). Although there was some decrease in comprehension at the 1 in 12 ratio, it was only at the 1 in 6 ratio that there was a reliable decrease in comprehension. Kameenui *et al.* (1982) found that ratios around one low frequency word in fourteen running words (7 per cent) gave a reliable decrease in correctly

answering inferential questions based on the text. The answering of literal questions was not significantly affected.

Research with foreign-language learners has not provided an answer to the ratio question. Holley (1973) tried to find the best ratio experimentally. She investigated the relationship between new word density (i.e. the ratio of unknown words to the total length of a text) on the one hand, and vocabulary learning, reading time, comprehension, and student rating of difficulty and enjoyability on the other, using a 750-word text with a glossary. Instead of finding a favourable new word density beyond which learning suffered, Holley found that 'vocabulary learning continues to increase even up to a new vocabulary density of one new word per fifteen known words' (7 per cent) (p. 343). Scores on reading time, comprehension, and student ratings of difficulty and enjoyment were not significantly related to new word density.

A reason for Holley's finding may be that her text was short, 750 words, compared with the length of most simplified reading books which are several thousand words long. In Holley's short text, a high ratio of unknown words to known may be acceptable because the total number of unknown words is not high. In a longer simplified reading book, this high ratio would result in an unacceptably high total number of unknown words.

It is likely that only a study involving a large amount of material and a representative range of prose types will provide useful answers to the question of unknown word density. Until there is further research it is still wise to follow the guideline suggested by West (1941, p. 21) of a ratio of no more than one unknown word to fifty known words (2 per cent).

2. *In what ways do low frequency words affect comprehension?*
Freebody and Anderson (1983) examined the effect of placing low frequency words in the important parts of the text as well as in the unimportant parts. The effect of putting difficult vocabulary in important parts of the text was not clear, but seemed to result in a general drop in comprehension over the whole text. The effect of difficult vocabulary in unimportant parts of the text resulted in more adult-like summaries. A 'parsimonious explanation of this result is that students did not process many of the unimportant items, lightening the load in terms of length, and helping them focus on more important items which would be more useful in the formation of summaries' (p. 35). This indicates that readers' reaction to unknown words may be simply to skip over them if they do not seem to play a crucial role in the text.

The effect of pre-teaching vocabulary

Kameenui *et al.* (1982) in two studies found that pre-teaching vocabulary had a significant effect on comprehension. The pre-teaching involved mastery learning where the meaning of the low frequency word was given and the learner answered questions which used the word in a sentence context. As soon as the teaching was completed the learners sat the comprehension test. In an earlier experiment, Pany, Jenkins and Schreck (1982) found only negligible effects of vocabulary training on reading comprehension. Kameenui *et al.* (1982) looked at the effect of redundant information in the text and suggested that the positive effects of this could mask the effects of vocabulary learning. Stahl (1983) found that two of his three groups showed comprehension gains as a result of vocabulary pre-teaching.

Beck, Perfetti and McKeown (1982), McKeown *et al.* (1983) and Omanson *et al.* (1984) examined the effect of vocabulary teaching using a variety of procedures on reading comprehension. The following conclusions can be drawn from their studies.

1. If vocabulary 'instruction is to influence comprehension it must go beyond establishing accurate responses to words' (McKeown *et al.* 1983, p. 17). It must develop fluency of access to word meaning and must integrate the learned words into existing semantic networks.
2. Such instruction takes considerable time. In the McKeown *et al.* (1983) experiment, 104 words were taught over a five-month period in 75 thirty-minute lessons. About 80 per cent of the words were learned.
3. Repetition of the words affected learning with more repetition having some effect on some learners. The minimum number of repetitions in the study was around ten, and this was enough to have an effect.
4. The pre-teaching of vocabulary has an added effect of increasing the saliency of a word when it is met during reading. This meeting gives 'rise to parallel processing in which the learning context of the instructed words is called to mind, which in turn improves the recall of propositions [in the text] containing the instructed words' (Omanson *et al.* 1984, p. 1266).

The studies on readability and pre-teaching indicate the important role vocabulary knowledge plays in reading. But they also indicate the difficulties in experimentally demonstrating a clear connection between vocabulary manipulations and comprehension. Vocabulary knowledge is only one, though an important one, of many factors that allow readers to get information from texts. If, for particular texts, vocabulary knowledge is insignificant, then a range of strategies and other sources of information is available to compensate for this lack. We will look at one of these strategies in the following section of this paper.

Learning vocabulary through reading

Nagy and Anderson (1984) conclude that 'even the most ruthlessly systematic direct vocabulary instruction could neither account for a significant proportion of all the words children actually learn, nor cover more than a modest proportion of the words they will encounter in school reading materials' (p. 304). Jenkins, Stein and Wysocki (1984) point out that 'learning from context is still a default explanation; evidence that individuals actually learn word meanings from contextual experiences is notably lacking' (p. 769). Indeed the very redundancy or richness of information in a given context which enables a reader to guess an unknown word successfully could also predict that that same reader is less likely to learn the word because he or she was able to comprehend the text without knowing the word.

Coady (1979) has argued that the successful ESL reader employs a psycholinguistic guessing approach (Goodman 1976; Smith 1982). That is to say, the reader samples the clues in the text and reconstructs a mental representation of what he or she thinks the text says. This analysis by synthesis approach to reading has also been described as a top-down model of reading. In contrast to this approach, the more traditional view of reading as decoding of letters into sound and ultimately meaning, is characterized as a bottom-up model. More recent theorizing in schema-theoretic models of reading has claimed that both approaches are integral to reading (Adams 1982).

Typically, ESL learners are poor decoders since their vocabulary knowledge is weak while, at the same time, they are already literate in their mother tongue, and are familiar with top-down processing. Therefore, it becomes important to consider whether our instruction should emphasize top-down or bottom-up processing, as well as an appropriate emphasis on the use of context.

Adams and Huggins (1985) claim that word recognition abilities are the single best class of discriminators between good and poor readers. They investigated the sight vocabulary knowledge of second through fifth graders, and proposed a stage theory of sight word acquisition, wherein at the most sophisticated stage the word is 'securely represented in the reader's visual lexicon' (p. 275), i.e. sight vocabulary; the second stage comprised words not recognized in isolation but only in context, and finally words not recognized at all. Note that sight vocabulary is quite distinct from listening vocabulary where there is no internal mode of the word in its written form. Perfetti and Lesgold (1977, 1979) have argued that when a reader's efforts at word recognition are especially slow and laboured, short-term memory is so taxed that the reader cannot take full advantage of context. In sum, these researchers are arguing that a good reader has a sufficient command over the language so that words are recognized automatically – sight vocabulary – or recognized in context. Poor readers do not have enough sight vocabulary to take advantage of the context. This would seem to imply that successful instruction of ESL readers will have to take into account their vocabulary knowledge and especially their sight vocabulary.

What is context?

Context can be viewed as morphological, syntactic, and discourse information in a given text which can be classified and described in terms of general features. This is the context within the text. But the reader also has background knowledge of the subject matter of a given text, i.e. the general context. Good readers take advantage of such background knowledge in processing the text, and in creating an expectation about the kind of vocabulary that will occur. Hayes-Roth and Hayes-Roth (1977) and Abramovici (1984) have found that lexical information persists in memory representations of meaning; that is to say, good readers tend to remember the words they encounter as well as their meanings.

In an experiment on the facilitating effect of previous knowledge, Adams (1982) found that giving learners information about the topic of a passage before they read it resulted in significantly higher scores on guessing the meanings of nonsense words in the texts. Learners reading in their mother tongue gained higher scores than those reading in a second language, French.

Learning from context

In the research and literature on guessing words from context, a distinction is often made between getting the meaning of a word from the use of context clues, and the learning or retention of this meaning. Studies on getting the meaning give their attention to the types of clues available in context, learners' success or failure in using available clues, and the effect of training on using clues.

Studies on learning words from context sometimes consider the presence of clues, but are most interested in what has been remembered of a word from meeting it in context. Failure to remember information from context can result from failure to get the meaning or from failure to retain the meaning. It is important to note that studies on learning words from context have not shown the large amounts of learning we might expect, considering the rates at which first-language learners seem to increase their vocabulary. (See Anderson and Shifrin 1980).

Jenkins *et al.* (1984) presented low frequency words in very informative contexts in two, six or ten passages read over several days. 'Half of the unfamiliar words were informally taught before their appearance in the passages. Word meanings were learned from context, and more frequent presentation in context increased learning' (p. 707). However, Jenkins *et al.* were surprised that the amount of learning from context was not as great as was expected. Pre-exposure to some of the words by seeing them listed on a sheet with synonyms and a sentence context had a marked effect on learning from context.

Nagy, Herman and Anderson (1985) argue that the failure of Jenkins *et al.*'s study to show substantial learning from context results from the experimenters' failure to consider truly the incremental nature of learning from context. As a result their measures of word knowledge were not sensitive enough to reveal small increments of learning. In their study, Nagy *et al.* used multiple-choice and interview measures which were designed to show small amounts of learning if they occurred. As a result of their research, Nagy *et al.* estimated the probabilities of learning a word from context after just one exposure to be between .10 and .15. Although this seems low, when it is seen in relation to the hundreds and perhaps thousands of unknown words a learner meets, this could result in learning a substantial number of words. And, of course, repeated exposure to a word should have some incremental but as yet undetermined effect.

The rate of success in guessing

What are the chances of success in guessing from context? Ames's (1966) study gives the clearest indication of this because the many words to be guessed were chosen on a random basis. His doctoral level students successfully guessed 60 per cent of the unknown words. Liu and Nation (1984), working with advanced second-language learners, found that the high proficiency learners guessed between 85 per cent and 100 per cent of the unknown words. The unknown words were all the low frequency words in the texts which were not in *A General Service List* (West 1953), and *A University Word List* (Xue and Nation 1984). The important corollary is that if the learners cited were able to guess a majority of the words, then the necessary clues are there for other, perhaps less gifted, learners to use. It is not an unrealistic goal to expect learners to guess between 60 per cent and 80 per cent of the unknown words in a text if the density of the unknown words is not too high.

Sternberg and Powell (1983) distinguish between clues to the meaning of an unknown word in context, and variables that facilitate or hinder the use of these clues. Density, that is the ratio of unknown to known words in a text, is one such variable. Other variables include the number of times the same unknown word occurs in a text and the variety of contexts in which it occurs in the text, the importance of the unknown word to understanding the context in which it is embedded, the closeness of the contextual information to the unknown word (Carnine, Kameenui and Coyle 1984), and the usefulness of prior knowledge.

A few experiments on training learners to guess from context have shown some improvement in guessing (Hafner 1965, 1967; Carnine *et al.* 1984). Teaching a strategy is one way of providing training.

A strategy for guessing from context

The following strategy is an elaboration of one described by Clarke and Nation (1980). It represents a procedure learners can use to ensure that they are making good use of the available context clues. As will be seen later, it is expected that as the learners become more proficient in the use of the clues, they will not need to follow the steps of the strategy so rigidly.

The strategy presupposes two things; firstly that the learners are able to follow the ideas in the text they are reading, that is, that they have sufficient command of vocabulary, grammar and reading skills in order to achieve basic comprehension of the text, and secondly that the learners bring some relevant background knowledge to the text.

This strategy consists of five steps:
1. Finding the part of speech of the unknown word.
2. Looking at the immediate context of the unknown word and simplifying this context if necessary.
3. Looking at the wider context of the unknown word. This means

looking at the relationship between the clause containing the unknown word and surrounding clauses and sentences.
4. Guessing the meaning of the unknown word.
5. Checking that the guess is correct.
Initially the strategy is a major interruption to the reading process while learners develop familiarity with the range of clues available.

Steps 1 and 2: Focusing on the word and its immediate context
The first two steps of the strategy focus on the word itself and the pattern it fits into with the words close to it. Aborn, Rubenstein and Sterling (1959) investigated native-speakers' prediction of words missing from isolated sentences. They concluded that 'increasing the context beyond ten words does not increase predictability. The length at which context attains maximum effectiveness lies between five and ten words' (p. 179). They also found that having context on both sides of a gap was superior to a longer context on either side. If the immediate context is difficult to interpret because of other unknown words, however, then guessing is affected.

Studies of incorrect guesses (Haynes 1984; Laufer and Sim 1985) show that many learners are unable to make use of the immediate context and are often misled by the form of the unknown word.

Step 2, immediate context, can be elaborated by listing possible sources of information that learners can look for:
1. Use the context to answer the question 'What does what?' about the unknown word.
2. Make use of any related phrases or relative clauses.
3. Remove *and* or *or* and make two or more simpler sentences.
4. Interpret punctuation clues such as italics (showing the word will be defined), quotation marks (showing the word has a special meaning), dashes (showing apposition) or brackets (enclosing a definition).

Step 3: Using the wider context
Clauses and sentences in texts enter into relationships with surrounding clauses and sentences. These relationships include cause and effect, contrast, generalization – detail, exclusion (*on the contrary, instead*), explanation (*in other words, that is*), time (*before, subsequently, finally*), and arrangement (*in the first place, secondly*). These relationships may be signalled, but most often they are left for the reader to infer. Helping learners make use of these relationships usually involves making the implicit relationships explicit (Nation 1984).

The wider context can also be elaborated by citing possible sources of information for learners to make use of:

1. Make use of any reference word clues like *this*, *that*, *it*, etc.
2. Complete any comparison clues.
3. Choose and interpret the appropriate conjunction relationships between the clause or sentence with the unknown word and the preceding and following clauses or sentences.

Several researchers have developed lists of the clues which are available in context to help in guessing the meaning of an unknown word. Usually these lists were made to guide teachers in helping their learners develop the guessing skill. The lists were developed in several ways:

a) by analysis of texts (Artley 1943; Dulin 1970);
b) by getting learners to describe the clues they used on words they selected themselves (McCullogh 1943, 1945, 1958);
c) by getting learners to describe the clues they used to guess words which were randomly chosen by the experimenter (Ames 1966).

The lists can be divided into two main types – those based on features of semantics or meaning and those based on sources of clues. Sternberg and Powell's (1983) list is an example of the first type. The list contains eight items and is suited particularly to guessing the meanings of nouns. It acts as a checklist for learners to use to see if the related information is available in the text. Sternberg and Powell suggest that when the learners are trying to guess a word they should look for temporal clues regarding the duration and frequency of the unknown word, value clues, class membership clues, etc. Sternberg and Powell's list describes the type of information to look for, but does not indicate what form that information can take in a text.

The most thoroughly researched list of sources of clues is that produced by Ames (1966), which contains fourteen items. One of these, clues derived from language experience or familiar expressions, does not apply to true guessing from context, because it presupposes that all of the familiar expression is already known. Of the other thirteen items, four can apply to step 2 of the guessing strategy (modifying phrases or clauses, words connected or in series, preposition clues, non-restrictive clauses or appositive phrases), and nine apply to step 3 – the use of wider context. These nine include definition or description, comparison or contrast, synonym, tone, setting and mood, referral, main idea–details, question–answer, and cause–effect.

The aim of most guessing strategies is to make learners aware of the range of information available from context so that after practice they have no need to keep to any rigid guessing procedure.

Step 4: Guessing
Step 4 consists of the actual guess made by the learner using the clues obtained in steps 1–3. This guess may be made in the mother tongue or in English.

Step 5: Checking the guess
There are several ways of checking the guess:
1. Check that the part of speech of the guess is the same as the part of speech of the unknown word.
2. Break the unknown word into parts and see if the meaning of the parts relates to the guess.
3. Substitute the guess for the unknown word. Does it make sense in context?
4. Look in a dictionary.

When the learners have used the available context clues to guess an unknown word, they then can use additional information to check that their guess is correct. The first way of checking is to see if the part of speech of the unknown word is the same as the part of speech of the guess. A surprising number of wrong guesses are a different part of speech from the unknown word. If the learner checks and the part of speech is not the same, then another guess should be made.

A second way of checking is to use the form of the unknown word, particularly prefixes and stem, as a clue to its meaning. For example, *presentiment* can be broken into three parts, the meaning of which can be used to compare with a previous guess of the meaning of the word. It is very important that the use of the word form comes after the context clues have been used. A common source of error with untrained learners is guessing using the form of the word rather than the context (Looby 1939; Gibbons 1940; Haynes 1984; Bensoussan and Laufer 1984). For example, *habitat* was guessed as *habit, enormous* as *abnormal, offspring* as *the end of spring, on the grounds* as *on the earth, uniquely* as *unequally*.

When learners make an incorrect guess based on word form, they then try to interpret the context to support the incorrect guess. If they learn to delay using word form clues until after using contextual information, then one of the most difficult parts of the strategy has been mastered.

One important reason why learners rely heavily on the form of the word when guessing is that their vocabulary knowledge is so poor that they cannot interpret the surrounding context (Laufer and Sim

1985). Thus the only source of information they can use is the form of the unknown word. In the Bensoussan and Laufer experiment (1984) many of the learners had to guess at a density of one unknown word in every eleven running words.

However, Laufer and Sim (1985) and Gibbons (1940) showed that even the better readers among their learners made wrong guesses based on form. Haynes's (1984) study clearly shows that second-language learners are likely to let the form of an unknown word take priority over syntactic clues.

Similarly, second-language learners are more adept at making use of syntactic clues than they are at using discourse level clues. Research on reading by Cziko (1978) supports this conclusion. Gibbons (1940), working with university graduates who were native speakers of English, found that 33 per cent (78 out of 234 freshmen) were unable to guess *itinerant* in the following context, and 91 per cent were unable to guess *vicarious*.

> In the beginning the teacher travelled from one locality to another to meet the students, thereby bringing into existence the *itinerant* school master.

> Part of our education is obtained directly through actual experiences; *vicarious* experiences which come through reading, pictures, lectures, art and music are equally important, however, as a means of extending real experiences.

Studies of incorrect guessing show the importance of getting learners to delay making use of word clues until they have made full use of the available context clues. For this reason, in a guessing strategy, information based on word part analysis is best used as a way of *checking* context-based guesses. In addition, guessing making the widest use of context clues is encouraged if the context is understandable. If the frequency of unknown words is high, then learners are forced into a word-by-word reading strategy, and they guess by using word form clues rather than context.

Conclusion

In general the research leaves us in little doubt about the importance of vocabulary knowledge for reading, and the value of reading as a means of increasing vocabulary. The precise nature of these relationships, and how we can make use of them in our teaching, are still fruitful areas of investigation.

Points for further development

1. Nation and Coady's review of the research implies that, in spite of a long history of investigation into vocabulary and reading in a first language, and isolated studies in second-language learning, we are still forced to rely on our feelings and intuitions about how we can best deal with vocabulary for reading. In what ways have intuition and experience influenced your approach to the problem of vocabulary for reading? Do you follow any particular set of principles for dealing with vocabulary in the reading lesson?

2. Pre-teaching vocabulary has traditionally been recommended to help learners deal with a reading text. Nation and Coady claim that research indicates that this may be of doubtful value. Firstly, knowing the meaning of a word and readily accessing that meaning both require attention. Secondly, pre-teaching may result in the discouragement of strategies such as guessing, or ignoring unknown words. It may make learners give an importance to knowing the meanings of words in texts which discourages the use of other coping procedures. Research by Taylor (1986) nonetheless suggests that pre-teaching *is* useful and has an important role to play. Do research experiments still have a value for teachers, even when contradictory claims result?

3. There is evidence to show that too high a density of unknown words in a text has a negative effect on comprehension and vocabulary learning. The optimum density is probably a function of a variety of factors not the least being interest in the text. Statistical studies of vocabulary indicate that a relatively small vocabulary is needed to account for a very high percentage of words in a text (Kucera 1982; Nation 1983). If teachers ensure that learners master this important base vocabulary through a variety of approaches, and that reading material is roughly matched to vocabulary level, then comprehension and vocabulary learning activities will have more chance of success. Consider some of the texts you regularly use in your teaching in the light of these remarks.

4. The general conclusion to be drawn from research is that learning vocabulary through context must be the major way of increasing vocabulary knowledge. But it would seem that two complementary approaches are necessary to get this increase: the encouragement of a substantial quantity of reading and the development of the skill of guessing from context. How can we motivate learners who may lack the reading habit to do this 'substantial' reading, and thereby increase their vocabulary?

5. Good learners can guess a very high proportion of unknown words, perhaps 60 per cent to 80 per cent, providing the density of unknown words is not too high. Success in guessing is affected by variables such as the number of times a word occurs, the variety of contexts in which it occurs and the importance of the word in the text. This would still seem to leave the problem of judging the right density of unknown words to the teacher; are there any ways in which teachers can be assisted in this?

6. Nation and Coady suggest a practical strategy for guessing unknown words in texts, consisting of five steps:
a) find the part of speech of the word;
b) examine the immediate context;
c) examine the wider context;
d) guess the meaning;
e) check that the meaning is correct.
Can students be trained to the habit of using the five steps? We might also consider whether some steps are more crucial than others.

The role of dictionaries in language learning

Della Summers

Current attitudes in EFL to vocabulary and dictionary use

My aim in this article is to show that dictionary use is a valid activity for foreign learners of English, both as an aid to comprehension and production. I do not claim that the dictionary is the only, best, or easiest source of the linguistic knowledge needed to understand and write or speak English accurately, but simply that in addition to other learning strategies, such as making guesses about new words encountered in reading texts, asking the teacher for explanations, or asking help from their classmates, students can and should be encouraged to avail themselves of the substantial information contained in their dictionaries. This does not necessarily happen, however. Until very recently vocabulary learning has not received the primacy in EFL teaching methodology or in published coursebooks that might be expected. There have been changing trends – from grammar-translation to direct method to the communicative approach – but none of these has emphasized the importance of the learner's lexical competence over structural/grammatical competence.

Dictionaries for language learning have been largely ignored in the wealth of books and articles on language learning by linguists, psychologists, and language teachers. There is a strong insistence that words should not be thought of individually, or 'in isolation', and dictionaries are seen as reinforcing the students' tendency to learn individual words when acquiring a second language. (For example, see Bullard 1985 on individual word learning analysed in spoken contexts.)

An article by McCarthy (1984) argues for vocabulary teaching based on the findings of discourse analysis and the use of naturally occurring language. He says: 'The habit of viewing words as isolated semantic problems to be resolved by definition is one best discouraged from the start of the beginner course.' This opinion is far from being uncommon. It reinforces the prevailing view that newly encountered words should only be decoded by means of contextual clues. Although this is a widely agreed pedagogic principle, it cannot always be reconciled with what is possible for the native speaker, let alone the actual practice of the EFL student. In reality, unknown words within texts – whether in the form of a repetition, an encapsulation, a superordinate or subordinate term – are very often *not* deducible from contextual clues, and I cite the underlined words in the passage entitled 'Memories' quoted on p. 119 as evidence of this. Look for example at the word *dratted* in the passage, where there are no contextual clues of any kind to help a reader guess at its meaning.

Many of us would like to believe that teaching words in some systematic way would be helpful – whether in semantic sets, by collocational or semantic feature matrices, even by linking them via their etymology, morphology or phonology – but naturally occurring language is not easily systematized. Trying to deduce the meaning of an unknown word from the text is one valuable strategy in understanding language, and so is dictionary use, but it is only by repeated exposures that a word can enter a person's active vocabulary, whether in first or subsequent language acquisition.

Students of English as a foreign language often *are* confronted with words that they need to clarify before they can continue with the text they are working on. How important the meaning of the word is in the passage, the number of unknown words in the passage, the reason why the student is working on it – to write an essay, for a comprehension test, as background reading – all these affect whether or not the student may turn to the dictionary for help. If unknown words are stumbling blocks to comprehension, surely it is reasonable to encourage students to make use of that help?

Nonetheless, in recent years, ELT teachers have actively discouraged the use of dictionaries, particularly in class. Teachers' disapproval may be caused by students' using bilingual dictionaries too slavishly, especially small ones that they can carry around with them. Students do indeed work on an individual word basis, in the worst sense, expecting a one-to-one correlation between the words of their own language and English. If they do not get help over the collocations, typical context, and grammatical possibilities of the word, they may make errors.

There is also the suspicion that the use of any dictionary, (even a monolingual learners' dictionary, which does have examples to show collocation, typical context, and grammatical information) interrupts the flow of concentration when the student is reading a passage. This fear is compounded by the notion that the dictionary is too easy a solution – it is always better for students to work out the meaning of an unfamiliar word by using contextual clues. In fact, the student must have done some useful linguistic processing of the word in order to look it up at all – e.g. tracing an inflected form of a verb back to its base-form, then perhaps distinguishing the verb entry from the noun entry and so on. Although more and more teachers are realizing that vocabulary acquisition has been neglected in ELT, the main (approved of) method of acquiring vocabulary is still through reading, and reading without the help of a dictionary.

Native-speakers' use of dictionaries

There is a marked difference between the attitudes towards diction-aries of teachers of English as a foreign language and teachers of native-speaker students, and no doubt this arises from the different purposes for which a dictionary is used by foreign learners and native speakers. Vocabulary acquisition by children in a native-speaker situ-ation is similar to vocabulary acquisition in EFL, but not the same. The native-speaking child is exposed to words in a variety of different contexts, and so forms a well-rounded concept of the word's meaning and use. There are many excellent human dictionaries in the form of parents and teachers, who are frequently asked to give explanations for new words to children. In an EFL environment, there are few or no proficient speakers of English, and there is no constant verbal interaction as with native-speaker children.

Interestingly, research done by Longman into the use of diction-aries by native speakers in the UK showed that looking up meaning was actually the most frequent use for the dictionary in most house-holds, with checking for correct spelling coming second. Reference to the dictionary for word meanings was not for common words, but 'hard words':

1. words commonly confused or misused (e.g. *aggravate* being used to mean *annoy*, instead of *make worse*; *infer* being used instead of *imply*);
2. encyclopedic words – from science and technology, politics, econ-omics, etc.;
3. new words (e.g. *rate-capping, spreadsheet*);
4. rare or obsolete words (*abigail, pellucid*).

The dictionary, in our research project at least, was more commonly referred to for word games and to settle family arguments than for schoolwork or individual interest. Clarification about word meaning appears to be the main native-speaker requirement. Vocabulary acquisition from a dictionary by adult native speakers may be relatively rare, although I can remember clearly learning words from a dictionary myself, *ubiquitous* and *eponymous*, for example, both of which I was able to use immediately.

However, the use of dictionaries is generally expected and actively encouraged in most native-speaker schools and colleges in the UK and the USA. Training in dictionary skills is less common in ELT, as teachers assume such training has already been given for the mother tongue. The fact that ELT dictionaries have a great wealth of additional features, particularly grammatical information in the form of abbreviated codes, is not therefore attended to by very many teachers, although workbooks (e.g. Whitcut 1979; McAlpin forthcoming) are usually published to accompany such dictionaries.

Use of dictionaries in ELT

In 1980 the Longman ELT Dictionaries Department carried out a Needs Research project into the use made of the *Longman Dictionary of Contemporary English* (*LDOCE*) by intermediate students in secondary schools and colleges in the UK, Japan, Germany, the USA, Mexico and Nigeria. We analysed the relative use made of parts of the dictionary entry, and compared how often the dictionary was being used for reading as opposed to more active uses like essay writing. Again *LDOCE* was often referred to for checking spelling, but it was referred to four times as often to check the meaning, about 60 per cent of the total usage. Reference to other parts of the entry (examples, spelling, pronunciation, grammar or part of speech) could be assumed to relate to production activity or a need for more detailed comprehension than the immediate task necessitated. When a student of Hispanic origin in the USA wanted to check the meaning of *stuff* when reading a twentieth-century novel, he checked not only the meaning, but the spelling, pronunciation, and examples too. Perhaps when the student noted the spelling, it was to write in a vocabulary book of some kind. It appeared that the students in our Needs Research programme were indeed using the dictionary in some way to increase their vocabulary, although how the dictionary facilitated the process and how effective it was was not fully clarified in this research. In general, words that were looked up were not rare, technical, or 'hard', as in our native-speaker research; they were higher frequency words, particularly abstract ones.

Vocabulary acquisition

The term 'acquisition' raises the question of when we may regard a word as being truly 'acquired', and how we measure understanding of a word. We may ask whether cloze tests or multiple-choice questions are effective tools of assessment, or whether the learner's ability to give an accurate translation of the word in their L1 is the best indicator. On the other hand, we may wish to consider words to be only really 'acquired' if the learner can use the word actively and correctly, or has efficient recall of it in a variety of contexts. The evidence would suggest that there is a cline of acquisition, as there is a cline of need, ranging from a minimal idea of the typical context of the word through to very comprehensive capability. For example, it may be essential if you are a student reading an English newspaper to understand that a *spreadsheet* is something that presents calculations on a computer screen, but further detail may be quite unnecessary. In the reading passage quoted later, the word *skeins*, in the last paragraph, is almost certainly a 'throwaway' word, i.e. one that a student may feel he or she has to understand at the time of reading the passage, but which is very infrequent, and not worth the student attempting to remember. There is certainly little or no possibility of deducing the meaning of *skeins* from the context.

On the other hand, students clearly will be expected to use common words like *book, pencil, house, eat, drive, buy*, and so on, with near-perfect competence, so far as their commonest senses are concerned.

Between these two extremes is the vast bulk of the language, including polysemous words, like *run, set*, and *turn*, words having very many shifts of meaning, which together with their phrasal verbs (and their well-known attendant difficulties) and noun compounds, cause students widespread problems of decoding sense.

The traditional split of vocabulary learning into two parts – whether they are called decoding/encoding, comprehension/production, or passive/active – may ignore an intermediate stage, which might be termed 'deep understanding' or 'detailed comprehension': that is, not just what an unfamiliar word means within a particular text, but what it means in general, archetypally. To accept this notion, one must agree that words do have a basic fixed area of meaning that can be used in other texts: in other words, to believe that meaning is not always 'negotiated' or entirely dependent on the context and structure of the text in which it occurs. For example, in 'Memories' (p. 119), students might have deduced that *new-fangled* meant 'modern' in some way, but without understanding the range of possible referents (machines, ideas, etc.) and the attitude of the speaker (humorous or derogatory), they would be unable to understand the full implications of its use. Some linguists, however, would not even accept that *new-fangled* has the connotations specified here.

Although the text itself may give clues to the meaning of unknown words, when teachers and students need information for more productive purposes, such as essay writing, the dictionary may be the only help available. It is very unlikely that students will be able to guess collocations from the one or two contexts that they have remembered for a particular word, or to deduce grammatical regularities. They are much more likely to revert to their first language here, and produce interference errors. The dictionary should give concrete help to counteract such errors. Jain (1979) achieved invaluable results in an experiment he ran in India in which he presented *LDOCE* as 'the native-speaker on your desk'. In this experiment, the grammatical information in *LDOCE* was judged by the students taking part as more specific and therefore more helpful than the lexical information. For example, no dictionary was sufficiently clear to answer the question 'Which is right?' out of these options: *The non-cooperative movement broke out/emerged/sprouted*. Jain's report on how well *LDOCE* stood up to the title 'the native-speaker on your desk' has been a salutory reminder to us in our work. (See also Scholfield 1982.)

How can dictionaries help students to learn words?

The most obvious way is through providing further exposures for the word in other contexts, with different collocates and constructions, by making the student think about the words in relation both to the passage being read and the dictionary information. The meaning of the word as encountered in the passage is contextually bound or limited, a particular realization of the concept that the word expresses. There may be mismatches with the archetypal or prototypical meaning which would be shown in the dictionary, but the core is the same. In addition, the dictionary definitions and examples provide contexts which have been specially written to make it as easy as possible to infer the most likely meaning of the word.

In this way dictionaries present a powerful analytic tool in organizing language. When the definition provides an archetype onto which real-world realizations (e.g. a particular instance of *tail*) can be mapped, it does this by restating the concept behind the word, either in simpler terms that are more likely to be understood, as in example (1), or by breaking the concept down into constituent parts such as its appearance or typical functions, as in example (2). Johnson-Laird (personal communication) has argued that the mental activity involved in unpacking the definition would help to implant the word and its concept into the student's mind, especially when this is backed up by explanatory examples:

(1) **demise** /dɪ'maɪz/ *n* [U] *law or euph* death: *Upon his demise the title will pass to his son.* | (fig.) *the demise of a famous newspaper*

(2) **tail** /teɪl/ *n* **1** [C] the movable long growth at the back of a creature's body: *a dog's tail* | *a fish's tail* **2** [C] something like this in shape or appearance: *a comet's tail* | *We saw the tail of the procession* . . .

Differentiation from other similar words may be necessary for accurate comprehension. This is most obviously done in dictionaries by means of Usage Notes, for example, this one under **damp** in *LDOCE*:

USAGE **damp**, **humid** and **moist**. **Damp** is often used in a bad sense: *I can't wear these socks; they're* **damp**. **Moist** is used especially of food and parts of the body and often has a good sense (= not too dry): *a rich*, **moist** *cake* | **moist** *eyes/lips*. **Humid** is a more scientific word usually used of climate or weather: *It was hot and* **humid** *in the jungle.*

Drawing the user's attention to opposites or words with close meaning will also help fix new vocabulary in the memory. This is a definition of *feasible*, a word referred to in our 1980 Needs Research study:

feasible /'fiːzəbəl/ *adj* **1** able to be done; possible: *Your plan sounds quite feasible.* – compare PLAUSIBLE . . .

plausible /'plɔːzəbəl/ *adj* **1** (of a statement, argument, etc.) seeming to be true or reasonable: *Your explanation sounds quite plausible; I think I believe it.* – opposite **implausible** – compare FEASIBLE **2** (of a person) skilled in producing (seemingly) reasonable statements which may not be true: *a plausible liar* . . .

(From the *Longman Active Study Dictionary of English*, 1983)

Examples in dictionaries are of course absolutely essential both to extend the user's comprehension, and to provide models for students to remember and perhaps eventually produce, by putting individual words into a range of typical contexts and appropriate phrases. For example, these under **economy** in *LDOCE*:

to practise economy | *We're trying to make a few economies.* | *economy of effort* | *We had an* **economy drive** (= we all tried to spend less) *in order to save money for our holiday.* | *They are able to keep their costs low because of* **economies of scale.** (= the advantages of producing something in very large quantities) | *Buying cheap tyres is* **a false economy** – *they may cost a bit less, but they will wear out much more quickly* . . .

Some of these examples are based on sentences from a computerized corpus of authentic citations, but the actual examples in the citation base were substantially different, depending much more on the structure of the piece of discourse they are taken from, as one might expect. The dictionary examples have been shortened in order to clarify the meaning. As stated earlier, dictionaries deal with standard accepted meaning and use of words – with archetypal use, not all possible uses. ELT lexicographers do believe that it is possible, and advisable, to state the generalized meaning, including attitudinal restrictions, of words, using citational information, their knowledge of the language, and drawing on their experience as teachers of English.

A closer look at the effectiveness of dictionaries – the Longman APU Dictionary Experiment

In 1985, when we were about to revise the *Longman Dictionary of Contemporary English*, we instituted a research project intended to test the effectiveness of different entry organizations in presenting information both for comprehension and for production.

Dictionary editors at Longman have, for some years, been able to discuss their work with the Linglex committee, a group of linguists headed by Professor Sir Randolph Quirk. We were able to enlist the help of one of the members of Linglex, Philip Johnson-Laird of the Applied Psychology Unit in Cambridge, in this project, the principal aim of which was to test the proposition that an ELT dictionary consisting only of examples would be more helpful than the usual combination of abstract definition plus examples, to students at post-Cambridge-FCE level, in aiding comprehension and memory of vocabulary in production. (Here we must gratefully acknowledge the help of Alison Black, also of the Applied Psychology Unit, who structured the research for us, and Richard Rossner and Robert Hill and students of the Bell School, Cambridge, who took part in the actual tests.)

Description of the experiments

The reading passages
First, reading passages roughly equating to the level between FCE and those in the Cambridge Proficiency exam were selected. One class of students at the same level as the class to be used in the experiments were asked to underline the words they might want to look up in a dictionary and then rank them on a scale of 1 to 5 for difficulty. In this way, eight target words were selected for each of three texts. This is one of the three texts:

Memories

She smiled a little to herself at the thought of some of her childish escapades, the <u>scrapes</u> she and the Barnes boys got into, but apart from special days like today – the anniversary of her sixteenth [*sic*] birthday – she wasn't one for <u>reminiscing.</u> Not like Martha, the last of her old friends; she had been able to slip back into the past at will, happily re-running scenes and dialogues like one of these <u>new-fangled</u> videos.

Now even Martha with her caustic wit and <u>iron-clad</u> loyalty was gone, folded away, neat and tidy, in the little churchyard at the top of the hill. 'Don't you go coming to my funeral,' she had said dryly. 'If they see you in the churchyard, they might not let you out again.'

She had always made Pippin laugh; she would miss her – and her <u>dratted</u>, ever-lasting reminiscing.

The clock chimed and Pippin started. She would have to hurry. There was only an hour before the family began sailing in. And, much as she wanted to see them, she needed just a little more time to herself; time for simply remembering.

She quickly wrapped the rest of the apples, spaced them evenly and closed the drawer – they would keep well there, she knew that; the passage of time might wrinkle their smooth cheeks, but it would impart a mellow sweetness that honeyed on the tongue. Then, straightening her back, she reached up and twisted a <u>carved</u> knob at the back of the chest. A small drawer, cunningly concealed, slid open – Mother's hidden drawer, the secret of its existence <u>bequeathed</u> to her, and only to her, many years ago.

She took out a small package and as she unwrapped the yellowing tissue paper, a tangle of vividly coloured <u>skeins</u> of silk tumbled out on to the table; scarlets, greens and ebony black – poppy colours.

The sample entries

Three entries were written for each of the eight words, one consisting entirely of examples, another entirely of abstract definitions, the third type consisting of the normal abstract definition plus examples. The length of the information given was roughly the same for each of the three types. Here are the entries for *new-fangled*:

new-fangled *adj derog or humor* (of ideas, machines, etc.) new, but unnecessary or of no new value; more modern, but no improvement on the old ideas, machines, or way of doing something

new-fangled *adj derog or humor 'I don't like these new-fangled washing-machines', my grandmother always says. 'It's just as easy to wash the clothes by hand, and the clothes last longer.' | We need better teachers, not more new-fangled ideas of education! | To old Ned, even cars were new-fangled contraptions.*

new-fangled *adj derog or humor* (or ideas, machines, etc.) new but no improvement on the old ideas, machines, etc.: *'I don't like these new-fangled washing-machines', my grandmother always says. 'It's just as easy to wash the clothes by hand, and the clothes last longer.'*

Multiple-choice comprehension questions were written for each of the eight words. The different entry types were typed onto index cards and mixed so that each student received entries of all three types, in order to minimize the possibility of the different aptitudes of the students influencing the test results. Blanks cards to equate to the control condition, i.e. not having a dictionary to refer to at all, only the passages, were also inserted into each student's set of cards.

The first part of the experiment addressed the question of how successful each definitional technique was when the students retained the definitions for reference, and the second part measured success when cards were taken away prior to the test. This was an attempt to estimate the retention of information from the different dictionary presentations.

Both parts of the comprehension experiment showed that in the control condition (i.e. no dictionary definition at all) the students performed only slightly better than chance. This is the condition in which students were *only* able to make inferences from the text itself, in the way that their teachers would normally prefer. The general conclusion, however, must be that in *all* cases, comprehension was substantially improved by using the dictionary entries, together with the text, of course, but that there was no statistically significant difference between the success rates of the three different entry types:

	Definitions only	Examples only	Definitions + Examples	Control
Exp. 1	74	82	75	55

In the second experiment, when the dictionary cards were taken away but the students retained the passages, the scores were:

	Definitions only	Examples only	Definitions + Examples	Control
Exp. 2	67	67	64	48

Again the 'no-dictionary' control condition fared worst, with no significant differences between entry techniques. (The numbers quoted are percentages.)

Perhaps this is not surprising, if we examine the words underlined in the reading passage. How many of them are deducible from the context alone? *Scrapes* could be regarded as a repetition of *escapades*, except that perhaps only a native speaker would see it as a repetition

– because he or she already knows what *scrapes* means, and recognizes the phrase *get into scrapes*. The foreign learner might well fail to use the syntactic clue of apposition. *Escapades* was not one of the words underlined, i.e. rated as difficult, presumably because of its cognates in French, Italian, Spanish, and German. It seems that *iron-clad*, *dratted*, *carved*, and *skeins* also have little or no contextual support in the passage. Nor is it reasonable to expect the student to deduce the attitudinal restriction on *new-fangled*. In research by Oller (1975) even native speakers failed to guess accurately at unknown, but not necessarily infrequent, words from the context surrounding them about 50 per cent of the time, even when more than 100 words of context were given. The subjects failed to guess much more than 25 per cent accurately when fewer than 25 words of context were given.

The production test

A third experiment tested the value of the three different approaches by getting the students to produce nine of the words in sentences. The students' responses were marked by four separate judges for correctness. Each judge allocated each answer to one of four categories:

Correct and Original (O): The student clearly understood the word meaning and used it in a grammatically correct sentence which departs from the definition they were given.

Correct (C): The student's illustrative sentence is grammatically correct, but too similar either to the definition they were given or to the comprehension text, or alternatively, not informative enough to indicate that they have fully understood the word meaning.

Incorrect (I): The student has made an error of syntax, semantics, collocation, etc.

No response: (/)

This produced the following results over the selected words:

	Response	O	C	I	/
Entry condition	Definition only	17	24	41	7
	Examples only	23	20	44	4
	Definition + Examples	23	36	28	3
	Control	14	17	34	25
	Total	77	97	147	39

For production purposes, and of course this takes in the need for syntactic correctness, the mix of definition plus example would be seen as the most successful, being equal to the examples-only entry style in producing correct (O) sentences, but producing fewer incorrect sentences (28) than examples only (44). The productive power of examples is perhaps seen, as the more abstract definition was only slightly more successful than the control condition in which only the original passage was available for guidance.

Here is the result for *new-fangled*:

Response type	O	C	I	/
Definition	–	4	5	1
Example	4	1	5	–
Definition + Examples	2	4	4	–
Control	1	4	–	5

Entry condition spans the Definition, Example, Definition + Examples, and Control rows.

Most subjects correctly applied *new-fangled* to new inventions, technology, etc., but, in all conditions, failed to appreciate the derogatory connotation of the word. A student using the definition-only entry produced:

> They are constructing a lot of new-fangled avenues and bridges all over the city.

Some others using the examples-only produced:

> I always prefer buying new-fangled things.

> In this days is easier to make mathematic operations with all the new-fangled machines.

We were aware that aspects of the research were artificial, particularly in that students were asked to do production tests for words which they also needed to look up for comprehension. Particular words produced errors of a particular type. For example, errors for the word *reminisce* were always grammatical. Could this error be caused by the dictionary entry or was it just a typical error? Some errors might be guarded against in a dictionary by changes of presentation, once the likely errors were identified, which almost certainly could only be done by using an error corpus similar to collections of authentic examples already used by dictionary compilers. Overall, we did not feel that the examples-only approach would be an improvement in ELT dictionaries on the basis of these experiments, although the provision of natural, apt, generative model sentences was still of vital importance, particularly for production.

However, the experiments show that all three types of dictionary entry substantially improved student performance in all the tests, with the use of the dictionary for comprehension being much more successful than for production, at least at this level.

Conclusion

If we return to the central issue of whether dictionaries should be used in vocabulary learning, then it is apparent that, while the findings of research in reading and discourse analysis show the importance of context, establishment of topic and theme and so on in deducing the meaning of unfamiliar words, this should perhaps be seen as an aid to comprehension of the particular passage being worked on and as the basis for preliminary comprehension. In the specialized ELT dictionary, the student and non-native teacher have a powerful tool at their disposal, not always a perfect tool, but nonetheless a useful one, with which to gain further understanding of the range of use of new language, leading eventually to accurate production, mainly in writing. Yet, although the dictionary can 'put the student in charge', teachers often do not train their students in how to use the dictionary to best advantage. As dictionary-makers, we hope that the new awareness of the importance of vocabulary in language learning will go hand in hand with a greater appreciation of the dictionary's potential and that dictionary training will become an interesting and valuable new addition to the students' timetable.

Acknowledgements

I would like to thank my colleagues, Susan Maingay and Michael Rundell at Longman, and members of Linglex, Professor Sir Randolph Quirk, Dr Philip Johnson-Laird and Mr Philip Scholfield for their comments on this article.

Points for further development

1. Summers's paper argues for a corrective to the general tendency among language teachers to insist on teaching words in context. She points out that not all meanings *can* be inferred or accurately guessed or 'negotiated', and that some meanings are non-negotiable. Thus, we need to be alert to *both* the negotiable or inferential dimension of words *and* to a strict denotational dimension. It is always valuable

to keep questioning how words are best *retained* – whether they are learned in context or as a result of exposure to the isolated forms of the word encountered in a dictionary entry.

2. The more technical or specialized the field of discourse the more likely it is that meanings will be less negotiable and that greater reliance will have to be placed on dictionaries.

3. But when is a denotation not a denotation and when does it become a connotation? The use of *new-fangled* probably always carries fairly particular, even restricted meanings or associations. However, some very common words which would appear on the surface to have obvious referents or denotata (i.e. 'a basic fixed area of meaning', see p. 115) can acquire specific values in contexts of use. Learners also have to be taught to recognize and interpret such occurrences. For example, 'He's a *politician*' or He's a typical *man*' or 'She's a *diligent* student' can each acquire positive or negative connotations depending on context. A useful discussion of this topic, with particular reference to lexicography, is contained in Ayto (1983); but see also Chapter 5 and the paper by McCarthy in this chapter.

4. Reference to prototypical or fixed areas of meaning raises the issue of core vocabulary discussed in Carter (1987, Chapter 2) and elsewhere. But far more complex is the issue of core meanings, particularly of polysemous words. Can such meanings be isolated and, if so, should the range of meanings be explicitly taught? What role can the dictionary play here? Can definitions, rather than examples, best serve to reinforce prototypical meanings?

5. Summers notes that both teachers and students have a somewhat conventionalized view of the dictionary. How can the 'procedures' of the good monolingual learner's dictionary be brought into greater prominence in the vocabulary class? By, in particular, making greater use of the definition-plus-example method? Do we rely too much on what will be invariably random exposure to examples? Should more use be made of the extended but controlled examples dictionaries such as *LDOCE* supply?

6. Research reported by Summers shows that dictionary use appears to result more successfully in comprehension rather than production. Is it worth investing classroom time in teaching the codes used by particular dictionaries for the generation of accurate grammatical/ colligational patterns?

7. How can students be taught to recognize when the meaning of a word is essential for understanding a piece of text – and therefore has to be looked up or checked in a dictionary – and when it is less essential and can be safely ignored or, at least, known only in a generalized, 'pragmatic' way?

8. How do we best deal with lexical items which are either culture-specific or in some way gradable relative to the culture or part of the world we inhabit? How important are such 'meanings' or 'associations' in the learning of a second or foreign-language vocabulary? Should there be regional supplements to dictionaries which present the particular vocabulary of, say, Indian or Singapore Englishes?

9. Summers does not comment on the potential usefulness of etymological information or analysis in the decoding of the meanings of isolated words. Do teachers neglect this dimension? If so, why? See Ilson (1983) for useful discussion.

10. Summers concentrates largely on content words. How can dictionaries help in the provision of information concerning those items which are discourse markers or are, in some way, regularly discourse sensitive? See the discussion in Chapter 3, pp. 52–9 – which in particular, reports on the development of the COBUILD dictionary; see also Chapter 5 on discourse markers and text-structuring words.

Stable and creative aspects of vocabulary use

A. P. Cowie

1 Introduction

In recent years, the notion that the meanings of words and sentences are typically 'negotiated' through interaction between speakers (that is, created or interpreted by one speaker by cooperative adjustment to the assumptions and knowledge of another) has been strongly canvassed by proponents of a 'communicative' approach to language teaching, and now commands wide support among methodologists, teacher trainers and materials writers. This view is of course one reflection of a more general shift of interest within language teaching theory away from the formal features of language and towards the principles which control their appropriate use in normal communication (Breen and Candlin 1980; Brumfit 1985a and b; Widdowson 1978, 1979, 1983).

Within the wider debate, relatively little attention has been given to vocabulary use in particular, as compared with language use in general, though Widdowson (1983, pp. 92–3) has recently drawn a perceptive distinction between 'indexical' and 'procedural' vocabulary, one which echoes, though it does not exactly match, the much earlier division into 'encyclopaedic' and 'lexical' words made by Sweet (1899/1964). Nonetheless, it is possible either from direct references in the current literature to lexical meanings, or by inference from more general statements, to discover how vocabulary resources and their deployment are perceived by advocates of a 'transactional' view of meaning in use.

This paper will aim to show what these perceptions are. But it has a broader scope and purpose. In presenting their case for the negotiation of meaning through interaction between speakers, its advocates have provided, I believe, a far from complete account of the linguistic (including lexical) knowledge which they mostly agree is a prerequisite for successful communication. In specifying lexical knowledge especially, we need to do justice to the great variety of lexical units (including multi-word units) which can occur, and to their semantic and functional complexity. Only thus can we determine whether, or under what circumstances, the lexical resources which the speaker possesses can be negotiated from one context of use to another. In this paper I shall try to lay out some of the complexities, say where the evidence leads, and present an alternative view.

The case for negotiation has been forcefully, often eloquently, presented in various places, and merits careful and reasoned assessment, not cavalier dismissal. But there is no single 'communicative' voice: differences of substance and emphasis can be found in the work of one author, as well as from one author to the next. In what follows I shall try to reflect what appear to me to be significant differences of viewpoint.

Perhaps the first point to be made is that, with one important qualification, the notion that meanings are constantly readjusted, temporarily or more permanently, to suit the needs or pressures of the moment, is by no means new. Semanticists of an earlier generation, such as Ullmann, provided rich and varied evidence of semantic changes which have their roots in a culture or in the state of mind of an individual or social group at a given moment (Ullmann 1962, pp. 197–210). The influence of various extra-linguistic factors on semantic change has also long been the concern of professional lexicographers (Zgusta 1971, pp. 70–4). The remarkable series of slang dictionaries compiled by Eric Partridge, for example, show that in an attempt to rid the fearsome weapons developed in World War I of some of their terror, English soldiers compared them to familiar household objects: shells to coal-boxes, mortar-bombs to sausages and segmented hand-grenades to pineapples (Partridge 1961).

Nonetheless it is true, and this is the necessary qualification, that more recently a shift of interest has taken place towards a more systematic treatment of the conditions which have to be assumed if the interpretation of new meanings is to be explained. Following developments in the philosophy of language and pragmatics (Grice 1975; Leech 1983), applied linguists have turned towards more formal accounts of the principles which govern the creation of new senses, including those which later pass into more general use (Widdowson 1979, 1983).

Writing from within this theoretical perspective on the subject of the notional syllabus (which he characterizes as 'an inventory of units, of items for accumulation and storage') Widdowson speaks thus of communicative competence:

> ... communicative competence is not a compilation of items in memory, but a set of strategies or procedures for realizing the value of linguistic elements in contexts of use, an ability to *make* sense ... by the skilful deployment of shared knowledge of code resources and rules of language use.
>
> (Widdowson 1979, p. 248)

Here are two elements of key importance for the present discussion. First, it is recognized that existing 'shared knowledge of code resources' is essential: such knowledge is a necessary prerequisite for successful communication. Brumfit makes much the same point, with reference to vocabulary as well as grammar:

> 'we need our understanding of the vocabulary and structure of the language before we can negotiate meaning well'
>
> (Brumfit 1985a, p. 5)

But second, these resources are thought to be insufficient in themselves. As Widdowson remarked in the extract quoted earlier, competence is not simply 'a compilation of items in memory' but a set of procedures which can give those items value in contexts of use. Here, the precise emphasis can shift as between or within the work of individuals. In one paper originally published in 1980, Brumfit compared the linguistic resources deployed by the speaker to clay in the hands of a craftsman. The knowledge of forms which the speaker inherits, and shares with others, is reduced to a subordinate and manipulable element in the creation of meaning (Brumfit 1985a, p. 16). Elsewhere, Brumfit shares Widdowson's *interactive* view of the relationship between knowledge of linguistic elements and awareness of rules of use (Brumfit 1985b, pp. 150–1), while still indicating a fundamental concern with 'how language is made into messages, how it makes sense ...'. The interactive elements identified by Breen and Candlin, in a passage which makes no specific reference to lexical meaning or form, appear to be somewhat different:

> In any communicative event, individual participants bring with them prior knowledge of meaning and prior knowledge of how such meaning can be realized through the conventions of language form and behaviour.
>
> (Breen and Candlin 1980, p. 90)

Here meaning is contrasted with the 'conventions of language' (the forms) through which it will be realized, but the relationship is not as straightforward as at first appears. Since 'the conventions will be modified as they are used' ('negotiated'), Breen and Candlin have in fact assumed a position close to that of Widdowson and Brumfit.

It will be noticed in these various statements that linguistic forms and meanings are referred to in the most general terms: 'vocabulary and structure' (Brumfit 1985a), 'items', 'linguistic elements' (Widdowson 1979), 'meaning', 'language form' (Breen and Candlin 1980). Now it is precisely this lack of specificity in referring to the negotiable 'code' elements which makes the claim that such elements are not directly realized in use (or that they are typically negotiated in interaction) difficult to evaluate.

Once we begin to make specific qualifications to such terms as 'unit' or 'meaning' the precise scope and nature of negotiation will be found to vary with the qualification introduced. Consider, for example, the terminology of the specialist field of medical pathology, and in particular the items *osteoarthritis*, *meningitis* and *peritonitis*. Semantic shifts in the use of such terms, and especially nonce personal adjustments of sense are exceedingly rare. The terms are indeed monosemous, and given the need for precise and consistent communication among their professional users, semantic stability is to be expected.

The difference between technical and non-technical vocabulary (between 'terms' and 'words') is of course not clear-cut. One instance of the merging of the two categories is the existence of lexical items with scientific as well as non-scientific senses. Consider for example the item *iron*, which is both the term applied to the commonest metallic element (symbol *Fe*) and the word used to form various idioms (*rule with a rod of iron*, *strike while the iron is hot*) and non-scientific compounds (*iron-grey*, *Ironside*, *the Iron Duke*). Allowance must constantly be made in individual cases for overlap and interaction. Nonetheless, such criteria as the absence of exact synonyms and multiple-meaning do characterize many technical terms, and serve to set them apart from ordinary lexical items as a category resistant to semantic change.

Faced by the evidence of words which resist semantic adjustments altogether, one is prompted to ask what types of words lend themselves to negotiation of meaning from one context to another.

Two broad categories can be recognized, distinguishable at the centre but merging at the edges. The first consists of words with a small range of senses which mature speakers of the language perceive as distinct and firmly established. The qualifications are important, since they govern the extent to which the hearer's (or reader's) existing lexical knowledge is engaged in interpreting entirely new senses or in making an interpretative selection from established ('institutionalized') ones. Consider the case of a hearer faced with a fresh meaning of such a word: *wolf*, say, in the sense 'an avid consumer of reading material'. Here, his interpretative strategies will be engaged; but he will seek to interpret the sense partially in terms of an existing one, perhaps as an instance of its metaphorical extension (Leech 1983). The point is that the learner's informed awareness of the word's polysemy helpfully constrains his semantic options. Here, one might say, is a case where lexical knowledge and the skilful reading of contextual clues are equally crucial.

The other major category I wish to distinguish consists of such 'common-core' or 'heavy-duty' words as *top, bottom, side, edge, give, take, send, bring, light, heavy, long, short*. Such items have a high frequency of occurrence, are not restricted to the language of specialist activities or groups, and possess very low specificity of reference. The verb *take*, for instance, can denote the conveyance of a liquid, a solid mass, human passengers or abstract ideas. In all these respects 'common core' words contrast sharply with technical terms of the kind discussed earlier (Widdowson 1983, pp. 92–3).

The significance of these factors for the present discussion is not that they lead to a proliferation of established senses, making interpretation that much more difficult than in the case, say, of *compose, control* or *commission*, each of which is polysemous. It is in fact doubtful whether one can usefully talk of the sense divisions of heavy-duty words at all. Particular 'senses' of such verbs as *come* and *go*, that is to say, or such nouns as *top* and *bottom*, tend to lack the syntactic and morphological properties which mark off the musical sense of *compose*, for example (*a composer/the composition of a symphony*), from the sense which the verb has in *compose one's features* (cf. **a composer/the composition of one's features*). Specific textual clues must therefore serve to indicate which sense of *come* or *go* (or *top* or *bottom*) is intended at a particular time (consider *the bus/mail/inspiration/sense of urgency went; the top of the mountain/page/class/schedule*), and interpretation is thus heavily dependent on variable contextual factors.

Yet running counter to the semantic variability which is an undeniable feature of common-core items is a stabilizing force. Many meanings of such heavy-duty verbs as *bring* and *take* recur repeatedly; and they recur in the particular lexical contexts (the specific collocations) which are found to meet a routine communicative need. Thus various collocations incorporating common-core verbs cluster around everyday domestic activities: *clear the table, lay the table, dry the dishes, put out the cat, put away the car*. The stability of these two-word collocations is demonstrated by the fact that one seldom substitutes a synonym for the verb component: *?empty the table ?prepare the table*, (Cowie 1985).

Collocations of words in familiar literal senses are at one end of a broad spectrum of word combinations in English. At the other are idioms: combinations whose constant re-use in a fixed form has led to a radical change of meaning. The existence of many thousands of multi-word units across this wide range, and more crucially their recurrence over long periods in a virtually unchanged form, gives strong support to the view that stability is a pervasive feature of normal vocabulary use. It is this evidence which we must now turn to consider.

2 Composites and formulae

Evidence that complex word groups constantly recur unchanged in normal spoken and written communication comes from two sources in particular. First there is evidence which is broadly linguistic. Analysis of quite large bodies of authentic data, such as was undertaken for example when compiling the *Oxford Dictionary of Current Idiomatic English* (Cowie, Mackin and McCaig 1975/83), shows that thousands of multi-word units are quite stable in form across much of their range of occurrence, while thousands of others tolerate only minor variations, which are themselves regular and predictable by native informants (Mackin 1978). Examples of the first type are *keep the pot boiling*, *kick one's heels* and *kill or cure*; examples of the second are *keep/break one's word*, *know one's onions/stuff*, and *know/be up to all the dodges/tricks*.

Linguistic analysis is clearly needed to isolate fixed and semi-fixed expressions from their surrounding context, and to provide a framework of categories (based among other criteria, on degrees of internal variation). But it cannot explain their pervasiveness, or their well-known tendency to fuse, or congeal, into single semantic units – into idioms.

It is questions such as these which have come to interest language acquisition specialists investigating the nature of the units which children internalize when acquiring a first or second language (Hakuta 1974; Krashen and Scarcella 1978; Peters 1983). Peters's book-length study of the problem is of special interest. Drawing on a number of investigations, she shows how young children first extract multi-word units ('speech formulae' or 'prefabricated routines') from the flow of speech to which they are exposed, store them, and then after later segmentation redundantly retain them both as components and as wholes (cf. Bolinger 1976).

Of more direct relevance to the present discussion, however, is

Peters's attempt to account for the proliferation of multi-word units in adult language, and their economizing role in speech production. According to Peters, their usefulness is explained by an imbalance between memory capacity and processing speed in the human brain (1983, p. 86). Storage of ready-made expressions (those already in general use) and the creation ('fusion') of new expressions serves as a short-cutting device: it enables the speaker, for example, to focus on social (as opposed to linguistic) aspects of interaction, or to concentrate on the organization of longer stretches of discourse (1983, p. 3).

This important research provides a convincing explanation for the widespread occurrence of fixed expressions. But does it explain the increasing idiomaticity of some of them? Referring specifically to language acquisition among children, Peters notes the invariant form of certain phrases, for example such social formulae as *good morning* and *how are you*. She goes on: 'This invariance makes these phrases more likely to be perceived as units and concomitantly less susceptible to analysis' (1983, p. 11).

This is a crucial point. The invariable form of many multi-word expressions has the effect, in time, of draining away referential meaning from their constituents and transferring it to a new focus. Peters's choice of examples suggests that this focus is the discourse function of the expression concerned. Thus *good morning* will be perceived as a greeting, and *how are you* as a polite enquiry after someone's wellbeing (cf. Coulmas 1981, p. 4).

But consider *how are you* in comparison with *kick one's heels*, say. Both have become less susceptible to analysis in the sense intended by Peters: neither now has a meaning which can be clearly derived from those of its constituents. But in becoming less analysable, *how are you* appears to have lost meaning (in the way already suggested) whereas *kick one's heels*, far from becoming meaningless, has acquired a new meaning, one which has the whole expression, rather than the parts, as its focus.

These examples suggest that word combinations can be divided into two major groups, which differ according to the kinds of meaning which their members convey and to the structural level at which they operate. The first category, of which *good morning* and *how are you* are members, have evolved meanings which are largely a reflection of the way they function in discourse (as greetings, enquiries, invitations etc.). In so far as those discourse meanings have stabilized, the expressions are *pragmatically* specialized (Leech 1983, p. 28). The second category, of which *kick one's heels* and *pass the buck* are examples, have developed more or less unitary referential meanings by virtue of their use as invariable units in grammatical constructions. To the extent that their meaning and form have stabilized in this way, the expressions have become *semantically* specialized, or *idiomatic*.

Let me pursue these distinctions a little further, beginning with units which have a discourse function. This category has come into prominence quite recently, chiefly through research into discourse structure, both in Europe and the United States (Alexander 1978; Coulmas 1979, 1981; Keller 1979; Yorio 1980) though there are earlier references to 'functional idioms' in the broadest sense in the work of Greimas (1960) and Makkai (1972). The more recent work focuses on fixed or relatively fixed expressions used to perform such speech-act functions as greetings, compliments and invitations, but also considers units employed in organizing turn-taking, indicating a speaker's attitude to other participants, and generally ensuring the smooth conduct of interaction.

A few examples from Keller's complex classification of 'conventional strategy signals' (Keller 1979) must suffice to illustrate the extraordinary range of expressions recurrently used by speakers to regulate spoken communication. Among 'communication control' signals, he quotes 'Are you following me?' and 'Is that clear?' (as checks on the listener's readiness or ability to receive a message) and 'Pardon me' and 'Would you mind repeating that?' (as signals that the interlocutor has failed to hear or understand) (1979, p. 229).

Such examples as these prompt two further comments on the nature of expressions used in a discourse function. The first is that though these particular 'gambits' (Keller's preferred term) are perfectly familiar (*pardon me* being rather more so to American than to British speakers), they mostly lack the fixity of form which is a precondition of complete specialization in a given discourse function. In this respect, *Are you following me* can be compared with *You can say that again*, which is used to indicate emphatic and often ironic agreement with a previous speaker's remarks (Cowie 1984, p. 163). Whereas the latter is invariable and a functional stereotype, the former is capable of being used in a larger construction and contributing to its referential meaning:

'I'm not at all sure you're following me.'

Such cases serve to show that pragmatic specialization is a matter of degree, a point I shall return to when reconsidering the second major category of word combinations – those with a purely syntactic function.

My second comment concerns the great diversity of grammatical patterns spanned by expressions used as discourse-structuring devices or as realizations of particular speech-act functions. Without exception, the items quoted earlier from Keller are, from the strictly grammatical standpoint, complete sentences. In other cases, the gambit or 'routine formula' (Coulmas 1981) is grammatically incomplete, and serves to introduce or round off a larger grammatical unit which is not itself fixed or specialized in the ways I have described. The expression *do you know*, for example, introduces a statement and signals that it will cause some surprise, especially in relation to facts which have been established earlier:

'I went to see father at 11 o'clock this morning.
Do you know, he was still in bed!'

Incidentally, it will be noticed that in order to use this formula successfully, the speaker requires knowledge of invariant form, syntactic position (initial rather than final) and intonation (fall-rise on *know*). It will also be noted that whilst the precise content of the final statement is contextually determined (and thus 'negotiable') the element of surprise is not. An alternative completion (e.g. '*Do you know*, he was reading his newspaper!') will still be interpreted as surprising by the hearer. (The speaker's elderly father has perhaps been fitted with new spectacles.)

There is much more general awareness of the second major category that I wish to discuss and which, following Mitchell (1971), I shall call 'composites'. Most popular discussions of fixed expressions focus on examples such as *blow the gaff*, *spill the beans* and *stop the rot*, all of which qualify as composites, and this tendency is reinforced by dictionary definitions of 'idiom' (for example those in the *Concise Oxford Dictionary* and the *Collins English Dictionary*) which make no reference to conversational formulae or discourse function. It is noticeable, too, both from the examples quoted and the dictionaries mentioned, that the difficulty of interpreting composites in terms of the meanings of their component words is seen as their essential defining feature. The truth, however, is that idioms in the strict sense make up only one, and not the largest, of a number of related types within a broader spectrum of composites.

Composites are word combinations, more or less invariable in form and more or less unitary in meaning, which function as constituents of sentences (as objects, complements, adjuncts, and so on) and contribute to their referential, or propositional, meaning. They are lexical building-blocks comparable in their syntactic functions to nouns, adjectives, adverbs and verbs. Thus *a dry run*, though not itself a noun, functions as a noun does, as the subject or object of a verb and as the object of a preposition:

A dry run had been organized for later that week.
We've just completed *a dry run*.
There was no more talk of *a dry run*.

There may, however, be syntactic restrictions which apply to individual composites. (These have to be acquired with other peculiarities of form or meaning, by native speakers and foreign learners alike.) Thus *a close shave*, though similar in structure to *a dry run*, tends to function as a complement after *be* or as a direct object after *have*:

That was *a* very *close shave*.
He had several *close shaves*.

At the beginning of this section, I cited evidence of written and spoken data (gathered in the case of the dictionary project I referred to from sources spread over thirty years) in support of a claim that thousands of word combinations in English survive constant reuse in an unchanged or virtually unchanged form. Later, I suggested that formal invariance over time was a major factor leading to a gradual reduction in the meaningfulness, or meaning, of component words.

In the case of composites, such reduction is accompanied by meaning change, which may eventually lead to 'petrification', a state in which the evolved meaning of the whole is no longer traceable to the original meanings of the parts. Of the three familiar examples quoted earlier, *blow the gaff* and *spill the beans* have undergone petrification and are idioms in the strict sense (Cowie 1981; Cowie *et al.* 1983; Gläser 1981; Klappenbach 1968).

However, at any one time a language such as English will include very many semantically evolved composites which are still partially analysable. Semantic change in composites often takes the form of figurative extension (as in the case of *stop the rot*) and a considerable number now have figurative senses (in terms of the whole combination in each case) while preserving a current literal interpretation. Among such 'figurative' idioms are *do a U-turn*, *close ranks* and *mark time*. That this group merges into the category of 'pure' idioms is shown by such examples as *beat one's breast* and (again) *stop the rot*. The literal senses of these idioms do not survive alongside their figurative ones in normal, everyday use and for some speakers they may indeed be unrelatable (Cowie *et al.* 1983, p. xiii).

The argument in this section has brought together insights into the structure, meaning and development of word combinations from two fields, lexicology and psycholinguistics. But the two perspectives are interrelated, as has perhaps been shown, by the reciprocal relationship which exists between expressions which are already recognized by a speech community (and so are likely to be recorded in dictionaries) and the speaker's predisposition to store specific word combinations for future use. On the one hand, the existence in a language such as English of very many institutionalized units perfectly serves the needs of adults (native speakers as well as foreign learners) who are predisposed to store and reuse units as much as, if not more than, to generate them from scratch. On the other, the widespread 'fusion' of expressions which appear to satisfy the individual's communicative needs at a given moment, and are later reused, is one means by which the public stock of formulae and composites is continuously enriched.

3 Conclusion

The arguments of the previous sections add up, I believe, to a strong case for regarding stability of various kinds as an omnipresent feature of normal vocabulary use. It characterizes the form of many multi-word units, and persisting over time contributes to their pragmatic and semantic specialization. Moreover, new formulae and composites are constantly coming into use, initially to serve the communicative convenience of an individual or group, later possibly to enter the general vocabulary as institutionalized word combinations.

The tacitly recognized fixed forms and contextually-bound meanings of composites may of course be broken into by a speaker or writer aiming at expressive or humorous effects, as when a contributor to the *New Statesman* writes:

> Manchester is a working-class city and remains so. The last has not been heard, nor the final chapter written on Manchester, a town with *a real touch of class*.

Here, the writer has conferred ambiguity on the noun *class* as used in the composite *a touch of class*, a context in which it is normally unambiguous. This is achieved by providing an earlier reference to 'a working-class city'. But such special stylistic effects depend precisely on the assumed invariance of composites and their meanings.

Widespread evidence of lexical stability must also have profound consequences for the way we regard the learning and teaching of vocabulary. I have no quarrel with the view that we possess, and must develop further, intellectual and social skills enabling us to interpret a new sense, or to confer fresh meaning on a word we already knew.

What is at issue, rather, is whether the lexical knowledge on which such strategies are assumed to operate is uniformly open to negotiation.

Let us suppose that lexical items were in all cases and at all times open to semantic and formal adjustment and that, moreover, language users were more inclined to create meanings than to reproduce them. In such circumstances we should be bound to establish the conditions in which verbal creativity and manipulative skill were best calculated to flourish (e.g. by encouraging free writing, language games, role play, and so on).

But the account of lexical form and meaning developed in this article encourages no such one-sided view of lexical knowledge or of its constant adjustment to changing contexts of use. It suggests, rather, that much of the lexical competence of mature native speakers has developed through exposure to precisely those established meanings and fixed word combinations whose recurrence characterizes day-to-day lexical performance. Part of the task facing language teachers is to create conditions which effectively compensate for the foreign learner's lack of such exposure, but which at the same time avoid recourse to sterile and discredited memorization techniques.

But there is a deeper challenge. Stability and creativity are complementary and interactive factors in vocabulary use. As one even-handed commentator has remarked: 'competent language use is always characterized by an equilibrium between the novel and the familiar' (Coulmas 1981, p. 2). The task therefore is to create a methodology for vocabulary teaching which accommodates this equilibrium. This is a task which we are only now beginning to address.

Points for further development

1. The shift towards the view that the meanings of words are 'negotiated' reflects the general move within language teaching to an emphasis on language use, but Cowie feels that this tendency should be counterbalanced by giving proper regard to stable features of vocabulary use. Cowie seems to be at odds with McCarthy's line (this chapter); are the two compatible?

2. The 'negotiative' view of language gives an incomplete picture of the lexical knowledge needed for successful communication. Even the view that communicative competence is a matter of strategies or procedures for the communicative use of language recognizes that there must be a basic, shared code underlying use. Lack of under-

standing of the varied nature and function of this code makes statements about negotiability difficult to evaluate. We must therefore look more closely at stable and negotiable features of meaning. This does raise the big problem, however, of how we get at and define the 'stable' meaning of items (cf. the discussions on the representation of meaning in Chapter 2).

3. Cowie does attempt to narrow down the question of stability of meaning by looking at different types of lexical item. One category resistant to semantic adjustment is technical and scientific terminology. Then there are words with a small range of senses whose meaning can be extended into new contexts, and which we can interpret by our knowledge of polysemy. Beyond these are high frequency items like *take*, *top*, *long*, *send*, etc., which seem to have different interpretations in a multitude of different contexts, and for which it is meaningless to talk of senses. Yet even this last group of words display features of stability in their everyday occurrences; the same meanings occur repeatedly. How can we best bring the attention of learners to the regularity of occurrence of basic, stable meanings for words like *top*, *take* and *long*?

4. Idioms also present strong evidence of stability. Thousands of idioms and other multi-word units are either quite stable or only tolerate minor adjustments. What is the best way to present idioms in a natural and non-artificial way to reveal these regularities? Could micro-concordances of the type used by Johns (see Chapter 3, p. 51) be one answer? They do seem to give learners the chance to study lots of examples of regularities in language through natural contexts.

5. The degree of 'frozenness' lexical units display varies; what adjustments can and cannot be made to them is part of our lexical competence. New formulae and composites are constantly coming into use and many become institutionalized. Take any recent newspaper or magazine text or advertisement and see how many 'frozen' units such as idioms and compounds occur. How many are new and how many are already 'institutionalized'?

6. Cowie claims that the evidence he presents should temper our view of vocabulary teaching and learning. The native-speaker's ability to reinterpret, to create and to confer fresh meaning is based on the assumed invariance of meaning of such things as composites, and this aspect of lexical knowledge does not seem uniformly open to negotiation. The negotiative view of language would tend to suggest teaching methods which encourage verbal creativity and manipulation

(games, role play, etc.). Cowie feels this tendency should be balanced by an attempt to compensate for the learner's lack of day-to-day exposure to the fixed, stable, routine aspects of meaning that native speakers enjoy. McCarthy (this chapter) argues for a negotiative view of lexis, as does Chapter 5. Summers (this chapter) takes the traditional line that words have independent meaning that can be stored in dictionaries; Sinclair and Renouf's data (this chapter) seem to question the notion of independent meaning. Can these distinctly opposite perspectives be resolved into the equilibrium Cowie sees as desirable in vocabulary teaching?

A lexical syllabus for language learning

John McH. Sinclair and Antoinette Renouf

1 The EFL syllabus

1.1 Introduction

An EFL syllabus is a set of headings indicating items which have
been selected, by a language planner or materials writer, to be
covered in a particular part of the curriculum or in a course series.
Its content is usually identified in terms of language elements and
linguistic or behavioural skills. Sometimes there is a methodology built
into it, although syllabus and methodology are in principle distinct.
(See Section 1.5 for further discussion of the role of methodology.)

The syllabus may be a simple list, or it may have a more complex
structure. The list may be prioritized according to some notion of
importance or usefulness; or it may be graded according to some
notion of difficulty; or hierarchically ordered.

The traditional view of a syllabus gives it an independence from
any particular course that follows it. It is not negotiated in the knowledge of the precise needs and expectations of a given individual or
group of students. At times when linguistic description is settled and
unchallenged, it is reasonable to consider abstractly what areas of
grammar and vocabulary should be covered in one or more years, and
regard the matter as settled.

Syllabuses, then, are usually presented as independent statements;
they may show a family connection with a prevalent theoretical
approach, because the terms they use indicate the orientation of those
who write them. But it seems that nowadays the syllabus is in fact
influenced by other considerations in the teaching spectrum and is
less independent. It should be noted that throughout this paper we
are using the word 'syllabus' to mean an official, explicit, public statement intended to control the teaching activity, and not the variety of
unofficial, hidden, incidental syllabuses which are adduced from time
to time.

Most syllabuses, but not all, are expressed principally in linguistic terms, and there are many different approaches to language that can be used as a basis. An English language syllabus generally used to be organized structurally, in that the briefest statement of it was a list of grammatical points – verb tenses, comparison of adjectives, etc. A closer look showed that there were also some secondary organizing features, in particular the introduction of vocabulary words. From this inspection one could appreciate the connection between the syllabus and the prevalent theory of language at the time. A summary statement of that theory would be: language consists of a set of rules for the combination of words into well-formed and meaningful sentences. A small number of frequent words are used to indicate the structural frameworks and these have no independent content. The frameworks provide places for the selection of content words chosen from a large lexicon. Pride of place is given to the grammar, and the vocabulary is clearly secondary.

In recent years, the specification of syllabus has changed. There is now a large group of notional, functional and communicative syllabuses which reflects a different theory of language, deriving not so much from traditional linguistics as from theories of discourse based on **speech act** philosophy. Language is viewed as a list of potential acts, and language behaviour is a succession of such acts. Syllabus headings look like a selection of verbs with pronounced illocutionary force, or nouns formed from them, like 'inquiry', 'comparison'.

There is no comprehensive theory of language in these terms available as yet, so such syllabuses rest on shaky ground. The partial descriptions of discourse that exist (see Coulthard 1985 for a review of these) suppose a hierarchy of functions rather than a succession of them, and offer structural frameworks that serve to organize the individual acts. In the new syllabuses, the structural frameworks are largely ignored, and no criteria are provided for distinguishing functions and other features which appear to overlap. There is no claim to provide a list of functions which is comprehensive in a given area.

1.2 Vocabulary in syllabuses

The measurement of progress in a language often includes an assessment of the number of words a learner knows. One of the clearest examples of this is a graded reader scheme, which produces word lists at several levels. The school syllabuses in several countries are similarly organized; on occasions the target word lists are the product of substantial research (Gougenheim *et al.* 1956).

However, in recent years there has been little interest taken in the lexical approach, and little apparent control exercised in published materials (McCarthy 1984). Different books which offer themselves as covering similar ground show widely differing treatment of vocabulary.

For example, an analysis of nine major EFL courses (Renouf 1984) shows that in the first book of each series, the number of different word forms introduced ranges from 1,156 to 3,963, which is a wide variation. Also the average number of times a word form recurs ranges from six to seventeen: this means that the pattern of reinforcement ranges widely too.

It is not clear what is signified by the presence of a word in the published word list of a coursebook. Many words which occur several times in the body of the book are not acknowledged at all, whilst official teaching words sometimes receive very little reinforcement, with some occurring only twice in the entire volume.

This suggests that the approach taken to the vocabulary has generally not been systematic and that there has been little coordination in establishing targets. The vocabulary is regarded merely as the means of exemplifying other features of the language. It serves all the other syllabuses, or syllabus strands. Therefore it is not normally organized in and for itself, and receives only partial attention.

An example is the word *give*, which is always included in courses, but with a restricted and different range of uses in each. As expected, in all courses it tends to represent the archetypal di-transitive verb, particularly in the forms *give* and *gave*, and in contexts such as:

/ give Tom this book/
/ he gave her some sugar/
/ here's the card. You gave it to me on Monday/
/ Mary is giving Arthur a cup of tea/
/ what shall we give him?/
/ you've got my phone number. Give me a ring/
/ give my love to Jill and Carole/

Perhaps less obviously, in most courses the forms *give* and *giving* also play a significant role in the meta-language, in instructions to the learner as to how to proceed, such as:

/ give more answers like this/
/ give facts to describe: a lake, a city, a river/
/ give another word or phrase to replace the following/
/ and say when things will be ready, giving time limits/
/ write giving details of likely length of stay/

In nine major course series, one third of the total instances of *giving* are in fact devoted to this use.

In functional-notional courses, there is a common metalinguistic use of *give* and *giving* for categorizing speech functions. In this case, the di-transitivity is not fully realized. Typical examples are:

/ (ask for and) give information about x/
/ give (instructions and) advice/
/ (ask for and) give directions/
/ giving and receiving instructions/
/ giving directions/
/ giving advice/

In the same nine course series, every second instance of the word form *giving* is used in this way.

Other uses also occur in language courses, and altogether it is clear that each course presents a different profile of the word *give*.

1.3 Mixed syllabuses

Statements of syllabus can be mixed, so that a grammatical list and a lexical list may together constitute a syllabus. There will be no indication of how these are to be coordinated, so it must be assumed that they will be focused upon in separate sessions.

Of course, it is almost impossible to teach grammar without in passing teaching some vocabulary. Vocabulary fleshes out the structures, introduces variety and promotes practice of the structure in question. The vocabulary is not the organizing force, but many teachers feel that this kind of teaching covers an adequate vocabulary.

In the same way, a class devoted to expanding its vocabulary will not be able to avoid syntax, assuming that it is not exclusively committing lists to memory. And for the same reason, the structures will not be controlled, being those that arise in passing. It is exceptionally difficult to teach an organized syllabus of both grammar and lexis at the same time.

In the activity of text explication, there is often a good balance between grammatical and lexical focus, but this does not constitute an organized syllabus in either field. The points come up as they occur in text, and that is the only organization.

The newer notional-functional syllabuses, of which the *Threshold Level* is a notable example (van Ek 1977), are not usually a simple list of headings, but are related to grammatical and lexical features. Typically, each notion or function is presented with a range of linguistic expressions that are held to be appropriate realizations. The latter constitute a partial syllabus, but once again the vocabulary is not organized for its own sake and, in many cases, the words are principally grammatical.

There is another type of syllabus which has some popularity. Language proficiency is expressed in terms of levels of proficiency in reading, writing, speaking and listening – the four skills. Skill-based syllabuses may be free-standing, or may be mixed with others, or partially coordinated. For example, a reading skills syllabus may be coordinated with a graded vocabulary, or a speaking skills syllabus with a range of speech functions. *Reading and Thinking in English* (Widdowson 1979–80) is based on a series of syllabuses like these.

Since the mid-1970s, there has been a growth of interest in the task-based syllabus. This is not expressed in linguistic terms at all; syllabus items refer to activities in the world, like 'interpreting a time-table', or 'changing a wheel'. A judicious selection of tasks will provide a varied learning environment, and the language engendered will be quite natural. This type of syllabus was in operation on a large-scale teaching project in Jeddah (Harper (ed.) forthcoming).

A task-based syllabus is not normally mixed or coordinated with any other, because it is held that, properly designed, such a syllabus will cover a sufficient range of vocabulary, grammar, notions, functions and skills. In relation to language, then, a task-based syllabus is a contradiction in terms. Obviously there is no linguistic theory which corresponds to a non-linguistic syllabus. Some check on the basic assumption could be provided *post hoc* by field research, involving the recording of a series of actual classes constituting a course, and the analysis of the language which occurred. This would be extremely laborious, however, and one such exercise would be no real guide to what might happen in the next.

In most modern coursebooks, there is evidence of an attempt to coordinate several parallel threads of syllabus (see, for example, the *Cambridge English Course*, Swan and Walter 1984–5). Sometimes the structure is stated explicitly and elaborately. Typically the books contain a recurrent series of activities which imply a syllabus that mixes skills, structures, lexis, notions, functions and tasks. The variety is often bewildering, and the actual coordination minimal.

But the books give expression to a point of view which is probably held fairly generally – that no one method of organization is adequate for a balanced and comprehensive course. Language has many facets, and corresponds partially to many different patterns of organization. True, it can be represented substantially as a set of structures and a list of words; true also that it can be seen as performing a variety of functions. Or the learner can be monitored through the skills or through a set of tasks. Some teaching from each of these points of view is necessary to make the teaching effective and efficient.

1.4 Eclecticism

Some language teachers favour an eclectic approach to the planning of work, which can be a different position from adopting a detailed pre-set mixed syllabus. Instead, they prefer performance targets to be set, and to have a fairly free hand in how the targets are achieved. They thus take on themselves the responsibility of devising a reliable syllabus.

Most language teachers, however, do not have the choice, but are obliged to use a textbook and nothing else. This state of affairs is dictated often by economics, sometimes by politics and religion, sometimes by educational tradition or bureaucracy. In our experience, there is generally very little resentment from the teachers, because the language they have to teach is quite tidily presented through a textbook, particularly if it has been specially composed for them.

Although there are exceptions, particularly in the UK, there is for language teachers in state schools and private organizations increasingly no distinction between syllabus, methodology and coursebook. All are blended in an officially blessed publication from which it is imprudent or illegal to deviate.

1.5 A methodology is not a syllabus

The profession of English Language Teaching in recent years has seen the rise of methodology to a dominating position. The content of language teaching – the specification of what has to be taught – has been relegated to a secondary role. The assumption seems to be that plenty of the right sort of activity will provide a sufficient framework for language learning to take place. The exact nature of the content, the sequence of events and the pattern of coverage will not be specified fully.

In extreme cases, such an approach to methodology denies the relevance of a content syllabus – in task-based learning, for example, or in the communicative approach. Such confidence in method renders syllabuses unnecessary.

It also implies a lowering of confidence in the reliability and usefulness of independent syllabuses. Lists of structures and vocabulary words are reminiscent of teaching methods which are not currently in fashion; notions and functions are not exhaustively specified and do not of themselves constitute a comprehensive syllabus.

This point of view is in line with a shift of interest away from language data which has characterized the profession recently. The British Council's 50th Anniversary Conference in 1984 was entitled

'Progress in English Studies'. So little progress was reported, however, that the resultant conference record has a different title: *English in the World* (Quirk and Widdowson 1985).

1.6 A coursebook is not a syllabus

A coursebook is essentially a set of instructions concerning operations in the classroom. Whether or not it contains one or more syllabus statements, or refers to an external syllabus, the bulk of it is an elaboration of only one of many ways in which coverage of the syllabus may be achieved.

There is a tendency at present for syllabuses to be incorporated into coursebooks – both in the large number of national textbook projects, and in the fairly free area of international publishing. The danger is that the syllabus could be confused with other aspects of the teaching-learning apparatus, and be little more than an appendix.

For a syllabus to have an important role in education, it should either pre-exist or be devised independently of other elements like course materials, methodology, and assessment. It should be as independent of linguistic or pedagogical theory as possible, and the theoretical background should be seen primarily as a vehicle for the clear expression of the syllabus. A syllabus which is negotiated in advance of being taught shares many features with an independent one.

A syllabus which is dependent on a particular coursebook is a degenerate syllabus, not very much different from the table of contents. It might even have been composed after the materials rather than before.

2. The lexical syllabus

2.1 A word list is not a syllabus

A simple list of words is not nearly explicit enough to constitute a syllabus. In order to construct an adequate syllabus, it is necessary to decide, in addition to which words we want to include in our syllabus, such things as what it is about a word that we want to teach, and what counts as a word.

2.2 What is a word? – word and word form

Syllabus designers and coursebook writers as a whole have conducted relatively little empirical research into the nature of lexis, and consequently the concept of 'word' remains blurred. The conventional view is an inclusive one: that the term 'word' denotes a unit of language comprising a base form, such as *give*, and an 'associated' set of inflexions, such as *gives, giving, gave, given*. Sometimes derivations will be included, e.g. *gift*. This concept of 'word' is also an established one in computational linguistics, where all forms, including the base form, can be subsumed under the term 'lemma'.

Where a word list accompanies a particular language course, it will typically consist of abstractions derived from the base form of a word group – *go* will stand for *go, goes, going, went, gone*, and so on. Unless there is an indication to the contrary, the implication will be that all forms of the word **go** are covered in the material. However, this is not necessarily true, nor is it necessarily desirable. It is not actually the case that all forms of words in a given word list are shown in use in a language course, even taking into account the various levels of progress. *Hold* and *holding* may appear, but not *holds*; *stand* and *stood* may be exemplified, but not *stands*. There is no evidence that such omissions are based on principle, and in any case, the principles involved would not be lexical.

From a lexical point of view, it is not always desirable to imply that there is an identity between the forms of a word. Textual evidence shows that an inconsistent relationship holds between such elements. Sometimes all forms of the word – for example, *get, gets, getting, got*, and the singular and plural forms of many nouns – share a similar range of meanings and usage patterns, and it is justifiable to indicate this. But often, particularly with the commoner words of the language, the individual word forms are so different from each other in their primary meanings and central patterns of behaviour (including the pragmatic and stylistic dimensions), that they are essentially different 'words', and really warrant separate treatment in a language course.

The morphological pair *certain* and *certainly* is one case in point. Consider the following contrast in their uses, listed in order of importance as they are shown in the 7.3 million word Birmingham Corpus which forms part of the Birmingham Collection of English Text (Renouf 1984):

certain
Function 1. (60% of occurrences) Determiner, as in:
/ a certain number of students/ in certain circles/
Function 2. (18% of occurrences) Adjective, as in:
/ I'm not awfully certain about . . ./ We've got to make certain/
Function 3. (11% of occurrences) Adjective, in phrase 'A + *certain* + noun', as in:

/ ... has a certain classy ring/ there is a certain evil in all lying/

certainly
Function 1. (98% of occurrences) Adverb, as in:
/ it will certainly be interesting/ He will almost certainly launch into a little lecture ... /

There is one area of overlap between the two, where *certain* appears in contexts like:

/ there is certain to be water here/

which is arguably paraphrasable by 'water will certainly be here', or 'there is certainly water here'. But this use of *certain* occurs rarely.

Other pairs of this kind include *easy* versus *easily*; *near* versus *nearly*; *real* versus *really*; *particular* versus *particularly*; *vain* versus *vainly*; also *west* versus *western*; *use* versus *used*; *one* versus *ones*; *detach* versus *detached*.

2.3 Which words? – criteria for lexical selection

Whilst the question of lexical selection has passed many course writers by, there have been attempts made through the years by a number of individual linguists to establish criteria for creating lexical inventories for teaching purposes. These will not be gone into here, though we acknowledge the efforts of such people as Ogden (1930), Thorndike and Lorge (1944) and West (1953), and the existence of selectional criteria identified in terms of 'disponibilité' (Gougenheim *et al.* 1956), 'familiarity' (Richards *et al.* 1956/1974), 'coreness' (Carter this volume), and in various terms by others.

All these people have been concerned with the problem of identifying the lexical items which should be introduced into an all-purpose programme for teaching English for general purposes. The needs of a specific group of learners are usually easier to identify.

It seems reasonable to us, in the absence of any specific guidelines, to propose that, for any learner of English, the main focus of study should be on:
a) the commonest word forms in the language;
b) their central patterns of usage;
c) the combinations which they typically form.

In the Birmingham Corpus the list of top-ranking word forms looks as follows. It is in fact not particularly controversial, confirming largely the intuition of the language teacher about which words should be in any course, and it continues to be familiar for the first 800 or so items.

First 200 word forms in the Birmingham Corpus, ranked in order of frequency of occurrence:

1 the	51 out	101 most	151 another
2 of	52 them	102 where	152 came
3 and	53 do	103 after	153 course
4 to	54 my	104 your	154 between
5 a	55 more	105 say	155 might
6 in	56 who	106 man	156 thought
7 that	57 me	107 er	157 want
8 I	58 like	108 little	158 says
9 it	59 very	109 too	159 went
10 was	60 can	110 many	160 put
11 is	61 has	111 good	161 last
12 he	62 him	112 going	162 great
13 for	63 some	113 through	163 always
14 you	64 into	114 years	164 away
15 on	65 then	115 before	165 look
16 with	66 now	116 own	166 mean
17 as	67 think	117 us	167 men
18 be	68 well	118 may	168 each
19 had	69 know	119 those	169 three
20 but	70 time	120 right	170 why
21 they	71 could	121 come	171 didn't
22 at	72 people	122 work	172 though
23 his	73 its	123 made	173 fact
24 have	74 other	124 never	174 Mr
25 not	75 only	125 things	175 once
26 this	76 it's	126 such	176 find
27 are	77 will	127 make	177 house
28 or	78 than	128 still	178 rather
29 by	79 yes	129 something	179 few
30 we	80 just	130 being	180 both
31 she	81 because	131 also	181 kind
32 from	82 two	132 that's	182 while
33 one	83 over	133 should	183 year
34 all	84 don't	134 really	184 every
35 there	85 get	135 here	185 under
36 her	86 see	136 long	186 place
37 were	87 any	137 I'm	187 home
38 which	88 much	138 old	188 does
39 an	89 these	139 world	189 sort
40 so	90 way	140 thing	190 perhaps
41 what	91 how	141 must	191 against
42 their	92 down	142 day	192 far
43 if	93 even	143 children	193 left
44 would	94 first	144 oh	194 around
45 about	95 did	145 off	195 nothing
46 no	96 back	146 quite	196 without
47 said	97 got	147 same	197 end
48 up	98 our	148 take	198 part
49 when	99 new	149 again	199 looked
50 been	100 go	150 life	200 used

Certain of these word forms will not warrant separate treatment, but can be subsumed under their base form or full form in a teaching list. Others, according to the criterion of textual frequency, will also be eliminated from the final list. Among the top 650 items, *clothes* will appear, but not *clothe*; *building*, but not *build*; *roughly*, but not *rough*; *simply*, but not *simple*; *suddenly*, but not *sudden*.

A few word forms appear here which are perhaps less expected – *back, own, life* and *great*, for example. But a look at their use in text explains their prominent status in the corpus: they are in frequent daily use, but probably largely at a subliminal level. Let us try to account for the prominence of *back* and *own*:

back
Function 1. Adverb, as in:
/ are you getting the bus back?/ I've just come back from C/ afterwards we go back to sleep/
Function 2. Noun/Headword, as in:
/ Brody put his left hand behind his back/ will you three sitting at the back please move round/
Function 3. Adverb, as in:
/ into the car without looking back/ she moved back a little/ I turned back to Mary/

own
Function 1. Adjective or Phrasal Element, as in:
/ I can say that my own childhood was unhappy/ a ... unit of my own/ both phrases will do though I prefer my own/
Function 2. Noun/Headword, as in:
/ Oh, I'm not on my own, then/ he didn't like sitting on his own and reading about it/ he had developed it on his own/

These are surely everyday uses which need to be reflected to some extent in a course.

To base a selection of words on a study of native-speaker usage is not, however, to imply that there is an identity between the worlds of the learner and the native speaker. There are already signs that specialized corpora will be established, to serve the needs of the major English language learning communities.

The statistics of word occurrence are vindicated when usage is examined. But it would be difficult to construct a motivating course based entirely on the 200 words listed above, and ludicrous, say, to try to start with the top fifty. Hardly any text of any length, spoken or written, will be found with such an impoverished vocabulary. The list must be extended to include some lower frequency items.

In this way, the materials writer will have some flexibility, and there will be a reasonable range of topics which can be covered, and a chance that the work will be lively and interesting.

The additional list will probably include, among other things, words relating to domestic reality, such as days of the week and kinship terms, and other common lexical sets; also further words to refer to physical sensations and personal emotions, and to use in making evaluations. These additions should be monitored carefully, so that the final word list contains items of maximal utility and power. A balance has to be achieved, however, between natural usage and utility.

As said, the introduction of whole lexical sets is not justified by the criterion of frequent use, and evidence shows why it is that some set members feature more centrally in the language. This is sometimes due to facts in the real world – for example, that Sunday is the most cited day of the week; it sometimes reflects the extent of metaphorical usage, as in the case of certain colour terms. Set membership is also only one of the roles played by many common words. In the case of *black* and *white*, for instance, their sociological reference is actually far more common today than their physical one. All this needs to be taken into account in the selection of such words, and the spurious tidiness of language that one achieves by listing words and phrases that are like each other should be viewed critically.

2.4 What to teach? – central patterns of usage

Moving on from the selection of a word list to the idea of basing a syllabus on normal mainstream usage, the everyday core of the language, the question is how to establish what this is. There has not until very recently been any way of reliably doing so.

Now there are a small but growing number of large, computer-held banks of text, such as the Birmingham Collection of English Text, that can provide evidence of typical language use. The retrieval systems, unlike human beings, miss nothing if properly instructed – no usage can be overlooked because it is too ordinary or too familiar. The statistical evidence is helpful, too, because it distinguishes the commoner patterns of usage, which occur very frequently indeed, from the less common usage, which occurs very infrequently.

The human being, contrary to popular belief, is not well organized for isolating consciously what is central and typical in the language; anything unusual is sharply perceived, but the humdrum everyday events are appreciated subliminally. Let us take as an example the word *see*. Textual evidence shows us that the first and second most frequent uses of *see* are those found in the familiar phrases *you see* and *I see*. The first is an indication of interactive concern in spoken discourse:

> / – I thought they were all away, you see – /
> / well, you see, I have to like her, you see, because she's invited . . ./
> / Yes I know but, you see, computers might rule the world one day/
> / You see, my wife's nervous when she's left alone/

and the second is a response with a wide range of meaning, to some extent controlled by its intonation, and falling within the semantic area of 'understand':

> / '. . . and one as you leave the country, you see.' 'I see, and how long is that?'/
> / '. . . It's Saturday to Sunday,' 'Oh, I see.' 'cause you don't count your first night . . .'/
> / . . . Oh, I see. Well, that's as good a reason as any for . . ./

Most native speakers, despite accepting the truth of the above, would probably say, as we did, that it is the *see*ing through one's eyes which is surely the major use/meaning associated with *see*. Lyons (1977 p. 247) explains this kind of disposition by reference to the concept of 'salience', psychological or biological.

It is most important that the evidence of very long texts is not dismissed without careful thought. Language text is the record of linguistic choices, but it is not necessarily a completely comprehensive and reliable record of the way the choices are made. No claim is made here that frequency of occurrence is the only relevant factor. Equally, no description of usage should be innocent of frequency information.

In view of its prominence in natural text, the interactive function in discourse of word forms like *see* above tends to be under-represented in coursebooks. In nine courses, instances of *you see* and *I see* together account for only 10 per cent of all occurrences of *see*, as opposed to 53 per cent in the Birmingham Corpus.

The conventional view of the words in a language is that they either have lexical meaning or are confined to syntactic functions in the sentence. Hence usages which are discoursal or pragmatic, which carry out functions to do with the larger patterns in texts, are often missed. For example, the humble and exceedingly frequent word *to* has a discourse function which is important and valuable to a user. It often occurs at the beginning of a move or sentence, and indicates that the comment which it introduces is an evaluation of the main part of the utterance. Some of these uses have become familiar phrases, like 'to be honest', 'to cut a long story short', and the contrast between this function and the use of *to* as if it was 'in order to', can be seen in the ambiguity of the following (constructed) example:

To be fair, Tom divided the sweets evenly

In one of the meanings, the person who is fair is the person speaking or writing, and the phrase is a judgement on Tom.

Delexical verbs

A major feature of the language is not specifically taught in current coursebooks. It is the phenomenon known as 'delexicality', the tendency of certain commoner transitive verbs to carry particular nouns or adjectives which can in most cases themselves be transitive verbs. In general, the more frequent a word is, the less independent meaning it has, because it is likely to be acting in conjunction with other words, making useful structures or contributing to familiar idiomatic phrases.

A clear example of this is *give*, which is most commonly used ditransitively in conjunction with certain nouns, particularly *look*, *information*, and *advice*. In Section 1.2, we showed that this delexical use of *give* does occur in language courses, but primarily in the rubric of the text, which is apparently not part of the teaching programme.

Have has a range of delexical uses, and combines with various classes of abstract nouns. *Look* is the single most common collocate. The nouns are commonly modified, as for example in *a good look, minor doubts, a deep longing, a heart to heart talk, a strange feeling, legitimate expectations*.

In contrast, the delexical contexts for *have* in most coursebooks are somewhat more concrete. The frequent occurrence of *look* here reflects natural usage, but otherwise there seems to be an obsession with having a drink, a bath, or a shower, in that order. An exception to this is the reference in some books to 'words which *have* the same or different *meaning*', and so on. But again this occurs only in the rubric of the text.

Textual evidence now shows us the extent to which the phenomenon of delexicality occurs. The primary function of *make*, for example, is to carry nouns like *decision/s, discoveries, arrangements,* thereby offering the alternative phraseology 'make your own decisions' to 'decide on something'; 'make her travel arrangements' to 'arrange her travel,' and so on. Which of the two formulations to choose is obviously a strategic matter in text creation, but the delexical option is firmly there. Since it complicates the syntax, it must provide an overriding facility to justify the complexity. Other verbs which operate in this way are *take*, with e.g. *care of, note, action*; and to a lesser extent *put*, with e.g. *question*. Aisenstadt (1981) has noted the importance of delexical verb combinations for vocabulary teaching and learning.

2.5 What to teach? – typical word combinations

In the two previous sections, we have made reference to the fact that words combine, or collocate, with each other in certain characteristic ways. With the benefit of a corpus of real text, we can now be clearer about what these preferences are, and be more systematic in presenting them to the learner of English.

The combinations are often lexical collocations, where two words occur next to each other, e.g. *happy marriage* or *accidental death*.

Sometimes the combinations have grammatical restrictions, and the words are regularly found in a particular syntactic pattern, such as 'accede to X's demands', where a different pattern, such as 'X's demands were not acceded to' is unlikely to occur.

Even common grammatical words have collocational patterns. *Each*, for instance, occurs significantly with units of time – *hour*, *day*, *week*, etc. Similarly, *of* collocates frequently, in its left-hand context, with *kind*, *part*, and *sort*.

Common grammatical words also combine with each other, often in discontinuous frameworks, such as *a ... of*. In turn, they attract particular lexical words, so that the *a ... of* framework typically encloses the following: *lot, kind, number, sort, couple, matter, bit, series, piece, member*, in that order of frequency.

In these ways, the essential patterns of distribution and combination in modern English will be included in the lexical syllabus. It is not possible here to present a full account of the field, but it is clearly one of the growth points of research which will feed into language syllabuses for many years to come.

3 Implications of a lexical syllabus

3.1 Vocabulary

The approach to a lexical syllabus which is taken above highlights the common uses of the common words. The common words are very common indeed, and mastery of them is rewarding in practice. Typically they are found each to have a few very common uses and a number of minor ones that can be given a low priority in the selection of items to be taught.

The is approximately 4 per cent of all text; *and* and *of* make up another 4 per cent. The top ten words in the list printed earlier in this paper account for about 17 per cent. The little words that make up the structural framework of the language and that are the recurrent elements of phrases are found to dominate the frequency lists. Only *time, people, new, know, man* and *little* bring any great semantic content into the top hundred. After that, familiar lexical items come in much faster.

Almost paradoxically, the lexical syllabus does not encourage the piecemeal acquisition of a large vocabulary, especially initially. Instead, it concentrates on making full use of the words that the learner already has, at any particular stage. It teaches that there is far more general utility in the recombination of known elements than in the addition of less easily usable items. The more delicate discrimination of meanings which is accessible to someone who commands a large vocabulary is postponed – at least from the business of the first few years of English.

It is important to recognize that this is not so much a point of view about how to teach a language as a statement about the nature of modern English. Other languages may be different; English makes excessive use, e.g. through phrasal verbs, of its most frequent words, and so they are well worth learning.

3.2 Relation to other syllabuses – implementation

In the construction of a balanced and comprehensive course, the designer will no doubt keep a tally of structures, notions and functions, as well as vocabulary. But in the presentation of materials based on a lexical syllabus, it is not strictly necessary to draw attention to these check lists. If the analysis of the words and phrases has been done correctly, then all the relevant grammar, etc. should appear in a proper proportion. Verb tenses, for example, which are often the main organizing feature of a course, are combinations of some of the commonest words in the language.

This is different from attention to combinations of the four skills, and the use of tasks to practise effective communication, about which the lexical syllabus is neutral. It is an independent syllabus, unrelated by any principles to any methodology. It may suggest that certain types of teaching practice can readily adapt to it, but that is not a principled connection, just a similarity in philosophical approach.

Whenever it occurs that the learning process would be improved by introduction of, say, a grammatical table, that does not disturb or interfere with a lexical syllabus – it merely sheds light from a different angle.

3.3 Efficiency

One big advantage of a lexical syllabus is that it only offers to the learner things worth learning. Variations are not built in, as they are in conventional presentations of language structure, but are introduced when they are necessary. So instead of building up phrases, the learner will be gradually breaking them down, sensing the variability. Needless variation can lead to ungrammatical expression, as we know from the common phenomenon of over-correction.

On the other hand, there is no suggestion of the stifling of creativity; not only is it possible to teach to a lexical syllabus just as creatively as to any other, it is likely that sensitivity to the rule margins, where so much linguistic creativity lies, will be greater than in conventional presentations, which are about as sensitive as a fruit machine, and espouse a similar theory of message structure. It sometimes appears to teachers that a syllabus based on observation of language is somehow backward-looking, giving licence only to what has occurred. The lexical syllabus is just a much more detailed inventory of the possibilities of the language.

3.4 Utility

The argument for utility in a lexical syllabus is not confined to the exploitation of common words. What are exposed are the *uses* of those words, and prominent among those are devices, signals, and strategies in discourse, both spoken and written. The emphasis shifts from constructing messages to delivering them, and delivering them to maximum effect, and to achieving communicative goals.

The description of discourse has brought out clearly that language text is simultaneously organized on at least two different dimensions, or 'planes'. One of these is used for constructing and elaborating messages, and another is concerned with commenting on, labelling, evaluating and generally negotiating the messages interpersonally. Because language teaching has not until recently recognized the importance of the purposes, intentions, objectives, etc. of language users, the second of these planes has been largely neglected. If the teacher stops the talk and the class waits for a student contribution, the student is unlikely to learn how to get an opportunity to speak, or to recognize the structures and vocabulary that will express his intentions.

3.5 Statement

One form which a lexical syllabus of the kind discussed could take is shown in a sample below (an abridged version of the original). The syllabus in this case is several hundred pages long and forms the linguistic specification for a new English course (D. and J. Willis forthcoming).

Lexical syllabus extract for the word 'by'

No. of occurrences in the Corpus: 21,916

CAT 1: used to indicate the person or thing that performs or causes the action mentioned; usually preceded by a verb in passive voice (prep) [53% of occs]
Henry was surprised by *the* plopping sounds in the water/ the daily business is still announced by *the* procession of the speaker/ Another survey carried out by *the* University of Florida/ He was brought up by *an* aunt/ He had been poisoned by *a* mushroom/ he found himself touched by *a* bittersweetness/ worker-elected directors have been accused by *their* former colleagues/ Carlson was interviewed by *a* major television station/ they are protected by armour/ the first atom bomb was manufactured by famous men with bogus names/ it was bought with his own money by *his* own cook/ The affection with which it is regarded by *its* old pupils is evidence of its success/ an investment of 12 million pounds by Courtaulds/ attacks on EEC ministers by *a* commission member/ I see this change in position by Reagan/

CAT 1.1: used to show who is the author or artist of a particular work (prep) [4% of occs]
Three books by *a* great and original Australian writer/ An article by J. B. Priestley in the New Statesman/ he bought great numbers of paintings by Hook, Millais, Orchardson/

CAT 2: used (with the present participle of a verb) to show that you perform a particular action and to indicate that something happens as a result of this action (prep) [11% of occs]
Holmes became WBC champion by beating Norton/ They were making a meagre living by selling artefacts to the tourists/ You win by being older/ dared to take the law into his own hands by evicting a tenant/ as a bird changes direction by dipping one wing and lifting the other/ is an artificial way of making the child learn by doing/ you'd be amazed the places you can get into by just looking confident/

CAT 2.1: used to indicate the means used in order to achieve something, or to introduce the circumstances which lead to something happening [9.5% of total occs in sample concs]
The contest was settled by *a* practical test/ The rabbit escapes once by *a* last-second change of course/ There will be a lift to go *up* and

down by/ approached by *a* most imposing flight of steps/she was plucked to safety by *a* helicopter/ which arrived by chance/ washing our dinner dishes by hand/

CAT 3: **beside something and close to it** (prep) [3% of occs] She lingered by *the* door/ I sat by *her* bed/ We sipped tea by *a* hot stove in his living room/ the pilot with his arm full and the red can by *his* feet/ Ralph was kneeling by *the* remains of the fire/ We moved down by *the* river/

Phrases and miscellaneous:
i) *by myself, himself,* etc [1.5% of occs], meaning 'alone'.
ii) Used in reference to times and dates [1.5% of occs].
iii) Used of standards, rules, etc. [1.5% of occs], e.g./ by British standards/

Notes:
i) In CAT 1, 48 per cent of occurrences occur in the passive; 5 per cent occur after nouns with transitive verbal counterparts (see last three examples).
ii) Some passive forms also occur in CAT 2.1.

Immediate collocates

RIGHT HAND	LEFT HAND
the – 5130 occs	*and* – 380 occs
a – 1321 occs	*up* – 222 occs
his – 327 occs	
an – 293 occs	
their – 233 occs	

Acknowledgements

The authors would like to acknowledge their debt to colleagues in English Language Research at Birmingham University, in particular to members of the COBUILD project teams. Much of the evidence reported here has arisen from the project, which is largely financed by grants from William Collins Sons and Co. Ltd., publishers. Without such support, this paper could not have been written.

Points for further development

1. Sinclair and Renouf take as their point of departure the notion of a syllabus as an explicit statement, not dependent on methodology, controlling what is to be taught in a language course. Many current approaches to syllabuses lack rigour and proper control over lexical content, even though they may appear to be highly organized in other respects. Consider the syllabus you are working to in the light of their remarks.

2. Most published courses, according to Sinclair and Renouf, are inconsistent with regard to how lexis is presented. They work with word lists of base-forms of words, but then use inflected forms of those bases in a way that often does not correspond to natural language use. What is needed is a careful consideration not only of what words occur in natural use, but in what forms and in what patterns they typically occur. Sinclair and Renouf clearly feel that coursebooks let us down in this respect; is there any evidence that the coursebooks you use take cognizance of natural language use?

3. The lexical syllabus should be devised independently of considerations of course materials, methodology and assessment. But it is not enough simply to construct a word list. First we have to be clear what we mean by *words* and *word forms*; it may not be desirable to include all the possible forms of a word in the syllabus. Textual evidence shows that word forms (e.g. *certain/certainly*) often behave quite independently of each other in terms of meaning and usage patterns; this fact seems rarely to be recognized and yet affects a vast number of word forms. The problem would seem to be how to break the traditional expectations that all forms of a word are equally important and that all will behave in the same way; consider restrictions such as the following:

> He owns a factory in London.
> He is the owner of a factory in London.
> He runs a factory in London.
> *He is the runner of a factory in London.

Should vocabulary teaching explicitly deal with such areas?

4. The basic principles for word selection are commonsense ones of frequency and centrality of patterns of usage, along with observations of the typical combinations that words form. An interesting activity is to make a list of about twenty words by sticking a pin at random in a dictionary. When, if ever, might you want to teach these words? What criteria are you using for accepting or rejecting them?

5. Frequency is useful, but language teaching cannot, of course, proceed with only the 200 or so most common words, most of which will be semantically 'empty' function words. Words relating to everyday domestic reality should be added, words for classroom procedures, etc. What would be the 20 or 30 most useful words in addition to the top 200 for your teaching situation?

6. In deciding what are the central patterns of usage of items, computers are often more reliable than native-speaker intuition, and often produce evidence that goes counter to expectations. Such evidence should not be ignored in the preparation of syllabuses. Should teachers be demanding more access to computer evidence? Can dictionaries and coursebooks afford to ignore such evidence?

7. The kind of evidence computer corpora can give us is illustrated by the case of delexical verbs (*have, make, take*, etc.), which do heavy duty in the formation of idioms and other multi-word combinations in English. How are these verbs dealt with in the materials you use?

8. The lexical syllabus does not foster massive vocabulary acquisition in the initial stages, but encourages learners to make full and extended use of words they already have by recombining elements. Compare this with the stance of the post-war structuralists such as Fries discussed in Chapter 3.

9. In the lexical syllabus, such things as lists of structures and notions and functions would be secondary, and would come out of the implementation of the lexical syllabus rather than constrain it. A coursebook based on this syllabus would be radically different from conventional ones and would almost certainly meet resistance at first; the residue of the structuralist position is still very potent (see McCarthy 1984).

Vocabulary, cloze and discourse: an applied linguistic view

Ronald Carter

1. Introduction

Cloze procedure has been around for a long time. A recent article in *English Language Teaching Journal* (Soudek and Soudek 1983) reviews a range of applications for this procedure in language teaching. Over a period of thirty years, cloze procedure has been used for error analysis, as a measure of readability, as a tool for informal group-based prediction and discussion activities, for oral language development, for teaching stylistic sensitivity in the literature class, and so on. It is also widely employed as a device for testing language competence. Cloze procedure conventionally involves routine deletions from sentences or longer texts into which a student inserts an appropriate lexical item. The deletions can be random (though they are usually between every eighth or twelfth word) or can be more specifically directed at teaching or testing linguistic features such as particular grammatical categories. It is a procedure which is, however, regularly used to develop vocabulary.

The main aim in this paper is to explore the extent to which insights provided by some recent models of written discourse organization can assist the employment of cloze techniques. One focal area of concern is: can cloze procedure be made more sensitive to patterns of discourse in texts and thus provide a basis for more cohesive and coherent writing? In particular, what are the most effective ways of underlining the important role played by vocabulary in connectivity? The immediate goal is one of language development rather than language testing, and the focus is on second-language learners of English, although there are, hopefully, clear implications for the teaching of writing in mother-tongue classes, too.

2 Cohesion

Halliday and Hasan's *Cohesion in English* (1976) represents one of the most developed models we have for understanding the connectivity of texts. Its first forays into the language classroom were accompanied by hopes that it could be used by the teacher as a cure-all for those 'illogical' and 'ill-structured' essays students are sometimes wont to produce. In practice, the model does no such thing; and this is, of course, an unreasonable expectation with which to approach any system of analysis, since models usually only describe limited sub-systems within larger systems and, in the analysis of extended texts, usually only allow partial understanding of aspects of their organization. Halliday and Hasan's account of inter-sentential cohesion draws attention to the important role in connectivity of surface markers of linkage, such as conjunctions and pro-forms, and of devices such as substitution and ellipsis. In terms of the uses of cloze, this can serve to show students the importance of such cohesive ties by encouraging them to explore the kinds of connecting items which obtain between clauses and sentences. For example:

1. The man walked slowly down the road . . . he was late (although, when, because, while).
2. I waited for the train. . . . was late (it, he, but).
3. The trains always run on time in Holland and so . . . the buses. (do, run, can)

Here, items can be selected from lists of alternatives (in the manner of a multiple choice) or as a standard cloze procedure of filling a gap. They can be graded for difficulty. Possibilities also exist for class discussion of the semantic differences between the respective choices. We should also note here that there is nothing random about the deletions; they are targeted to a specific end.

One limitation to the above operations is that the emphasis is mainly on the function of grammatical words; there is little attention to the specific role of lexical words in the organization of a text. Thus, the substitutions are made from a finite store of mutually exclusive 'closed' grammatical items. In terms of Widdowson's distinction between text and discourse, cloze based on the above cohesive relations would be a text cloze and not a genuinely discourse cloze (Widdowson 1978, p. 23). Although there is much of value in this domain which can be exploited by the teacher, it is within the semantic networks established by lexical cohesion that teachers might find more extensive ways of using cloze to exploit the discourse structure of written language.

2.1 Lexis, cohesion, and chains

It would be inaccurate to give the impression that in *Cohesion in English* Halliday and Hasan do not consider the part played by lexis in cohesion. In fact, they devote one chapter to this topic, and recognize two main categories of lexical cohesion: reiteration and collocation. **Reiteration** refers to different types of lexical item which, some in a more general sense than others, share the property of being related to a single common referent (or a referent in a connected field of discourse) which has occurred in the preceding text. In this function, the role of repetition of a word (same item), synonyms, super-ordinates and general words are evaluated. (For further discussion of 'general words' see pp. 206–8). **Collocation** is an aspect of lexical cohesion which embraces a 'relationship' between lexical items that regularly co-occur. The central insight here is into the ways in which long cohesive chains can be built up out of lexical relations. In a text these relations can be realized by different referents (e.g. *boy/girl*; *Monday, Tuesday, Wednesday*) but the items are systematically related to form a semantic network which can extend into a cohesive chain. Sometimes the networks between words are associational; for example, *candle, flame, flicker* or *hair, comb, curl*, where the pattern is no more than one of a habitual co-occurrence of words in the same lexical environment. Halliday and Hasan conclude, however, that: 'the effect of lexical, especially collocational, cohesion on a text is subtle and difficult to estimate' (1976, p. 288).

One problem with a separation of lexical from grammatical cohesion is that within either domain it remains difficult to account for the overall *coherence* of an extended text. For example, Van Dijk (1985) cites the following text:

> This morning I had a toothache
> I went to the dentist
> The dentist has a big car
> The car was bought in New York
> New York has serious financial troubles

Here, there is lexical cohesion as a result of reiteration and by collocation (*toothache/dentist*) but the text lacks a coherent global organization. For further discussion see Petöfi 1985; Morgan and Sellner 1980; Carter 1986. In Carter (1986) the following piece of writing is cited as an example of a text which is cohesive in terms of grammatical cohesion, but which likewise lacks coherence:

Then we found our way outside from the cloakroom. Next we went
outside and we practest fire drill in the pleasants making sure we were
quick to line up in the pleasants. Then we went back through the
cloakroom. Then we had break and Jill dropped the crisps. We could go
into the dining room or go outside and eat our food.

(Joanna, aged 11)

Here the overt markers of connectivity (*then*, *next*) testify to its
cohesive properties, but we have to conclude that cohesion is a
necessary but not a sufficient condition for coherence.

However, there are a number of interesting exercises which draw
on insights provided by Halliday and Hasan's work on lexical
cohesion, and which utilize the categories of reiteration and collocation. Some useful exercises are illustrated in McCarthy (1984) and
in Morrow (1980). One example (from McCarthy 1984) is that of
inviting students to make connected sentences (in this case, two
sentences) from the following 'text':

The sofa is covered in leather.
Lilac is very nice.
The footstool is too.
Cloth is not half as nice.
There's one in bloom just over the porch.
The scent is heavenly.
The suite is very plush.

Its purpose is to make students aware of the cohesive power of lexical
relations when the more obvious signals of linkage are absent.

2.2 Coherence and cohesive harmony

Subsequent development by Hasan of the 1976 model into a more
semantically-based framework attempts to account more systematically
for the underlying coherence of a text (see Hasan 1984; Halliday and
Hasan 1985). And it is this later model which might be especially
suggestive for the teaching of vocabulary development through cloze
procedure. In this model Hasan assigns a more even distribution to
the role of lexis and grammar, and recognizes more explicitly their
necessary interdependence and interaction in longer stretches of text.
Cohesion is now seen as operating within three modes; **co-reference**,
co-classification and **co-extension**. Co-reference is a relationship
which holds between two cohesive ties which refer to the same item,
for example, an anaphoric pronoun referring to an antecedent noun.
Co-classification involves reference in which the things, processes or
circumstances referred to belong in an identical class, although the
items at the two ends of the cohesive tie may be distinct; for example:

The *boy* fell out of the tree
But *boys* are like that

Co-extension obtains between two referentially different lexical items which either create a network of association between them, or which exist in a tighter structural semantic relationship. This category subsumes collocation in the earlier model, but underlines that similar semantic domains are activated by the occurrence of co-extending lexical items. In the following (constructed) text:

Buildings in Asia are unusual. The hotels are too warm; the restaurants are too cold.

warm and *cold* (antonymy) and *buildings*, *hotels*, *restaurants* (hyponymy), are co-extending items.

In extended texts patterns of co-reference create **identity chains** (same referent); patterns of co-classification and co-extension create **similarity chains** (different referent). For Hasan, the existence of *both* identity and similarity chains is necessary for a coherent text. Since identity chains will rely considerably on grammatical cohesion and similarity chains rather more on lexical cohesion, their maintenance across a text will do much to ensure coherence.

We must now ask, however, what is the exact nature of the co-existence of identity and similarity chains? How is the relationship between them produced in coherent text? How does one chain make contact with the other?

The interdependence and interaction of lexical chains is a crucial feature of Hasan's account of coherence and cohesive harmony. In other words, Hasan now goes further than regarding cohesion as being simply the relationship between single items:

Although the chains go a long way towards building the foundation for coherence, they are not sufficient, we need to include some relations that are characteristic of those between the components of a message. This is the relation that I refer to as CHAIN INTERACTION.

Thus,

The relations that lead to chain interaction are the very ones that exist between the constituents of a clause or of a group, for example, doer, doing; sayer, saying; doing, done to; or quality, qualified, etc.

For Hasan, it is a minimum requirement for chain interaction that *at least two members* of one chain should stand in the same relation to *two members* of another chain. This can be illustrated from the following example:

Mrs Brown took the car out of the garage so that she could go
shopping. In the town she went into the supermarket where she bought
some food. Then she drove home.

A cohesive chain is set up between *Mrs Brown* and the following
pronoun *she* (an identity chain). These cohesive ties confer unity on
the text. But there is another kind of unity in the text. Mrs Brown
is consistently reported as doing certain things, and this consistency
of relationship between Mrs Brown and the things she does, brings
coherence to the text. This (following Hasan) can be shown diagrammatically:

1. Mrs Brown   took   the car ⎤
2. Mrs Brown   could go   ⎥
3. Mrs Brown   went   ⎥
4. Mrs Brown   bought   ⎥
5. Mrs Brown   drove   the car ⎦

There are also lexical relationships between *go* and *went*; *took* and
drove. These similarity chains give semantic connection to the whole
text, and it is just this sort of cohesive relationship that Hasan's term
attempts to capture.

3 Remediating discourse errors: using cloze

In this section some real data are examined with a view to applying
aspects of the above cited work on cohesion and coherence to texts
produced by students of English which are less than coherent.[1] The
following text was written by a nineteen-year-old student from
Pakistan, who has lived in England for about eight years. There are
obvious second-language problems in tense, etc. but we will not be
concerned with these, except in so far as they affect the cohesive
structure of the text:

Captain Box was wondering something did happen to Mr. Donald
Crowhurst, and when he was sailing his small yacht. No-one would
abandon a beautiful yacht in the middle of the sea. The sea rescuers
searched for several days, and still no sign of him or his dead body.
They stopped searching for him. Captain Box was confused while he
read the log book for several times, and still confused. After several
hours studying the log book Captain Box seemed to understand the
complex sentences. Donald wasn't an ordinary yachtsman, his occupation
was an electrician, and sailing was his hobby. He entered this
competition just to have time off from his work to sail around the world.
(Kamal, aged 19)

If we draw up a diagram of the chain interactions in this text, we can
show that the chains are diverse and vary too much between subjects.

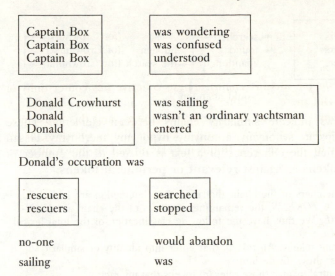

In such a diagram we can see that there are cohesive chains set up, but they shift from one topic to another rather too much. We shall re-write the passage in a (hopefully) more coherent way:

> Captain Box was confused about the fate of Donald Crowhurst, who was sailing his small yacht around the world. Surely, no-one would abandon a beautiful yacht in the middle of the ocean, he thought to himself. The rescuers had searched for several days, yet they had still found no sign of him or his body, and now they had abandoned the search. Captain Box had become more perplexed as he read through Crowhurst's logbook, but after some hours re-reading, he was beginning to unravel the mystery behind Donald Crowhurst. Crowhurst, it seemed, was no ordinary yachtsman, he was an amateur, taking time off work to sail around the world.

If we make a diagram of the chains in this, we get:

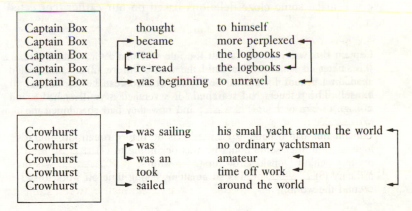

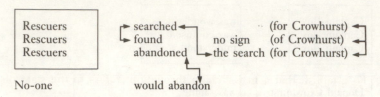

The arrows indicate similarity chains between elements. These relationships are synonymy, antonymy, hyponymy, meronymy. Hasan proposes that the coherence of a text is related to the number of **central tokens** as against **relevant** or **peripheral tokens**:

> Those members of the chain that enter into interaction are known as *CENTRAL TOKENS*; the remaining members of the chain are *NON-CENTRAL*. We thus have the following classification of the total lexical tokens of a text.
> 1. Relevant tokens. All tokens that enter into identity or similarity chains; these divide into:
>   a) Central tokens; those relevant tokens that interact;
>   b) Non-central tokens; those relevant tokens that do not interact;
> 2. Peripheral tokens; all those tokens that do not enter into any kind of chain.
>
> (Halliday and Hasan 1985, p. 93)

From this, Hasan goes on to define 'the correlates of variation in coherence':

1. The lower the proportion of the peripheral tokens to the relevant ones, the more coherent the text is likely to be.
2. The higher the proportion of the central tokens to the non-central ones, the more coherent the text is likely to be.
3. The fewer the breaks in the picture of interaction, the more coherent the text.

> (Halliday and Hasan 1985, p. 93)

We will make some cloze deletions based on our earlier 'corrected' text:

> Captain Box was confused about the fate of Donald Crowhurst, (1)_____ was sailing his small yacht around the world. Surely, (2)_____ would abandon a beautiful yacht in the middle of the ocean he (3)_____ to himself. The rescuers had searched for several days yet they had found no sign of him or his (4)_____, and now they had abandoned the (5)_____.
> Captain Box had become (6)_____ as he read through Crowhurst's logbook, but after some hours he was beginning to (7)_____ the mystery behind Donald Crowhurst. Crowhurst, it (8)_____, was no ordinary (9)_____, he was an amateur, taking time off work to sail around the world.

These deletions have two main text processing purposes:
1. To separate out the participants so that the particular cohesive chains can be clearly established as referring to (a) Captain Box, (b) Donald Crowhurst, (c) the rescuers.
2. To establish that a major chain throughout refers to the state of mind of Captain Box and is maintained through a similarity chain (i.e. co-extension).

The deletions

A *Referring to participants:*
  (1) **who** A straightforward anaphoric pronoun which functions to make clear that it is Donald Crowhurst who is sailing the yacht not, as the previous writer might have suggested, Captain Box. Chain interaction is achieved with the last sentence of the passage, 'taking time off work to sail around the world'.
  (2) **no-one** A substitution item cohesively linked with Donald Crowhurst by the inference 'not even Donald Crowhurst'. The word 'surely' emphasizes the certainty on the part of Captain Box that no-one including Crowhurst would just abandon a yacht.
  (4) **yacht** Part of the following chain interaction
    the rescuers searched (for a yacht)
    the rescuers did not find a yacht
    the rescuers abandoned the search (for a yacht)-
  A co-extension tie of synonymy and lexical repetition which produces a similarity chain.
  (9) **yachtsman** Completion of chains
    He was an ordinary yachtsman
    He was an amateur
    He was taking time off

B *Referring to Captain Box's state of mind:*
  A major topic in this text is the state of confusion of Captain Box. This is reflected in the chain interactions. The clause 'Captain Box was confused' is in interaction with:
    Captain Box had become more perplexed (6)
    Captain Box was beginning to unravel the mystery (7).
  (3) **thought** Again, an item to do with Captain Box's state of mind. The original text does not mark that the phrase 'no-one would abandon a beautiful yacht' is a thought of Captain Box and not an opinion of the writer.
  (6) **more perplexed** In interaction with chain 'confused' in opening sentence.

(7) **unravel** In interaction with chains 'confused' and (6).

(8) **seems** Continuing the idea that Captain Box is speculating about Donald Crowhurst, thus part of the semantic field of Captain Box's confusion.

In some cases, other words would be acceptable as completions, the criteria in these cases being that the similarity chains are semantically maintained; for example, (6) 'more perplexed', 'more confused', 'more mystified', etc., would all be acceptable. The important point is that these completions would be relatable to the chain interaction in the opening sentence, for example, 'was confused'. In diagrammatic form, the chains appear:

A *Referring to participants:*

who (Crowhurst)	was sailing his small yacht (around the world)
no-one (Crowhurst)	would (not) abandon a yacht
Crowhurst	was an amateur
Crowhurst	took time off work
Crowhurst	to sail around the world

rescuers	searched	for Crowhurst and yacht
rescuers	found	no sign of yacht
rescuers	abandoned	the search for Crowhurst and yacht

B *Referring to Captain Box:*

Captain Box	was confused
Captain Box	thought to himself
Captain Box	became more perplexed
Captain Box	was beginning to unravel the mystery
it seems	(also related to supposition, for instance, mental process)

The use of cloze procedure in this instance is designed to direct the student's attention to the lexical constituents of his text and to underline the part played by particular items in its coherent organization. It may be a useful principle to begin such sensitization on a text which students have produced themselves first. Subsequent development can involve deletions from items performing similar discourse functions in other written texts, such as familiar reading material and, at later stages, from texts which will not previously have been read. Another extension to the procedure would be to delete items which are instrumental in the style of the passage. This leads to consideration of the role of vocabulary in register maintenance and in the construction of lexically appropriate *genres* of writing. This relationship between 'core' vocabulary and genre is examined in the next section. More extensive experimentation is required, however, before the following questions can be answered systematically.

1. Are items in identity chains, which mainly comprise items from closed grammatical classes, easier to predict (or teach) than those in similarity chains?
2. In similarity chains should grammatical subjects or object complements be deleted? Which categories work most directly to enhance sensitivity to the coherence and cohesive harmony of the text?
3. If alternative items for substitution are supplied by the teacher, how many should there be?
4. Is there an optimum number of deletions from any one chain or from a passage as a whole?

4 Core vocabulary, cloze and discourse

Interest in the notion of core vocabulary has been activated recently by work in applied linguistics which has attempted to identify lexical items which are the most central, 'nuclear', or 'core' in the lexicon (see, for example, Stein 1979; Quirk 1982; Stubbs 1986b; Carter 1982b). The aim has been to provide a linguistically defined set of items which might form the basis of a lexical syllabus of key words for language-learning purposes. The potential advantages and disadvantages in pedagogical contexts of such an inventory are discussed in more detail in Carter 1987a and b. What is of relevance here is that the development of specific linguistic tests for core vocabulary do demonstrate that certain items have greater degrees of structural, semantic, and pragmatic coreness than others, and that coreness is systematically related to what is neutral or unmarked about the item. For example, *thin* is a generally more core word than other items from the lexical set such as *skinny*, *slim*, *slender*, *emaciated*, *scraggy*, *lean*, of which it is a member. (The other items exhibit specific positive or negative values.) Research has tended, however, to focus on the isolation of core lexical items as individual words rather than to explore the nature of their relationship as connected items in a coherent text. It will be clear that examination of this relationship has particular relevance for cloze procedures grounded in an understanding of the operation of key lexis in discourse.

Preliminary investigation of core vocabulary in discourse reveals that at least two broad distinctions have to be drawn. There is a level of core vocabulary which is 'core' as far as the organization of the lexicon as a whole is concerned; and there is a level of core vocabulary which is core to a particular field or subject. Subject-specific vocabulary will always be non-core as far as the language as a whole is concerned. This is because it is not neutral in field and is immediately associated with a specialized topic. And, in terms of vocabulary development, it is naturally important that pupils acquire appropriate subject-specific core vocabularies. They need to know that words like *pungent, residue* and *solvent* inhabit chemistry texts or lessons; otherwise, there will be a restricted access to the languages of a curriculum, (for helpful discussion of subject lexis in reading materials, see Perera 1982; Cassells 1980).

There is also another dimension to the notion of subject which may be relevant in the study and development of writing across the curriculum. The two levels of core vocabulary described above both embrace vocabulary which will be neutral. That is: **core vocabulary** will be neutral by not indicating degrees of intensity or formality, or by being neutral in field of discourse; **subject-core vocabulary** will be only expressive of a particular field; it will be neutral as far as the domain of the discourse is concerned. Writing development will, however, be limited if expressivity in the use of words is wholly replaced by expression which is neutral. For however important particular academic subjects and their attendant vocabularies may be, there is another issue to do with the subject in writing. Subject in this sense refers to the individual subject, the subject pronouns *I* or *we*, and with this sense is connected the individual *expressivity* of the learner as a producer of language and a recorder of experiences (for seminal discussion of expressive writing in a framework of language in education, see Britton *et al.* 1975). Use of vocabulary *by* the subject, as opposed to *for* the subject, necessarily involves more extensive deployment of non-core items. The relationship can be represented diagrammatically as follows:

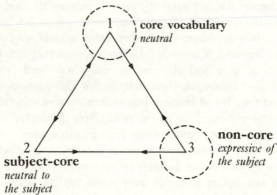

FIGURE 1

(The dotted lines here at 1 and 3 indicate that measurement of core vocabulary reveals *degrees* of coreness, rather than an unequivocal determination. At point 2, where more specified lexis is involved, a more precise relationship is possible.) The arrows between all three points constitute what I have argued elsewhere to be one of the most important of principles in writing development across the curriculum (Carter 1985). The principle is that a balance should obtain between writing appropriate to an academic subject, and writing which is expressive of the subject of the writer; in other words, a balance between neutrality and expressivity. The realization of this principle depends on the provision of writing opportunities and strategies such as cloze, which effect regular translation between 'genres' appropriate to the three 'vocabularies' of the triangle.

4.1 Vocabulary and genres of writing

A basic assumption underlying this section is that there is a relationship between core vocabularies and genres of writing. **Genre** here is used in a particular sense. The term is generally used to refer to speech events relative to particular contexts of use which are controlled in language structure by an intersection of field, mode and tenor of discourse. The term is more widely used in literary criticism; a genre of sonnet, for example, would be one traditionally restricted to *fields* such as love or prayer or religious speculation, would be in a formally elevated *tenor* and in a *mode* of written discourse which is marked by particular rules of lineation, pattern of rhyme, and so on. Literary genres are intrinsically more variable and subject to patterned reformulation for creative purposes; genres of a more stable kind might include recipes, car maintenance instructions, weather forecasts, etc., and, in this regard, may be indistinguishable from what linguists also term **registers**.

As far as genres of writing across the curriculum are concerned, it may be more productive to distinguish genres which, in their stylistic constitution and organization, transcend particular subject-specific discourses. For example, recipes are conventionally marked by a lexis of food and cooking. But a genre such as a report or argument would not necessarily be restricted to any particular field. To put it another way, a 'report' in biochemistry and a 'report' in zoology will differ in field and will, therefore, differ in register, but they are still in the same 'genre' of report. It may be useful to term such categories of writing **discourse-genres**.

Examples of such discourse-genres would be: *summary, report, recount, argumentation, narrative, description, explanation, instruction* (see also research by Martin and Rothery 1981). These genres are general in that they apply to writing in different subjects, though it should not be claimed, of course, that they are all equally necessary in all curricular domains. Thus, if we are studying English literature, then we may have less need for competence in the genre of instruction than in the genres of *narrative, description* or *argumentation*. Similarly, students of science may not need to be as proficient in reading and writing *narratives* and *descriptions*, as in *report* and *summary*.

In the linguistic and structural properties of these 'macro-genres' lexis is, of course, only one level and only one organizing component. There are, for example, syntactic formulations characteristic of the genres (for example, passivization in *report*; nominalization in *summary*; absence of pronominalization in both *report* and *summary*). But it is necessary to observe the extent to which different lexical relations obtain in these genres. And in these relations the coreness of particular lexical items is an important feature.

Initial research suggests that the presence of **core**, **subject-core**, and **non-core** lexical items (see Figure 1) can be connected with particular discourse-genres. The following correlations between lexical coreness and genre can be observed:

Summary		Instruction	
Explanation	} core	Report	} subject core
		Recount	

Argumentation		
Narrative	} non-core	
Description		

In a small-scale research project, Carter (1985) reported on teaching exercises designed to encourage cross-generic writing, for example, from one genre to another. The focus was on *report, explanation*, and *description*, and involved cooperation between a teacher of English and a teacher of physics. Samples of writing, verified by the teachers as appropriate to the relevant category, were produced. The following examples written by a fifteen-year-old are selected to illustrate the nature of the lexical choices in each macro-genre:

Report (subject core: physics/science)

A <u>bimetal bar</u> is taken. The bar is <u>composed</u> of two layers of metal. There is brass on the outer layer and iron on the inner. When heat is <u>applied</u>, the brass layer bends the iron over. This <u>demonstrates</u> that brass expands <u>at a faster rate</u> than iron.

Description (non-core)

I once saw two metals have a fight. They fought in <u>sweltering</u> heat. The metals were iron and brass and they were on either side of a piece of metal. As they got hotter and hotter, the brass began to win. It grew larger and the iron became <u>feeble</u>. Finally, the brass <u>wrestled</u> the iron. The iron <u>surrendered</u>.

Explanation (core)

You <u>take</u> a strip of metal. Half the strip is brass and half the strip is iron. Then you <u>heat</u> it. The bar gets longer and then <u>bends</u>. The curve <u>outside</u>, which is brass, is longer. This <u>shows</u> that brass expands more quickly than iron.

(Sikina, aged 15)

The underlined items illustrate relative degrees of coreness in the respective texts. For example, *heat* is more core than *apply heat*; *bimetal bar* is a more subject-core item than *strip of metal*; *sweltering* is non-core and so on. The tolerance of metaphoric items in the discourse-genre of description raises, because of the subjective nature of response to such texts, potentially awkward questions concerning assessment; but the more direct involvement of the subject, and an attendant expressivity in the use of vocabulary, may be as important an element in lexical development as the acquisition and appropriate use of the relative cores. In terms of fostering vocabulary development, in terms of maintaining a balance between writing to learn and learning to write, and in terms of mastering the genres of writing across a curriculum, teaching which facilitates regular translation between genres, or re-writing from one genre to another, could be claimed to lead to more productive writing in the fullest sense of the word. In Britain, in particular, there has been a tendency in the last fifteen years to encourage expressive writing at the expense of writing non-expressive genres; by contrast, work in ESL may have encouraged writing in a range of genres leading to language proficiency in a subject, but denying a measure of expressivity to the subject as a writer.

The foregoing discussion once again necessarily entails more extensive research, but this need not prevent classroom exploration of discourse-based cloze procedures which attempt to develop sensitivity to the roles of lexical items in different discourse-genres. Here one way of effecting recognition of lexical cores might be by juxtaposing passages which are thematically related but generically distinct. That is, students might be given a list of lexical items and invited to insert them in two generically separate passages. The particular task here is not exclusively that of locating an appropriate syntactic or semantic environment, but of selecting lexical items appropriate to each discourse-genre. Sensitivity to the coherence of each text at the level of lexical coreness can also be developed by a focus on a selection of consistently appropriate core items across an extended text. Another useful strategy, as mentioned above, would be to encourage re-writing from one genre to another, using a different set of core items, which can be supplied or withheld by the teacher, depending on the adjudged level of students' competence.

5 Conclusion: opening up cloze

Hasan's model of coherence and cohesive harmony does not account for all that is significant in textual connectivity; the notion of discourse-specific core vocabulary also captures only certain aspects of lexical organization and appropriacy in written discourse. By using insights generated by this lexicological work, cloze procedure can become more sensitive to discourse structures, and can begin to aid specific areas of writing development. It has been a main aim of this paper to underline the importance of discourse sensitivity in the use of cloze procedure. However, several limitations to the above discussion need to be acknowledged. First, the view of applied linguistics has been a predatory one: take and apply whatever appears to be of use in a model. There has been no real attempt to use the experience of practice to feed back into possible refinements of the models/descriptive frameworks. Second, there are other models which account for other features of lexical patterning and organization in discourse, and which have implications for the uses of cloze procedure for pedagogical purposes. Some of the models and their possibilities are discussed in the *Points for further development* section at the end of this paper. Third, problems with cloze procedure itself have to be acknowledged. Some of these, such as deletion ratios, have already been cited.[2] The remainder of this section briefly isolates one particular problem in the use of cloze as a teaching procedure for dealing with 'real', naturally occurring text.

We must recognize that not only is there more to connectivity than the above frameworks suggest, but also that there is more to language than connectivity. Language is used to make meanings and, although incoherent text can impair meaning or, at least, make readers work very hard to establish it, cohesion or coherence or appropriate degrees of coreness in lexis do not secure meaning. In order for meanings to be created by writers and by readers, language has to be in more than a merely formal static set of relationships. Each point of connection in a text has something unique about it, because connections in the world are themselves unique in time and space. Each lexical item in a text can be, and usually is, part of a formal stable relationship, but it is also part of a process of dynamic, unstable 'slippage' which can make different interpretations possible. Relations between words in texts are, therefore, regularly *instantial*, that is, they make unique partnerships or combine or associate to produce meanings specific to that individual text. In fact, the term 'instantial' is one used by Hasan, who recognizes that precise repetition or precise structural semantic relations such as synonymy, antonymy, etc. are not always feasible in texts, and in such cases terms such as 'equivalence' or 'semblance' should be preferred. The same point is made in Chapter 5, and in the article by McCarthy in this volume, in which McCarthy suggests that categories of 'equivalence', 'opposition' and 'inclusion' are needed to capture the dynamic nature of much lexical interrelation. The problem for the teacher using cloze procedure and inserting the (albeit very useful) knowledge of connectivity provided by linguistic models, is one of creatively intervening in a student's engagement with a text in such a way as to preserve the text's dynamic as well as its more static organization. An additional problem is that cloze makes it almost impossible to reproduce the conditions of *spoken* discourse. It invariably presents us with product rather than process; that is, the recipient of the text can see what comes after as well as before the deleted item. In utilizing cloze for teaching spoken discourse comprehension, or for improving listening skills, this can mean that more use might need to be made of lexical prediction in which ESL learners, in particular, need to be encouraged to use *post-* as well as *pre-item* clues. (For specific techniques which encourage such prediction see the oral 'Guided response vocabulary tests' in McCarthy *et al.* 1985.)

Cloze is not a perfect replica of the language-making process by any means; but, in spite of the above difficulty, cloze comes close to aligning with natural processing abilities, and especially when used in a discourse-sensitive way. More ways of allowing fuller negotiation of meaning need to be developed, experimented with, and researched further. And more ways of utilizing developing lexically-based accounts of product-oriented discourse organization should be found, too, for these relations provide essential scaffoldings around which meanings and generically appropriate styles are constructed. Cloze should, and will, continue to be opened up. It has been around for a long time, and there is a lot of life left in it yet.

Notes

1. I am grateful to James Bones for supplying me with some of these data, and for discussing some of them with me, as well as for commenting on the article in the light of his own work in this area reported in Bones (1986).
2. Clarke and Nation (1980, p. 217) ask the following questions about guessing words from context. Their list is especially relevant for supplementing any discussion in this section concerning lexical cloze procedure:

> Does the skill (of guessing words from context) transfer from one language to another . . .? Will practice in guessing in the mother tongue automatically result in improvement in guessing in the foreign language and vice versa? Is a score on a cloze test a reliable measure of how well a learner can guess word meanings? How much does practice with cloze tests develop the skill of guessing word meanings? . . . certain parts of speech are easier to guess than others. Is there an optimum density of new words to known words which will help guessing?

Further debate about alternative strategies and about theoretical perspectives is usefully summarized in Foley (1982).

Points for further development

1. As we have seen, Hasan's chain interaction analysis is particularly helpful in cases where writers shift topic or theme too often, and degrees of incoherence result. The question of *theme* may, therefore, repay further analysis by teachers. For example, does the fact that a lexical item is a theme in a sentence make it a more significant item to delete? Fries (1983) proposes that theme is the *first* item of a sentence, and that in cohesive harmony with other themes, this signals the 'method of development' of a passage. Should greater attention, therefore, be given to deleting themes in order to develop in students greater awareness of thematic development in a text? If certain texts establish similarity chains which lead from initial position, then deletion of items along the chain can also aid awareness of its conceptual progression. This may be especially useful in those genres where arguments are compared and contrasted.

2. It is a frequent strategy in texts which contrast and compare that they are based on sets of similar points being gathered together, and then contrasted with other sets; yet, other comparing texts contrast individual items in contrasting pairs. How useful is it to delete items such as *however, for example, and so, and yet*, which serve to propel arguments forward or signal semantic relations between sets of propositions? Is the deletion of such items, especially as they tend to be

in clause or sentence initial position, more or less important than deletions from lexical chains which constitute thematic and propositional development? Is the significance of particular items relative to text-type or genre?

3. Certain words do regular service as general discourse organizers. They organize the other words of the text, acting as lexical signals of where the text is going and where it has come from. As suggested in (2), they can be especially significant when in theme position or when marking the arrangements of semantic domains across a text such as hypothetical/real or problem/solution (see especially, Hoey 1983; Crombie 1985). A particularly widely deployed group of such words is that known variously as 'anaphoric nouns' (Francis 1986) and 'general words' Halliday and Hasan (1976): that is, items such as *this view, these reasons, the argument* summarize whole chunks of preceding or subsequent discourse. Are such items of even greater significance? Are there particular strings of words in certain genres which form lexical set relationships, for example, *this view, looked at from another angle, at first glance, upon closer inspection*? How might the use of such relationships be taught by cloze procedure? Compare Nattinger's suggestions for teaching lexis in metaphoric sets (pp. 73–5).

4. When using cloze procedure how necessary is it to delete only single orthographic words? Can whole units of language or whole themes be deleted? The article by Cowie in this volume may be particularly instructive here. Does it matter if items are not exactly retrieved and only a general sense is maintained?

5. Deyes (1984), in an article specifically devoted to *discourse cloze*, is another suggestive source for ideas for further classroom-based investigation and research. Deyes draws on Prague School linguistic analysis of 'communicative dynamism' and 'functional sentence perspective' to point out which elements in sentences and text carry new information (generally termed *rheme*) and which refer to already mentioned topics (generally termed *theme*). Deyes's classroom experiments which explore theme/rheme relations conclude that rhematic elements are generally less recoverable. But are some rhemes more or less predictable or recoverable than others? Are themes always more easily arrived at?

6. How far is both theme and rheme recovery dependent on the reader discovering or inferring appropriate 'schemata' or frames of reference? Do some passages supply appropriate frames? Do some rely entirely on world knowledge? What are the implications of this for

assessment of difficulty and a progressive sequencing of cloze exercises?

7. Cloze may be an especially productive procedure in the literature class, and need not necessarily be confined to more advanced levels. In genres such as poems, cloze can be used to exploit the multi-layered networks and functions and the text-instantial semantic densities which lexical items can acquire. In literary texts, chain inter-actions are regularly multiple, and thus, cloze can be employed to demonstrate the creative, dynamic process by which some words break with more formal and stable semantic networks. See Carter (1982b) and for a number of practical examples, Carter and Long (1987).

8. And, finally, a more theoretical and epistemological question. Is cloze no more than a sophisticated guessing game? If so, how do we ensure that semantic choices are genuine? Genuine semantic choices will also interlock with the semantics of the discourse, and it should be a continuing goal in the teaching of discourse-based language to develop ways of highlighting for students the several instances in which words can be *core* to a discourse. Is it more difficult merely to guess core-items than it is themes or items in a chain relationship?

Some vocabulary patterns in conversation

Michael McCarthy

Introduction

Two parallel developments in the last decade within the fields of
applied linguistics and language teaching converge in this paper: the
revived interest in vocabulary and the emphasis on the teaching of
languages communicatively. I have stated my commitment to the first
of these two elsewhere, and provided what I hope is a useful summary
of the arguments (McCarthy 1984); the second is a *fait accompli* whose
internal debates are too vast to be entered here, apart from a general
need to reiterate one of the implications of communicative language
pedagogy: that spoken, not written, data should be the model where
the teaching of spoken language is concerned.

Studies of the *written* language have in recent years acknowledged
the importance of different types of vocabulary patterning. *Lexical
cohesion* forms a significant (though not fully developed) part of
Halliday and Hasan's (1976) model for the analysis of surface links
over clause and sentence boundaries, and lexical signals play a key
role in the clause-relational approach to written text (Winter 1977;
Hoey 1983). These developments are discussed in Chapter 5 of this
book. Both of these approaches to written text can be directly applied
to vocabulary teaching and learning (see McCarthy *et al.* 1985 for
some examples). What is lacking is a similar approach to natural
conversational data. The rest of this paper is a tentative step in the
direction of filling that gap, and is a report of continuing research
into vocabulary in discourse.

Theoretical basis of the study

Vocabulary in conversation, as in written text, can be viewed from
two points of view, the transactional (content) and the interactional
(how this content relates to, is received by the listener and fed back
and how the conversation is 'managed' and steered to its outcome). This paper deals mostly with the second of these two

approaches, but it may be as well to dismiss one potential misunderstanding at this point: the separation of transactional and interactional is not in order to set up two different *kinds* of vocabulary; it is between two different ways of viewing the simultaneous functioning of lexical patterning on both planes. The patterns that will be focused upon here are those that seem to have important interactive functions in talk, which is not to say that the items realizing the patterns do not contribute to the developing content of the discourse. The type of analysis developed for this study is intended to highlight how speakers use words in a systematic and patterned way for interactive purposes. The passing back and forth of the content of messages in talk is not a unidirectional operation, and requires constant monitoring, feeding back and signalling the 'state of play' on the part of participants. The precise discourse *value* of items (for it is this rather than an abstract notion of *meaning* which discourse analysis seeks to illustrate) has to be established among participants, and speakers project *assumptions* as to such values, assumptions which are open to challenge or renegotiation; predicted or typical relations between items can be re-formulated, and many other subtle mechanisms are activated by interactive lexical 'management'.

The data

The data for the present study come from the Survey of Spoken English (SSE) data published in Crystal and Davy (1975) and Svartvik and Quirk (1980). In addition, eighty minutes of conversation from the Collins/University of Birmingham COBUILD corpus were consulted on tape and unpublished transcript and the relevant parts labelled for intonational features (see below). The SSE data come from fourteen whole conversations (over 17,000 tone units) recorded over the period 1964–1975; the COBUILD conversations are more recent, recorded over the last few years. The subjects of both corpora are academics, students, university secretaries and other educated and professional people; the majority of the time, most participants did not realize they were being recorded; certainly no participant could have anticipated the nature of the data the present study was interested in. While the participants are not widely representative in a social sense, the data have a great variety of age groups, subject matter, situations and settings, suggesting that they are reliable sources for attaching significance to lexical phenomena that occur throughout all of the conversations. No claims are made as to the absolute generalizability of the vocabulary features illustrated here for all dialects, varieties or sociolects of English. The corpora referred to are, however, full of the type of middle-class, standard British English to which much English language teaching aspires.

Analytical approach

An immediate and appealing approach was to work with the model of lexical cohesion proposed by Halliday and Hasan (1976), with due respect to later revision (Hasan 1984). Their model picks up reiteration in the form of repetition, use of synonymy and hyponymy, etc. over clause and sentence boundaries, and can reveal interesting patterns. But, being designed for written text, it misses much (this is not to say it *cannot* be used for spoken transcripts, see Halliday 1985). The model does not distinguish between lexical reiteration over a clause/sentence boundary and reiteration over a turn or speaker boundary, which for the present study is an important feature of the interactive management of talk. In natural conversation, lexical reiteration options can sometimes be taken up by the same speaker, a second speaker or a third speaker, and each speaker may realize their choice in a different way. More importantly, though, a model derived from written text does not account for the part played by *intonation* choices in signalling the existential, here-and-now lexical relationships projected by speakers. Whether an item is to be understood as equivalent in discourse value to another item or contrastive with it will crucially depend on whether it is phonologically prominent, whether it is realizing a contrastive choice of phonological key, and so on. It is with these additional kinds of language choice that speakers assign local value to vocabulary items and negotiate with one another the range and limits of meaning potential that are being exploited. Understanding and manipulating *value* is a discourse skill a language learner must possess for the full accomplishment of fluency in the target language, and it is one concern an applied linguistic model for lexical interaction must address if we really are interested in language in use. The present model therefore incorporates a *communicative* theory of intonation, that of Brazil (1985a and b).

Brazil's account of intonation begins with a discussion of the significance of *prominence* (put at its simplest, salient or 'stressed' syllables as perceived by a listener, and their opposite, non-salient syllables). A prominent syllable gives the lexical item it occurs in the status of *selective*, chosen from a list of possible alternatives. An item that has no prominent syllables, on the other hand, is signalled as non-selective, assumed and shared common ground, and a member of a paradigm where there is no real choice of alternative senses in the here-and-now discourse. The successive expansion and contraction of the lists of available items as the discourse progresses and speakers' worlds converge and diverge create what Brazil calls 'existential paradigms' (1985a, p. 41). What this means in terms of a model for the analysis of lexical choice in talk is, that in an example such as:

(1)   A: so you WANT to meet HArry
      B: YES and i'm dying to see BILL TOO

providing *dying* and *see* are non-prominent (indicated by lower case letters) they will be heard as largely synonymous with *want* and *meet* respectively. Their discourse *values* are the same. If *dying*, for example, were to be made prominent, as in:

(2)   B: YES and i'm DYing to see BILL

then the speaker would almost certainly be signalling a redefinition of terms, a new value-relationship between the items, since *dying* is now to be heard as selective. This new relationship could be an intensifying one, an increment or variation of some sort of the value of *want*. Furthermore, if the speaker wishes to signal clear contrastiveness between the two items, at his/her disposal is the system of *key* choices (high/mid/low; see Brazil 1985a, pp. 66ff.) and can change to a high (contrastive) key, indicated here by speech above the line:

                DYing
(3)   B: YES and i'm   to meet BILL

I have argued elsewhere that Brazil's theory of intonation is an indispensable element in a discourse theory of lexis (McCarthy 1987), and it seems inadequate to attempt to formulate a model for cohesion in talk without taking into account the effects of intonational choices. The surface elements of reiteration may be retrievable merely at the level of lexical form, but their significance, whether as reiterations of *sense*, or expansions and redefinitions of sense, must take intonation into consideration. Thus the present analysis distinguishes between change of item retaining the same value or sense, as in example (1) (for a precise explanation of sense, see Brazil 1985a, pp. 53ff.), and change of item for sense expansion, glossing, intensification or redefinition, as in (2) and (3), and such choices will have particular interactive significance both within and over speaker boundaries. The model then further specifies reiteration by a more general item for inclusion, and reiteration in the form of an opposing item, for opposition or contrast. This approach is designed to pick out significant interactive patterning in any occurrence of items which repeat, relexicalize, encapsulate or consciously contrast previous items in the discourse. Such occurrences are taken as illustrative of the negotiation and establishment of sense units among participants. The categories of analysis which resulted from the aims and constraints discussed above emerged as the following:

> Analytical headings (all are sub-divided into *same speaker* and *over speaker boundary*)
> 1. Change of item retaining same sense
> 2. Change of item for sense increment (e.g. glossing, expansion, redefinition, intensification)
> 3. Change of item for inclusive sense
> 4. Change of item for opposing sense

The model was applied to the data, and though categorization was, predictably, not always straightforward, even excluding questionable cases, there were enough occurrences under each heading to suggest that they may be generalizable to other data and to support the conclusion that lexical patterns of these kinds are illustrative of important conversational mechanisms which participants exploit in the management of talk.

Analysis and commentary

General

Throughout the data, speakers repeat, reiterate, set up value-relations between items and paraphrase items, both within their own turns and as an echo of another's previous turn, or even of some earlier turn of their own or of another. These repetitions and relexicalizations can be examined under the headings of the model.

A note on exact repetition

Exact repetition in the form of immediate ('sequential') repetition of the same item has been recognized as a feature of speech as well as writing (Persson 1974 is the most thorough account of the phenomenon). Speakers repeat themselves and one another. Exact words and sequences are repeated. Exact repetitions occur very frequently in speech and with a variety of conversational functions, but more striking are the occasions when content is repeated in a *non*-identical form, either re-formulated, re-structured or in some way given different lexical form, and it is in these *relexicalizations* that conversational management can be seen to operate most powerfully, and which are the basis of the types of lexical relations described in this study.

1 *Change of item retaining the same sense*
This category is concerned with how speakers re-state items of the discourse, using other items projected as equivalent in sense for the purposes of the situation in which they occur. That is to say, speakers often have the choice of what Brazil (1985a, p. 56) calls 'equally available words' which do not constitute a 'sense choice'; the words do not belong to those 'mutually incompatible senses' that comprise the existential paradigm from which a speaker may choose an item at any point in the discourse. Thus, in a concocted example such as:

(4)   A: have you HEARD joe SMITH'S got a new JOB he's LEAVing
      B: well i NEVer thought HE'D go

go represents a change of *item* but not of *sense*, and this assumption (for it is only an assumption or projection of how the message is likely to be perceived) is signalled by the speaker in making *go* non-prominent.

Changes of item retaining the same sense similar to (4) occur with significant frequency in the data, and Table 1 lists a selection of such occurrences.

TABLE 1

item	reiterated as	reference
same speaker pairs		
make it to	become	603: 553–60
turned up	came	824: 1136–45
clogged	cluttered	886: 883–4
shift	moved	841: 779–93
good	decent	628–9: 586–600
heard of	know of	90: 437–9
children	kids	833: 318–9
drive (a car)	take (a car)	C&D: 55: 23–7
sign of	confession of	C&D: 78: 15–24
write down	collect	COB: gs203
retrieve	get out	COB: gs204
marvellous	great	COB: gs204
different speaker pairs		
make a difference	affect	52: 1050–56
willing	pleased	839: 683–7
(they're) fun	like (them)	C&D: 28: 19–20
very	frantically	101: 1055–1061

same speaker chains

expounding views	bring forth (views)	
	came out with (ideas)	
	expounded*	159: 432–71
pack	bag*	
	packet	COB: gs204

different speaker chains (+ speaker designation: A, B, C, etc.)

work (B)	come in (C)	
	come floating in (A)*	
	working (C)	
	work (B)	131–2: 264–92
pleasant academic (exercise) (A)	purely an academic* (B)	
	simply a pedantic (A)	138: 649–54
trouble (A)	problem (F)	
	problem (B)	833: 352–6
conducted (A)	does (C)	
	gives (C)	143: 882–8
take it there (Z)	whip it in (Z)	
	took (it) (X)	
	took it in (X)	COB: gs203

Number only references are to page and tone-group numbers in Svartvik and Quirk (1980). C & D references are to Crystal and Davy (1975) with page and line numbers. COB references are to Birmingham COBUILD corpus. * denotes a change back to prominence on the underlined syllable.

The table is organized so as to bring out the fact that a speaker will vary his/her own choice of item for the same existential sense (*same speaker pairs*) and other speakers will repeat a first speaker's sense with a different item (*different speaker pair*). These are not always in simple pairs, but create subtle chains of recurrence, sometimes involving three or more occurrences, again either by the same speaker or by a second (and subsequent) speaker (*same speaker chains/different speaker chains*). Thus in the SSE data, a speaker talks of doctors *making* it to consultants and *becoming* consultants, in this case in one and the same turn, with *become* spoken non-prominently. The relexicalizations are given in table form to save space, but a typical occurrence contextualized would be something like the following:

> (5) B: EVery member of STAFF turned up but ONly six FInalists
>   C: OH GOD
>   A: well THAT wasn't so GOOD was it
>   B: the CHRISTmas at the CHRISTmas PARty we there was
>   STACKS of BOOZE and aGAIN all the STAFF came and
>   only ONE or two underGRADuates
>
> (Svartvik and Quirk 824: 1136–45)

(Speaker designations A, B, C, etc., are retained as in the original data transcripts. For the sake of clarity and simplicity in the presentation of examples, intonation choices such as prominence, key and tone will only be transcribed where they are directly relevant to the discussion.)

Here *turned up* is reiterated by the same speaker as *came*. This is a 'same speaker pair'. In the different speaker pairs the reiteration option is taken up by someone other than the first speaker, who signals equivalence by the same means.

To say that two items, of which the second is non-prominent, are equivalent, is not the same as saying they are semantically identical. A semantic feature analysis could undoubtedly illustrate differences in meaning *potential* (as items in the language *system*) between any two items, but discourse is not really concerned with such abstractions of meaning. Discourse is language in *use*, and the 'usefulness' of an item as a contribution to an unfolding discourse is a measure of its communicability in a given, here-and-now instance, where the semantic distinctiveness of an item may not necessarily emerge, and where its overlapping communicative potential with another item is the most important thing. Its usefulness as an equivalent to another item is a local, existential value and need neither undermine nor confirm the analysis of a semanticist; it is a statement about use, which is different in kind from statements made in a decontextualized, structural description of the lexicon. The label **equivalence** (as opposed to **synonymy**) attempts to point up this distinction: the paradigms from which these equivalent items are drawn are determined by here-and-now constraints. What items are and are not available in the paradigm may not coincide with the decontextualized sets codified in dictionaries, thesauri and taxonomies of lexical items such as occur in structural descriptions like those given in Lehrer (1974). What is available in use is not the same as what can be hypothesized as available in 'meaning', nor the same as what can be hypothesized as the structure of the psychological 'stored' lexicon of the competent language user.

To illustrate the complexity of this kind of situation-bound projection of sense and the negotiability of lexical value, the example of *work, come in*, etc. in the different speaker chains of Table 1 is worth closer consideration. The chain begins with a speaker raising the question of Saturday working:

(6a)   B: PEOPLE just don't WORK saturday MORnings ofFICially in LONdon

A short amount of talk (16 tone units) intervenes and then another speaker asks:

(6b)   C: does HE come in on saturdays

offering *come in* as equivalent to *work*. A third speaker (five tone units later) comments:

(6c)   A: well MOST of them SEEM to come FLOATing in on SATurdays because THIS . . .

This speaker signals *float in* as selective, perhaps to emphasize its 'expressive' and evaluative increment on the terms previously in play. C's and B's immediate responses are:

(6d)   C: well I quite enJOY working on SATurdays
        A: M
        B: well I always USED to when i was STILL at CAMbridge and ONE DID work SATurdays

where the sense of A's *float in* seems to have been absorbed in a progressive redefining of the sense of *work*. Evidence that C and B have indeed 'absorbed' the special expressiveness of A's *float in* are seen in A's apparent dissatisfaction in the subsequent talk with the value that has been established for the term. After continuing information from B and C concerning people who work in the department they are discussing, A intervenes:

(6e)   A: HOW many people in FACT FLOAT IN and out of the dePARTment

Her question is met by more information on staff who work there, but A is clearly not satisfied with the answer:

(6f)   A: YES i REalize THAT i WONdered just how many OTHER people SORT of came IN

(131–41: 264–760)

and then gets the information that satisfies her, on the drifting, temporary population of the department. The example illustrates how finely balanced the mechanisms of discourse negotiation are: mostly, equivalent terms are traded without difficulty or misunderstanding, but because prominence choices project assumptions they can be challenged. There is no reason why *work, come in* and *float in* should not be sense equivalents (as B and C perceive); nor yet is there any reason why they have to be (A's perception). The matter has to be resolved interactively.

2 *Change of item for sense clarification, expansion or redefinition*

This heading refers to the way items are reiterated, by the same or by a different speaker, in a different form and in a manner that signals that some increment of value is attached to the reiteration. Increments may be interpreted as adding features of meaning or expressivity, or merely saying something 'different', and what these differences are may not be immediately apparent or recoverable. The characteristic pattern is that second occurrence is phonologically prominent and spoken with a falling tone. Brazil (1985a, p. 107) assigns to falling tones a 'proclaiming' function (in contrast to rising tones, which 'refer' to shared knowledge or matter already 'given' in the discourse). The falling tone proclaims items as in some way forwarding the discourse, as 'world-changing' or incremental to the accumulated values and messages already present in the talk. The items in this category of the analysis therefore are on reoccurrence **selective** (because they are prominent); that is to say they are contrastive with other available items in the existential paradigm, unlike the non-prominent relexicalizations in category 1. A typical realization (in this case a same speaker pair) from this category is:

(7)   B: //. . . *p* it was SO HOrrible //
          . . .

                                      AWful
      B: //*p* it was   //
                                                              (634: 842–5)

(Here I use the conventions of Brazil 1985a: *p* at the beginning of the tone group indicates a falling tone on the underlined prominent syllable, while a shift to above the line indicates a change of relative pitch to 'high key'.)

Here we have the speaker exploiting the intonation system to the full: *awful* is selective, it is proclaimed, and its selection of high key projects it as **contrastive**, that is to say not of the same order of discourse value as *horrible*. Speakers do this frequently with previous items of their own turns (note how often high key is exploited in Table 2, p. 192).

Often, the intention of this type of relexicalization is to intensify or stress something:

(8)   A: HE'S a VEry nice MAN CHARming man

(169: 1031–2)

or else, as Brazil (1985b) indicates, prominence may be given even when the second item is to all intents and purposes discourse-equivalent and synonymous with the first, merely for insistence or dramatic effect:

(9)   A: I discovered that the MOther who had been THERE the day beFORE WASN'T IN it . . . just wasn't THERE which was VEry ODD

(C & D: 57: 48–51)

Another function of the prominent change of item seems to be a summarizing or segmenting function for stretches of talk of varying lengths, often quite small chunks:

(10)   C: i WONdered why he was so amazed when i came EARly
        A: YES
        C: I I have a nasty habit of being about
        A: M

            EARly   PRISED
        C: half an hour   and he SORT of seemed very sur
             about it

(130: 155–9)

Note the contrastive high key again on *surprised*. On other occasions the stretches summarized are quite long, with many intervening tone units. This is a very subtle kind of conversational management. (10) shows the frequent mismatch between decontextualized semantic accounts of scaleable words such as *surprised* and *amazed* (in which *surprised* is likely to be deemed a weaker form of *amazed*) and actual values in discourse. Real use, manipulating prominence, tone and key choices, gives *surprised* useful contrastive potential in relation to *amazed*, with clear incremental value. In fact, the data seem to suggest that with items such as *horrible/awful*, *frightfully/terribly*, *appalling/terrible*, *willing/want/longing*, and so on, actual discourse values are difficult to predict, and will be locally determined, subject to the assumptions speakers encode in their formal choices of lexis and intonation. It is no coincidence that many of the examples in Tables 1 and 2 are of the subjective-evaluative type of item, where negotiability and discourse sensitivity will be most salient. Discourse value is a feature of linear encoding rather than of a product model of the lexicon; the linear, process approach to meaning-in-use is what a discourse theory of lexis must be based on.

Table 2 presents a selection of examples of prominent reiteration, using the same sub-divisions as Table 1:

TABLE 2

item	reiterated as	reference
same speaker pairs		
horrible	^awful	634: 843–4
very	^awfully	37: 201–18
very	extremely	595: 63–4
pull down	demolish	832: 286–7
get on very well	^get on fine	156: 222–6
dormant	^stagnant	163: 708–9
certainly	definitely	818: 807–8
good	^brilliant	164: 746–9
amazed	surprised	130: 155–9
frightfully funny	^quite terribly witty	640: 1094–5
nice	charming	169: 1031–2
very funny	^absolute riot	627: 501–7
left	^buggered off	COB: gs203
drop	spot	COB: gs203
lucrative	well-paid	COB: gs204
strange	odd	COB: gs203
amazed	staggering	COB: gs204
great	terrific	COB: gs204
same speaker chains		
willing	want	
	longing*	837–9: 554–686
wild	^seething	
	^irritated	47–8: 793–812
different speaker pairs		
very	terribly	644: 1292–4
fairly	very	141: 787–9
appalling	terrible	819: 877–9
worse	disastrous	288: 161–7
horrendous	^nasty	COB: gs203
got dizzy	^felt faint	COB: gs204
awful	terrible	COB: gs204

different speaker chains

think (A)	certain (B)	
	certain (A)	52: 1054–6
prepared (A)	happy (A)	
	keen (B)	
	keen (A)	874: 181–8
nice (Y)	excellent (Z)	
	tasty (Y)	COB: gs203

(^ indicates change to high key. * indicates return to non-prominence for that item.)

Comparing Table 1 with Table 2 reveals interesting properties of intensifiers such as *very, terribly* and *awfully*. *Very* is essentially neutral: it can be used as a basis for intensification:

(11)   A: YEAH and VEry GENeral as WELL the QUEStions
           exTREMEly general

                                                    (595: 62–4)

or as itself an increment on a previous intensifier, and *equivalent* to a strongly expressive intensifier such as *frantically*:

(12)   A: but he's so BUSY
       C: M
       A: you KNOW
       C: yes he's VEry busy at the MOment
       A: YES well he's ALways frantically BUsy

                                                    (101: 1055–61)

Very can also operate as an intensifier where the intensified meaning is presupposed as part of the value of an item though not separately realized:

(13)   A: so it's INteresting to KNOW WHAT the state of the art IS
           . . .
       B: well and ALso very interesting is HOW as it WERE
           alTHOUGH people write . . .

                                                    (588–9: 777–99)

This does not mean that *very* is not available in other situations clearly to *proclaim* an intensification where none is presupposed:

(14)   C: GLAD to hear they're HUman
       A: YEAH
       B: well HE IS VERy human

                                                    (592: 939–41)

All of these uses are consistent with the view that prominence choices are decisive in determining lexical value.

3 Change of item for inclusive sense

In one respect, this category overlaps with category 1 (change of item retaining the same sense), insomuch as a more general item (i.e. an item retaining some basic features but losing some specifying features) can often replace an item and occur non-prominently, thus serving as a discourse equivalent. In Table 1, the pairs *make it to/become*, *turned up/came*, *conducts/does* can all be seen in this way: the second may be more general in meaning potential but equivalent in local value to the first. The test of discourse equivalence is reversibility. If we return to example (5), it is clear that *turned up* and *came* are interchangeable. However, things are not quite so simple. Allerton (1978) has suggested that the entailment that exists between a superordinate and its hyponyms (e.g. a *rose* is a *flower* but the reverse is not necessarily true) can make reversibility problematic:

(15a)　he PICKED up a BEETLE and TOOK the insect to his DESK

(15b)　? he PICKED up an INsect and TOOK the beetle to his DESK

(15b) sounds odd, since *insect* does not necessarily entail *beetle*. The data certainly contain examples of this predicted sequence of specific item referred to anaphorically by a general term; in a discussion on libraries we find:

(16)　B: I'VE found it necessary to join a PUBlic library on theobald's ROAD ...
　　　　A: well VEry good inITiative on YOUR part to FIND a place on THEobald's ROAD

(811: 409–20)

But the mechanisms of discourse inclusion are very subtle, and, as with all cases of value assignment, depend on the projected assumptions and presuppositions of speakers. A speaker's assumptions about context *can* enable the abstract entailment rules to be apparently reversed. If a speaker assumes that a *specific* sense is contextually shared knowledge, then the general item can precede the specific and the specific be non-prominent, a situation considered problematic in (15b):

(17)　C: but I had TROUBLE GETting my PApers i eVENtually got a work permit after about a FIVE month deLAY

(146: 1060–61)

The subject of conversation is the bureaucratic difficulties of working in the USA. Neither *papers* nor *work permit* have previously occurred in the discourse but the sense of *work permit* is so strongly predicted that it is *equivalent* to *papers* (the only papers at issue being work permits) and so *work permit* occurs non-prominently, as equivalent to its semantic superordinate. Something akin to a renaming or re-definition of 'papers' has taken place, not the introduction of a new sense. Inclusion works at several levels, and items can be signalled as equivalent to a general term and subsequently referred to by an even more general term. Consider the progression *wood, sticks/logs, things* in (18):

(18) A: we DON'T seem to have very much WOOD
      B: YES THAT'S a POINT YES M
      A: well i supPOSE if we went into the PARK we MIGHT
         collect a few STICKS but it's NOT quite like having LOGS
         IS it ... BACK in the MIDlands we would KNOW if you
         KNOW WHERE we could GO and GET all these things
         from but ...

                                                    (C & D: 29: 41-8)

This is a particularly good example of what is meant to be illustrated by opposing the discourse label **inclusion** to the semantic notion of **hyponymy**. In this conversation, *wood* is projected by speaker A as being a term that might include 'sticks'. In the C & D transcript *sticks* has a proclaiming (falling) tone which suggests that it is not assumed as inherent in the talk about 'wood'; in fact there is the impression that 'sticks' are somewhat undesirable in this situation. 'Wood' is also projected as including (more preferably in the speaker's mind) *logs*. The *referring* tone indicates that the speaker assumes this to be a *shared* view of the issue of what is included in the notion of 'wood'. But there is no reason why, in another situation, *wood* should not be projected as including other items (to the exclusion of 'sticks' and 'logs'). Two concocted examples might illustrate this:

(19) (builder to his mate)
      A: //p we need some WOOD//
      B: //r well there's some TWO by FOUR //p on the LOrry //r and
         the PLANKS //p are already HERE

(20) (making a fire on house-clearance site)
      A: //p we need some WOOD //
      B: //r well there's some BOOKcases //r in the YARD ... //p OH
         //p and there's some BOXES //

(19) and (20) illustrate the role of *tone*-choice here in projecting the times that are presumed to be included in 'wood'. (20) is like (18), in that it has a *p*-tone for *boxes*, so much as to say 'we may not have assumed boxes to be understood by 'wood' but in fact they could be,

and I offer them as a candidate'. *Boxes* with an *r*-tone would simply have projected the assumption that both parties accepted 'boxes' as viable candidates for firewood.

In (18) *things* (non-prominent) is then an equivalent for *wood* (understood as meaning *sticks* and *logs*). Thus the notion of discourse *inclusion* seems crucially dependent not on an item being prominent but on the accompanying tone choices. Where non-prominence occurs, regardless of semantic components, we are dealing, for discourse purposes, with *equivalences* once again.

4 *Change of item for opposing sense*

In this category are mostly short-span re-selections of items of opposing sense. Antonymy in semantics raises a problem of possible misentailment as Lyons (1977, p. 278) has noted with regard to sentences such as 'Is X a good chess player?', which, if it gets a 'no' answer could be ambiguous; the possible implicature that X is bad can be removed by saying 'no, but he's not bad either'. In talk, inexplicit antonymy might leave too open the question of what is being opposed to what, since speakers need to engage with existential senses for lexical items. The data suggest that speakers often cover themselves by making explicit the opposing terms that the existential set contains. Most commonly this is by a process similar to what semanticists have called 'metalinguistic negation' (see Horn 1985), except that sometimes the opposing item is specifically negated, even though it has not actually occurred:

(21)   A: //*p* he's a THOUGHTful man //*r* he's NOT a ⎯HASty⎯ man //
                                                                    (44: 597–8)

(22)   A: //*p*+ AND so it's GROWing //*r* rather than di ⎯MINishing⎯ //
                                                                    (156: 247–9)

(*p*+ is a rise-fall tone, with the same 'proclaiming' meaning as *p*. See Brazil 1985a, pp. 148ff. for precise differences.)

Choice of high key in (21) and (22) reinforces contrastiveness, and the choice on the opposing item of an *r* tone (fall-rise: *'referring'* tones; see Brazil, 1985a, pp. 106ff.), projects an assumption that it is shared knowledge that *hasty* and *diminish* are the existential opposites of *thoughtful* and *grow*, respectively, and further, an expectation that *hasty* and *diminish* might have been the listener's evaluation of the situation.

Oppositional relations occur over speaker boundaries too:

(23) C: //p HOW did you get <u>ON</u> // r+ WERE you <u>SHY</u> etcetera //

NERvous

A: //p i <u>WASN'T</u> // r+ <u>AC</u>tually // p i was comPLETEly un
about the whole thing //

(492: 58–60)

(r+ is a simple rising tone, with the same basic *'referring'* meaning as r.
See Brazil 1985a, pp. 132ff.)

In (23), A proclaims *unnervous* (with high key) and is therefore not
projecting the complete assumptions of shared knowledge that were
found in (21) and (22). A deems it necessary to assert the terms of
the opposition and to defy the listener's expectation. Sometimes the
antonym plus a negative marker simply creates discourse equivalence
and is, appropriately, non-prominent:

(24) B: HOW OLD is he cos I found this very difficult to GUESS
on LOOKing at him. . .
B: he's NOT he's NOT easy to GUESS ACtually

(152–3: 40–56)

Over a turn boundary opposing items can be used for agreement or
concurrence:

(25) Y: so they SHOULDn't alLOW you to eat so MUCH
X: it should be forBIDden

(COB: gs203)

As with the other value relations, terms in opposition will be locally
determined, and precise relations will be projected by speakers using
the systems of intonational choice to encode their projections. There
should be no automatic expectation that these local values will match
semantic feature analyses in uncontextualized words or sentences.

Summary and conclusions

The purpose of devising a model of analysis and applying it to
conversational data was, it was stated at the outset, an applied
linguistic one. I began by claiming that looking at real data was the
proper way to understand how vocabulary works interactively in
conversational English. This paper has only looked at one aspect, one
small corner of how speakers use lexical items, but certain things are
clear, and are unquestionably applicable to any study of vocabulary
in discourse.

All the findings of this paper point to a need to reassess what we mean when as language teachers we talk of such things as 'synonyms' and 'antonyms', or when as materials writers we work with the notion of lexical sets. While some observers of language (e.g. Brown and Yule 1983, p. 9) seem to suggest that, since there is a high incidence of fairly simple, general vocabulary in talk, the lexical demands on speakers are relatively low, the patterns of vocabulary illustrated in this paper would suggest that quite subtle functions are fulfilled by *varying* lexical choice within and over turn boundaries. This actually suggests a demand on the learner to understand and exercise lexical variation which may be greater than we think, and which only close examination of data can reveal.

If vocabulary teaching is to take on the same communicative approach as has become established for the functions of syntax, then the communicative functioning of lexical choice needs to be as explicitly incorporated into materials as the functions of syntax are, especially given the welcome trend towards a multi-syllabus approach (e.g. Swan and Walter 1984). The question of the universality of discourse functions can be addressed by saying that if lexical discourse functions such as those described here are *not* universal, then we do the learner a disfavour to ignore them. If they *are* universal, then we must at least give our learners the linguistic means to perform such communicative acts, and the best way to offer the means is unquestionably to present vocabulary in discourse contexts where it is performing those communicative functions. On the more conscious teaching/learning side, there is some justification for taking a linear approach rather than a 'product' approach to pieces of data in the class, and asking learners to consider just what items are 'available here and now', what are the existential lexical sets from which choices are being made, what equivalences and oppositions are being set up in *this* discourse, what the intonation choices are doing, and so on. There is certainly a justification for building lexical variability in at even comparatively early stages, perhaps once survival level vocabulary has been dealt with, and for not subordinating lexical skills too much to the demands of the grammar, even if only from the point of view of preparing the learner to tackle without panic the harsh realities of natural talk, and even if only from a comprehension point of view.

One could sum up the whole problem in one statement: the communicative approach to language teaching will always be incomplete as long as it only principally considers the communicative acts performed by syntax; the interactive management of talk, the signalling, segmentation and feeding back of messages involves lexical as well as grammatical skills.

Points for further development

1. McCarthy sets out to demonstrate that, in casual conversation, speakers regularly and systematically vary their vocabulary choice and do not simply repeat items; they vary items in their own turns and offer variations on items from other speakers' turns, and these variations set up patterned relations between items. He claims that we cannot effectively capture these lexical relations using the traditional terms of decontextualized semantics such as synonymy, antonymy and hyponymy. Are you aware of any language-teaching materials that tackle patterns such as those McCarthy is describing? Can they be easily applied and built into current approaches to teaching?

2. McCarthy uses the terms **value** and **usefulness**. These seem to have echoes of other terms used in communicative theory, such as **illocutionary force**, and **pragmatic force** (Candlin 1981). We cannot decide on the value of an item by looking at it in isolation, just as we cannot judge the illocutionary force of a decontextualized sentence; whatever we say about words, then, when we take their dictionary definitions, will have to be supplemented by discussing their local values in the discourses where we find them. Can this view be reconciled with Summers's (this chapter)?

3. Items in discourse enter into relations which McCarthy calls **equivalence, opposition** and **inclusion**. These relations have certain things in common with synonymy, antonymy and hyponymy, but are discourse-specific, and the lexical sets which items are drawn from in talk are not the same as the decontextualized sets drawn up by semanticists; they are realized as the talk progresses, shifting, growing and contracting as the negotiative process unfolds. Take a piece of written or spoken discourse and see what sets and lexical relations emerge from it. Chapter 5 offers practical guidelines for such analyses.

4. McCarthy claims that models of vocabulary in use should take account of how lexical items are taken up from one speaker to another, and in what circumstances speakers exercise choices such as repetition and relexicalization. How can learners be trained to exercise such options, which do seem to be part of native-speaker lexical competence? If learners do not seem to be using these options,

it could be a cultural barrier, or simply that they lack a sufficiently varied vocabulary; how could we find out?

5. Value seems to be realized formally at two levels; item selection and intonation choices of prominence, key and tone. McCarthy offers Brazil's communicative theory of intonation as the most effective and illustrative tool for analysing lexis in conversation. Brazil's theory directly predicts occurrences of relexicalization of the kind McCarthy's data record; the message here would seem to be that vocabulary work in spoken language requires separate and additional procedures to vocabulary teaching using written texts.

6. The general pedagogical implications of McCarthy's paper are that we need to reassess the dominant role semantics plays in vocabulary teaching, and to bring in a pragmatic, data-based approach. In this respect it is not out of sympathy with Sinclair and Renouf (this chapter); the 'lexical syllabus' might usefully include patterns of lexical relations taken from actual data. The resultant syllabus would counterbalance the traditional emphasis on decontextualized meaning.

5 Lexis and discourse: vocabulary in use

Introduction

Much of what has been written concerning lexis over the years has assumed that the proper place for discussion of the subject is within semantics. Chapter 2 of this book underlines that fact. The question now to be raised in this chapter is: what happens when we try to incorporate the insights of discourse analysis into our view of how the lexicon operates? What readjustments will have to be made to received wisdom on such matters as word meaning, lexical relations, the discourse-functioning of vocabulary and the nature of the lexical item itself? While we may not wish to reject the claims made by semanticists as to the nature and functioning of the lexicon, we may wish to add new dimensions to our view of vocabulary, and to attempt to integrate the best insights of semantics, corpus-based lexicology and discourse analysis. This chapter will therefore consider some of the ways in which vocabulary studies have been advancing across new frontiers in recent years, and will have some suggestions to make as to how discourse analysis could be applied in vocabulary teaching and learning.

1 Studies of lexical cohesion

Working initially within the framework of lexical semantics, several linguists have tried to show how stable vocabulary-relations such as synonymy, antonymy and hyponymy contribute to the 'cohesion' (or connectedness of meaning, the feeling that something is a text and not a random set of sentences or utterances) of discourse, over boundaries such as clauses, sentences, paragraphs or speaking turns. In other words, we recognize connectedness in discourse partly because we recognize relations between vocabulary items which would be valid even if those items were out of context. Thus in the following text-segment we can see relations of (near) synonymy between *aviation* and *flying* and antonymy between *amateur* and *professional*. Furthermore, there are strong collocational associations between *war* and *armistice* and *service*, and so on:

(1) In 1929 the air was full of noises. Aviation was at its amateur zenith. The fashionable and somewhat deliberately non-professional flying of young Edwardians like Moore-Brabazon, the Hon. C. S. Rolls and S. F. Cody had naturally lapsed during the war when it was disciplined by the service conditions of the R.F.C. but no sooner was the armistice signed than it broke out again with an intensity which was spectacular, and which the Press took every care to keep spectacular.

(Blythe, *The Age of Illusion*, 1963, pp. 90–1)

Such clear meaning relations in text have led linguists to see them as a systematic resource which writers and speakers tap in the creation of coherent discourse. Writers and speakers repeat themselves (see *spectacular* in the text above), and this is one obvious device of cohesion, but they also reiterate content in different lexical forms such as synonyms and antonyms or more general terms. What is more, they choose items to combine with one another which have a high degree of predictability of co-occurrence. Where they do not, we recognize creative, marked text or else deviance.

Halliday and Hasan (1976, Chapter 6) acknowledge this text-binding quality of lexical relations and categorize lexical ties in texts under the following headings:

1. Reiteration
   a) same word (repetition)
   b) synonym (or near-synonym)
   c) superordinate
   d) general word
2. Collocation

(Halliday and Hasan 1976, p. 288)

Collocation is left undivided, as a general relation of likely co-occurrence. This scheme makes for a convenient analytic tool for texts, especially written texts. Although similar patterns can be seen in spoken language data, McCarthy has argued in Chapter 4 of this book that the model needs considerable refinement to make it able to handle the complexities of conversation.

From an applied point of view, it should be possible to examine learners' written texts to see how they do or do not conform to native-speaker texts in the use of lexical cohesive ties. Certainly, one way of making notions such as synonymy and antonymy practically useful to learners is to show them how such relations occur over sentence boundaries in texts. In reading comprehension it is often important that the reader be aware of synonymy and antonymy between words which might occur sentences apart, and Chapman (1983, p. 46) argues that teachers of reading need to know more about the ability of skilled readers to perceive such cohesive links in texts.

Collocation, in the original Halliday and Hasan scheme, was left undivided. It thus became a sort of 'ragbag' category where associations (sometimes quite weak or difficult to define) between lexical items in a text could be recorded. Even texts with low levels of lexical reiteration in Halliday and Hasan's sense still seem to have multitudinous relations between their lexical items which carry across clauses, sentences and sometimes whole stretches of text. In the aviation text (1), we can see associations between *air/noises/aviation*, *zenith/fashionable/lapsed/broke out again/intensity*, *war/armistice*, and so on, associations difficult to define or label. Furthermore, we find that many texts simply do not have neat cases of synonymy and antonymy such as *flying/aviation* and *amateur/professional*, and that often, where we perceive quite strong lexical relations, they may not be valid or so strong once we remove them from their particular textual environment and view the items simply as members of the 'theoretical dictionary', as Leech (1974, p. 206) calls it. Hasan (1984), in her revision of the 1976 categories of lexical cohesion, concludes that it is necessary to distinguish between *general* lexical relations (those which belong to the language system, and which would still be valid even out of context), and *instantial* relations (those which are text specific). This distinction has in fact been long recognized (see Ellis 1966). It would seem a sensible division; indeed, to simplify matters, most texts could probably be handled by considering instantial relations under three headings (such as McCarthy has suggested in Chapter 4): **equivalence**, **opposition** and **inclusion**, which correspond roughly to **synonymy**, **antonymy** and **hyponymy** in the general relations, alongside the other headings proposed by Hasan. The relations we call instantial are then labels for lexical *value* rather than abstract meaning; they are the properties of particular texts. In the aviation text there seems to be an important set of oppositions established between the items *fashionable – lapsed – broke out again*, a chain of antonymy of a kind which would not necessarily be recognized in a dictionary or thesaurus, but which is clearly part of the lexical structure of the text.

This approach may hold the promise of a more complete description of lexical relations in text; it can illustrate the types of meaning or value relations that readers need to recognize for effective decoding (and, *mutatis mutandis*, the relations that frequently have to be encoded in well-formed text), but it still leaves some of the problems associated with cohesion unresolved. How *do* we recognize instantial relations? Is it accompanying syntactic structure, or some conditioning to text type and text sequencing? Some commentators have recently suggested that cohesion is not so much a set of overt semantic markers which signal a coherent chain of meaning in a text, as a set of meaning *potentials* which can only be realized when the reader/listener taps his or her knowledge of the world and of how situations characteristically manifest themselves in our experience. In other words, experience organizes itself into a series of *schemata* or mental constructs, whereby we continuously reclassify phenomena. Only when we activate the appropriate schema for a given language situation or text can we then ultimately extract a coherent message from the flow of speech or writing. Experience builds on experience; we make links between vocabulary items in a discourse because we are predisposed to do so; we are more or less looking for them once the appropriate schema has been activated. It is only then that we can process the cohesive elements of the surface text, as Steffensen (1986) argues. So surface cohesive ties such as synonyms should not be looked on just as interesting formal patterns, but as manifestations of how we are making sense of the message in the text.

If we look again at the aviation text, we can see a parallelism between a schematic representation of the content of the text and the lexical relations. To process the text successfully, we need to activate the appropriate schematic expectations of this kind of historical account. Questions we expect to have answered include: From when to when? What background features (or assumed shared knowledge) are the events pegged on to? Who were the protagonists? etc. The text presents its information linearly, but we process it according to the schema we are working with, and are thus able to 'sort' the information into categories. We could formalize it thus:

When?	background	protagonists	characteristics
pre-war	Edwardian	Brabazon & Co.	non-professional fashionable
war	war/armistice	R.F.C.	disciplined lapsed
post-war	1929	(amateurs)	amateur broke out again zenith

We can now observe that 'non-dictionary' relations such as *fashionable – lapsed – broke out again* and *non-professional – disciplined – amateur* are key sets of opposites predicated on the tri-partite time structure of the text, where events are matched and contrasted. This combination of a schema-based approach and a lexical relations approach to text would seem to have practical applications, not only for reading (see Carrell and Eisterhold 1983), but as a vocabulary-building tool too. Students can work with tables such as that above, filling in parts or all of the information categories, and can observe the lexical realizations and the relations between them, for different texts. The appropriacy or otherwise of a given chain of items as a cohesive structure for a particular text will be based on sociolinguistic criteria, including such things as addresser/addressee relationships, settings, goals and channels of communication. So for one text the structure implied by the chain *fashionable – lapse – break out again* might be suitable, but it might not be suitable for a text describing, say, the progress of an epidemic in a medical context; some or all of the items might be inappropriate to a text describing the popularity of the cinema. Lexis can also be conditioned by genre (see Fries 1983 and Carter 1987, Chapter 4), and awareness of genres can increase the reader's predictive power and ability to create coherence. In summary, the study of textual relations has many exciting paths to explore, and it represents a fertile area for application in vocabulary teaching and learning, with a bearing on reading and writing skills, and all other above-sentence domains.

2 Beyond cohesion: signalling in text and how language organizes itself

As well as the striking formal patterns created by cohesive lexical ties, we can observe all sorts of other vocabulary items in texts that seem to be doing important work at the discourse level. To understand what is meant by this, it may be worth considering an age-old distinction drawn by linguists and philosophers, one which most language teachers work with constantly, in however diluted a form. Ever since the time of the Ancient Greeks, a crude distinction has been made between words which have independent meaning and words which have no independent meaning, but which structure the meanings of combinations of the other words. Notwithstanding disputes as to exactly where the boundary lies between the two types of words, this distinction has come down through the ages and is firmly entrenched in modern theoretical and applied linguistics (surveys of the issue may be found in Carlson 1983 and Carlson and Tanenhaus 1984). The centuries of debate have provided different labels for the two types of words, but the distinction is fairly consistent. Words with independent meaning are variously called *lexical, vocabulary, content, full, contentive* or *open-system* words. Words which structure the other words in texts are called *grammar, function, empty, closed-system, functor* or *form* words. The first group comprises the bulk of the lexicon of a language like English; the second group includes articles, prepositions, pronouns, auxiliary verbs, etc. Such a fundamental division of the words of a language between grammar and lexis is a very powerful one, and most language-teaching texts hinge on it. It is a commonsense division and it has served us well, but there are problems. Firstly, the division between lexical words and grammatical words is by no means as clear-cut as may seem at first glance. Secondly, recent research in text and discourse analysis shows that whole classes of words over and above the grammar words seem to be doing jobs in texts comparable to those the grammar words have always been held to do, and that such words have less independent meaning than might be expected. Thirdly, computer-based research at the University of Birmingham (the COBUILD project) is suggesting more and more that language choice is conditioned by forces far more complex than the grammar/lexis division can capture, and that much language occurs in strongly-conditioned strings, weakening the argument for a slot-and-filler approach (Sinclair forthcoming). These three factors together force us to rethink the traditional distinction, to look at the role of *lexis* in structuring and organizing discourse (and not just being responsible for its information content) and, by these tokens, to rethink certain areas of vocabulary teaching.

A major reappraisal of the lexis/grammar distinction is found in the work of Winter (1977, 1978), who looks at a particular type of vocabulary that seems to defy easy labelling. This is best illustrated by a concocted (and deliberately unlikely) sentence:

(2) The reason for these occurrences depends on certain aspects of the problem.

This sentence does not seem to have much 'independent meaning', despite being syntactically well formed and containing both 'grammar' and 'lexical' words. To 'fill out' the words *reason, occurrences, depends, certain, aspects* and *problem*, we need to do something similar to what we do when we encounter words like *it, he* and *do* in texts: we either refer to the bank of shared knowledge built up with the author, look back in the text to find a suitable referent, or forward, anticipating that the writer will supply the missing content. Words of the type found in example (2) are common in written texts, especially technical texts, academic papers and newspaper reports. A random sampling of a newspaper (*The Guardian*, 8.4.1986) shows them at work (our italics throughout):

> (3) Rubbing salt into the wound, the liberals have released the *announcement* in the closing stages of the Fulham byelection.
>
> Hebditch says he reached his *decision* at Christmas and had intended to explain all in Liberal News at the end of this week.
>
> ... the Tynemouth MP, Mr Neville Trotter, said the men's *action* was 'beyond belief'.

Announcement, *decision* and *action* are all words that need to be filled out or 'lexicalized' with information so that the discourse can make sense. What was Hebditch's *decision* (to resign/to stand for election? etc.). Either the author/speaker must tell us, or there is a pool of shared knowledge so that we do not need to be told, such as is evidenced in statements like:

> (4) She's very angry over a certain announcement, and we all know which one ...

The detailed analysis of the role of such vocabulary items in texts is fully developed in Winter (1977), but most will find Winter (1978) a more succinct and useful version. Winter claims that inherent in the semantics of many words is a text-structuring function; these words signal the logic of a text, they link parts of texts to one another, they encapsulate chunks of text and refer back, forth and out into the world in a way comparable to how pronouns operate. Like the closed-system grammar words they seem to be finite in number, to carry 'logical' rather than 'content' meaning and seem to be non-free-standing. But like the open class vocabulary words, they seem to have a certain amount of content (at least apparently much more so than words like *the* and *at*), they occur in different word classes (*announce/announcement*, etc.) and, unlike pronouns they can be modi-fied and qualified:

> (5) When the Prime Minister said the pound would be devalued, the sudden announcement (*the sudden it) took the nation by surprise.
>
> (concocted)

So it seems there is at least one important class of words acting as a halfway-house between the grammar words and the lexical words of English. The list of these words given in Winter (1978) includes *achieve, addition, basis, cause, compare, differ, explanation, feature, kind, method, opposite, point, problem, result, situation, truth, way* and many more. They are words whose existence and occurrence is best defined in discourse terms, in a textual world outside of which they have little reality or meaningfulness. They are difficult to define in a dictionary, or in the language classroom. They are *signposts* in a text, signs as to the *value* of one sentence or clause in relation to another, and signal the interactive structure of the text (see also Francis 1986). Some of them, such as *problem*, can refer to very large chunks of a text; indeed a word such as *problem* will often be found in the same textual environment as words like *counteract* and *solve*, and the collocational chain taken together can represent in lexical form the whole macro-structure of the text. Hoey (1983) shows how 'problem-solution' structures are very typical of a large number of texts, and how writers use lexical signal words to make the text structure more overt to the reader.

One line of research which leads out of Winter's work is to look at actual occurrences of these text-structuring words and the environments in which they occur. It sometimes seems that a writer may choose one of them as a peg upon which to hang other types of word which function in signalling how the text is to be interpreted, for example, evaluating words, or words which instruct us to give more or less weight to particular parts of the text content, or words which commit the author to a particular course of action. The following extracts from a newspaper text illustrate these other types of vocabulary at work (our italics throughout):

(6)   *One significant difference* between the campaign against abortion and the campaign against Mr Enoch Powell's bill to ban experiments on human embryos is that this time the emotionalism is ranged more heavily in the other side.

The Powell bill may be imperfect in some of its detailed mechanisms, but it goes to *the central question*.

The Powell rules, they say, will have *two indefensible effects*.
(*The Guardian*, 6.7.1985)

Difference is a text-structuring word which predicts a contrast between two items within the text. But note that the author is committed to giving only *one* difference, whereas in the final extracted sentence, *two* effects require to be lexicalized for the text to be coherent. *One* and *two* are important *predictive* items in the text; they predict 'enumeration', to use Tadros's (1984) term. *Difference* is also modified by *significant*, and *question* is modified by *central*; these are 'weighting' terms, whereby the author signals that the items or chunks of text they refer to are seen to have great importance in the unfolding argument of the discourse. *Effects* is modified by *indefensible*, which is an evaluation on the moral plane of the effects which are to follow. The author manipulates our processing of the text by not giving us much choice as to how we evaluate or give weight to the arguments in question; the only option we have is to reject the text. Such lexical choices as these are a powerful tool in the expression of ideology, and data seem to suggest (though more work is needed) that the text-structuring vocabulary items of the type described by Winter are often important nodes around which cluster crucial organizational, evaluative and ideological features of text. Once again, it seems, we need to make the distinction between vocabulary as content and vocabulary as interactive, that is vocabulary organizing, structuring and evaluating messages.

Winter's work not only suggests a reappraisal of the grammar/lexis division, but it also makes us confront the possibility of dual or multi-functioning for large numbers of words in what otherwise might remain as an undifferentiated lexicon, an unsorted list consisting of everything not a 'grammar' item. English adverbials are one such case. Linguists have long recognized that adverbials often function above sentence level, describing items such as *also*, *incidentally*, *furthermore* and so on as devices for sentence connexion (see Greenbaum 1969, especially Chapter 5. See also Quirk and Greenbaum 1973, pp. 284ff., where attention is given to the role of adjectives such as *earlier*, *simultaneous*, *next*, etc. in textual linkage. See also Leech and Svartvik 1975, pp. 156ff., which has interesting examples from spoken English too). Equally there is broad agreement that a distinction must be drawn between occurrences such as:

(7) He smiled happily at her.

and

(8) Happily, we were able to contact her.

where (8) clearly has a discourse function of commenting on the significance of the sentence in relation to a whole text of events. Massive, data-based studies such as the Birmingham COBUILD project reveal in text concordances that this multi-functioning of lexical adverbs is all-pervasive (see Sinclair and Renouf's paper in Chapter 4). Words such as *broadly*, *vaguely*, *apparently*, *literally*, *briefly* and many others are regularly and systematically used as discourse markers, often much more frequently than with their expected values that occur when they are operating clause-internally. *Broadly* occurs frequently in the COBUILD data in the phrase 'broadly speaking', by which a speaker can emphasize the generality of a message and remain free from being committed to its absolute applicability or truth. Research into the general area of discourse marking, and how speakers frame their messages using the lexicon as well as the grammar, is growing; Stubbs (1986a) is a recent, significant example.

3 But what about the other 400,000 words?

At this point in our discussion this is a fair question. Even if features such as logical text connexion, information weighting and discourse marking are to be reassessed as within the lexicon, this would still surely account for at most only a handful of vocabulary items, however central to the way we structure our language these items are considered to be. So what can text/discourse studies tell us about the nature, organization and use of all of those thousands of items crammed into even the smallest of dictionaries?

In general, lexis in applied linguistics has been conditioned by two parallel views, the semantic and the 'lexical' (see Chapter 2). Both views converge in seeing lexical items as contracting relationships on the 'horizontal' or syntagmatic (left-to-right) axis (collocation) and relationships on the 'vertical' or paradigmatic axis (lexical sets). Lexis can be compared with grammar in the following way:

	syntagmatic	paradigmatic
grammar	structure	system
lexis	collocation	set

Examples of systems in grammar would be the closed set of choices between *this/that/these/those*, or the system of pronouns. Something similar is held to obtain in 'open' lexical sets, where words can be grouped together as realizations of meaning systems or 'fields'. In the cooking terms which Lehrer (1974) was interested in, sets can be found the members of which can be identified by their distribution and mutual exclusiveness (see Chapter 2). For example, food may be *grated, sliced, crushed, chopped, diced, minced, milled,* etc. in order to reduce it into smaller pieces. While the exact membership of the set may have somewhat fuzzy edges, most informants will agree on its central members. These items are in paradigmatic opposition to one another as *this* is to *that*. Items within sets will be seen to be in relation to one another either as co-hyponyms (as the cooking terms above are), synonyms or antonyms, and so on. Sets are powerful organizing principles, and have a strong psychological reality for language users and learners, as Channell's paper in Chapter 4 suggests. They are held to be effective teaching devices for vocabulary (*vide* Rudzka *et al.* 1981 and 1985) and lie behind part of our ability to recognize cohesive ties in text. Thoeretically at least, it should be possible to organize the entire lexicon of English along these lines, and *Roget's Thesaurus* is one attempt to do this.

However, there are difficulties in applying field and set theory to situated discourse. First there is the question of the nature of sets. Relations such as synonymy, antonymy and hyponymy seem to be shifting values in conversation (see McCarthy in Chapter 4) and the 'sets' which emerge from spoken data are somewhat fluid. But sets do have a psychological validity. Significantly, Saussure used the term 'associative' to describe the 'vertical' relations between words; it was Hjelmslev in the 1930s who rejected this term, preferring the term 'paradigmatic' in order to avoid the psychological connotations of Saussure's term (Hjelmslev 1938). Hjelmslev believed that the paradigmatic relations between words were part of the inherent system and structure of the lexicon, and not just part of psycholinguistic competence. But in some ways (and certainly for language learners) the psycholinguistic approach might be the most useful. Indeed, recent trends in vocabulary teaching emphasizing learners' individual responsibility for organizing their mental lexicons, and the positive value of even randomly organized lists, if their items are meaningfully related for the individual (Gairns and Redman 1986, p. 100) would suggest that a reassessment of the objectively verifiable, 'systemic' view of lexical sets is already under way. This is all to the good, for discourse certainly defies the neat categories found in the works of structural semanticists.

In most discourses, we rarely find that the so-called members of sets are in true paradigmatic opposition to one another. Put at its simplest, at any given moment in a discourse, a word may well be seen to be a selection from a putative set of alternatives, but these alternatives may be either a restricted sub-set from the general set, or items not closely semantically related at all. In example (9), the items *grate* and *mill*, and possibly others from our food preparation set, are excluded by the determining factor of *meat*, while in example (10), possible alternatives in any discourse to the word *secretary* seem many and varied and are entirely situationally determined:[1]

(9) (preparing a meal)
     A: how shall we do the meat?
     B: oh, let's mince it

(10) A: I told | a secretary | about it
              | your husband |
              | a newspaper |
              | everyone I met |

There is no useful way in which *secretary* can be seen to be a choice from the set of 'professions'. What the lexical selections encode in terms of what they are seen to be opposed to is a feature of the context of interaction, not of the language system. For this reason, Brazil (1985a, p. 41) chooses to call the paradigms of choice such as are represented in (9) and (10) 'existential' paradigms. The relevant question in studying language as discourse is not 'what are all the choices available in the lexical set of which this item is a member?', but 'what are the *actual* choices available to participants here and now at this point in the unfolding text?'

We have returned, from the learner's point of view, to the problem of vocabulary choice as part of sociolinguistic or pragmatic competence. This fact is recognized implicitly in Grice's (1975) set of conversational maxims, where cooperative speakers are enjoined to choose language that is informative, relevant, true and consistent. Cruse (1977) specifically relates Grice's maxims to vocabulary choice, pointing out that it is not sufficient to know that a relationship of hyponymy exists between the words *animal, dog* and *Alsatian*, but that one must know that in some circumstances it will be more appropriate to refer to a canine companion by one term rather than another. Thus, if we only have one dog and I say to my spouse 'I'll just take the Alsatian for a walk', this will be heard as an odd or marked lexical choice. Cruse shows how situational constraints shift the levels at which appropriate lexical choice may be made depending on participants' shared knowledge and moment-by-moment realignments of the discourse.

Arguments such as Grice's, Cruse's and Brazil's suggest that we should look at the notion of lexical sets and lexical selection as a context-bound affair. It might be useful to help develop the learner's awareness of the situational constraints (those of participants, goals, settings, etc.) that narrow vocabulary choice. Taking our model from Cruse, we might test learners' ability to gauge between what participants and with what communicative effect each of the following choices might be made:

(11)   A: what did you buy in town this morning?
       B: | a newspaper | | a garment |
          | *The Times* | | a jacket |

(12)   A: let's | go | down to Smythe's office
               | stroll |
               | amble |

(13)   A: then turn left and you'll see | a building | opposite
                                        | a cinema |
                                        | The Odeon |

Cruse is especially interested in levels of specificity in lexical choice (a problem closely related to the degree of informativity or 'quantity' demanded by Grice's maxims); example (12) shows that such choices also signal interpersonal factors such as degree of formality and social distance between participants.

A useful approach to discourse that tries to combine the socio-linguistic and contextual features of vocabulary with traditional lexical theory is that proposed by Benson and Greaves (1973 and 1981). They see text in a Hallidayan way, as being multi-layered, and are interested in how features of *register* (the field, tenor and mode of discourse) are reflected in lexical choice. They have a very simple, practical way of dealing with text, which is good for situated vocabulary work, and from which two useful applications emerge: the use of texts to generate actual lexical sets and to assist with comprehension of difficult items, and using sets as a means of access to 'institutional focus' (the sociolinguistic orientation of texts), which is manifested in the realization of different fields (roughly, subject areas) in texts.

Benson and Greaves suggest a simple device for tackling frequent unknown and (intuitively) central items in texts. Every time the key word appears it should be circled. Next, the two vocabulary (as opposed to 'grammatical') items before and after it are underlined. This is an arbitrary span, but one based on the weight of experience going back to Halliday (1966) and Sinclair (1966). These underlined items are then listed according to frequency of occurrence. Benson and Greaves (1973, pp. 56–7) illustrate this with a lengthy text, but a short text will suffice here as an example. If the word *document* is unknown, much can be learnt about its meaning and its value in this text by looking at its near collocates as an existential set:

(14) | Documents | to be produced
       Photographic copies of birth, marriage or naturalisation certificates or registration | documents | are not acceptable for passport purposes.

> These <u>tables show</u> which |documents| you should <u>produce</u> with
> your <u>application</u>. Please read all the sections that <u>apply</u> to you and
> make sure that you <u>submit</u> the <u>right</u> |documents.| |Documents| are
> not <u>normally needed</u> if you are surrendering <u>an unrestricted</u> blue
> British passport and all <u>details</u> are the <u>same</u>. |Documents| ARE
> <u>required</u> if a <u>British</u> Visitor's Passport only is being surrendered.
> (British passport application form, 1986)

We can see that documents are something we might have to *produce*
or *submit* when we are making an *application* for a *passport*, they are
like *certificates* and may be concerned with *registration*, and so on. It
should be possible by orientating towards this institutional set of items
and the field it betrays, added to the important situational clues of
the mode (written passport application) and the tenor (bureau-
cratic/official) to locate *document(s)* within a common social experience.
Benson and Greaves (1981) extend this notion of 'institutional focus'
and suggest applications for their lexis-based view of fields of
discourse. Fields of discourse are concerned with 'social actions
within an institutional focus'. Language is produced within institutional frameworks; readers must 'discover' the field by recognizing its
signals within the text. Fields are principally accessed through collocation, and collocational patterns are institutionalized over many years
and many hundreds of occurrences within their particular social
domain. The lexical sets which emerge from these institutionally-
focused occurrences are closely tied to characteristic patterns of
social action and features of events and situations. Taking this view,
Benson and Greaves remove lexical sets from the abstract, thesaurus
world of semantics and the psycholinguistic area of association, into
a domain where the internal structures of sets reflect social semiotics
and human interaction in varying degrees of institutionalization.

One of the most interesting insights a view of lexis, based on the
distinction between general lexical sets in the 'theoretical dictionary'
and actual or existential lexical sets observable in discourse, brings
with it is that the study of lexical patterning in discourse enables us
to throw light on world views or ideologies manifested in users' lexical
selections and in the negotiative process of interaction. Each participant brings to the discourse world views, standpoints, moralities,
prejudices and visions. Linguistic manifestations of these ideological
features can be seen in the matching (equivalence), contrasting
(opposition) and generalizing (inclusion) relations created in
discourse structures and formally realized as lexical selections. This
is another way of approaching the distinction between 'meaning' and

'value' (see McCarthy in Chapter 4) and is very much in sympathy with the discussion of the general difference between 'abstract sense and a concrete pragmatic force' in Candlin (1981), though here it is specifically the lexical strategies of users that will be of primary interest.

This chapter has throughout stressed the importance of viewing lexical sets as an *actual* or existential structure in discourse. In other words, whatever the validity of general or theoretical sets for the linguist, or their psychological validity for users, they do not exist as objectively verifiable sytems *a priori*, but rather are *realized* in inter-action. Each interaction will show users creating lexical relations of equivalence, opposition, etc. in line with illocutionary intentions and goals, and general overarching pragmatic and ideological consider-ations. A corollary of this is that the lexicon is not arbitrarily distinguished by a heap of 'stylistic' features, but offers users choices to express in varying levels of delicacy their motives and standpoints and to move purposefully towards outcomes. Also, it is of note that dominant speakers and speakers with more vested (or negotiated) rights and power can, in unequal encounters 'call the lexical tune' and impose a set of lexical relations within which contributions to the discourse will be defined and evaluated. The reference to unequal encounters is a conscious acknowledgement of the excellent applied linguistic work on pragmatic failure that has emanated from the University of Lancaster (e.g. Thomas 1983 and 1984), which has centred upon considerations of strategic issues in discourse, and which has suggested comparisons between the native-native situation of pragmatic failure and aspects of the foreign learner's situation and pragmatic competence.

As a starting point for exemplification of lexical strategy we might take the kind of polemic written text which represents the strong version of the unequal encounter and a fairly transparent vehicle of ideology. In such texts the author exercises freedom (within insti-tutionally focused norms in Benson and Greaves's terms) of lexical choice in realizing viewpoint and ideology. A type of text that frequently carries such features close to the surface is the popularized scientific text where a journalist evaluates a debate or division between opposing schools of thought. In these texts their authors select broadly from two institutionalized lexical stores, the vocabulary of scientists and the vocabulary of the popular narration of science. With most readers, the former vocabulary commands greater authority and is seen as closer to scientific practice and respectability. An author can play off the two vocabularies for ideological purposes and to achieve a goal. Consider the following text:

> **Germline**: Just as genetically based diagnosis of inherited disease is becoming a reality, so is the potential for treatment and even cure. Various approaches to therapy are possible. The most publicized, and least likely, involves the actual replacement of genes in sperm or egg – the germline – so that future generations will carry a specific change. Such a feat has already been achieved in the lab. Last fall, Ralph Brinster of the University of Pennsylvania and Richard Palmiter of Howard Hughes Medical Institute in Seattle implanted the rat gene for growth hormone into mouse embryos and produced a breed of 'Mighty Mice' up to 80 per cent larger than normal.
>
> This type of animal research is producing important basic scientific information. It has also fueled the alarmist fantasies of the superrace critics. In a recent book, *Algeny*, author Jeremy Rifkin invokes an ominous, scifi vision of perfect humans, designed in the laboratory through gene manipulation, that will 'redefine our concept of life'. A professional activist with little formal scientific background, Rifkin recently got dozens of religious leaders to petition Congress for a ban on human gene experimentation.
>
> **'Unrealistic'**: In truth, fashioning new kinds of people by tampering with the germline is the least likely outcome of new research, and critics like Rifkin needn't worry that gene therapy is about to change the course of human evolution. 'Germline therapy works OK in mice, but even to consider it for humans at this time is totally unrealistic,' says Palmiter. 'It's simply too inefficient.'
>
> *Newsweek*, March 5, 1984

In this text it is clear that the author supports Brinster and Palmiter and condemns Rifkin. This is done by a matching of interactive text structure and lexical choice. The text is structured round a situation (the growth of gene therapy) and two conflicting sets of hypotheses or predictions, one of which is dismissed. The latter part of the text may thus be seen as a 'hypothetical-real' structure (see Hoey 1983). The opening sentences set the situation within the following lexical contexts:

> *genetically based diagnosis* / becoming a *reality* / *potential* for *treatment and cure*

Strong lexical associations are thus set up. The next section of the text, on Brinster and Palmiter, presents these lexical items:

> *replacement* of *genes* / *specific change* / *feat. . .achieved* / *implanted* and *produced* / *'Mighty Mice'*

The key lexical link between this part of the text and the next (the set of predictions made by Rifkin) occurs in a replacement-for-opposition pattern:

(the research)	is producing	scientific	information
(the research)	has fueled	alarmist	fantasies

This set of lexical oppositions is crucial to the evaluative standpoint of the author. Rifkin's predictions are next. Significant collocations now are:

> *superrace critics / ominous vision / perfect humans / designed in the laboratory / gene manipulation / redefine concept of life / activist / little scientific background / religious leaders / petition Congress / ban / human gene experimentation*

Within this last set, key oppositions are established between 'manipulation' and 'experimentation', 'activist' and 'scientist', and, by collocation, between 'scientists' and 'religious leaders'. In the larger discourse structure, comparing this section with the previous one, 'manipulation' must now be seen as *not* equivalent to 'replacement', and 'superrace' as *not* equivalent to 'breed'.

Finally, the 'real' (or counter-hypothesis which is evaluated positively) brings members of the opposing lexical sets together:

Palmiter/Brinster	Rifkin
germline therapy	tampering with the germline
works	inefficient
humans	new kinds of people

The lexical choices have produced two sets: one is the vocabulary of scientific respectability, and is predicated upon Palmiter's and Brinster's work; the other is populist, emotively charged and less institutionally focused in terms of science. Each set has its own internal relations and associations and is in opposition to the other set. The piece is revealed to be anything but 'neutral' reporting and shows how a world view is reflected in lexical strategies at the textual level.

Discourse is goal-oriented, and our interpretation of lexical selection is made in the light of this knowledge. The interpretation of discourse by the foreign learner must ultimately also be based on such considerations, and the teaching of reading comprehension must surely confront the lexical dimension if the reader is successfully to 'unpack' the world view of the writer.

Spoken interaction, especially casual conversation, may be thought to be less amenable to analysis of this kind than the more obvious polemic written text we have looked at, with its convenient 'handle' of text structure and overt goal-orientation, but the text chosen above is simply a strong example of what is a universal phenomenon of lexical strategy. In fact, most spoken interactions are unequal encounters, and lexical options can frequently be seen to be manipulated by confident or dominant speakers (in casual conversation between 'equals', points where true equality is maintained are rare; dominant role shifts constantly between participants). Thomas (1984) shows, in her data of a demotion interview between a senior police officer and a junior officer, how the senior officer defines the useability of lexical items and their permissible range of reference. Similarly, in her data of a student/supervisor interview, the supervisor exercises lexical control:

(15) STUDENT: But it's not like that that's not that's just not the way people talk no-one talks like that really well maybe it's the way middle-class academics talk to people they've never seen before
SUPERVISOR: What you're saying then is Lamb is a bourgeois, Lamb is a hypocrite
STUDENT: I didn't mean to be rude
SUPERVISOR: Didn't you

(from Thomas 1984)

This is a case of 'pragmatic failure' brought about by a clash of world views, and linguistically realized by lexical selection that one party (the dominant) finds offensive. In the supervisor's view an opposition has been set up between *middle-class academics* and *people*, with the former term collocating strongly with *bourgeois* and *hypocrite* (to the extent of implied equivalence). This sort of conversational bind is difficult enough for the (non-dominant) native speaker; for the foreign learner it could be disastrous.

Lexical strategies can be seen at work in casual conversation, in the negotiation of lexical paradigms and the evaluation of terms in relation to one another. Example (16) is from the COBUILD corpus:

(16) A: oh yeah I forgot to say you know these hay fever tablets you know the new ones
B: the macrobiotic ones
A: the macrobiotic ones or whatever they are right I had a miserable day on Thursday cos I had you know streaming eyes the lot and I thought I was gonna die so I thought right you know I'll carry on with these cos I've got 480 left so on Friday I carried on every half hour taking four of these
B: four every half hour
A: yeah
B: is that what it said you . . . can't be very powerful then
A: well they're salts they're tissue salts I mean they're not they're not any sort of . . .
[A then recounts a bad attack of hayfever]

... I was bright red you know everything was red and thought
sod it so I just threw them away and I went and got some piriton
cos I just couldn't study at all and I was just sort of sitting and
oozing over a piece of paper so I'm back on piriton

B: none of this health food garbage

A: no and I'm gonna ... etc.

(COBUILD: gs 204)

The two participants (largely through B's challenging moves) have
negotiated a lexical set in which macrobiotic tablets, initially projected
as a hyponym of hayfever tablets, is 'shunted out' and redefined, to
enter a new lexical set as a hyponym of health food and no longer
as a co-hyponym of piriton. The world view (B's?) which has dominated may be formalized as the dominance of set a) over set b):

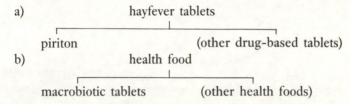

a)   hayfever tablets

    piriton   (other drug-based tablets)

b)   health food

    macrobiotic tablets   (other health foods)

Set b) is further denigrated by collocation with *garbage*.

This view of lexis is of interest to the linguist and applied linguist
alike. Language learners, in unequal encounters, will need to develop
the full range of lexical strategies used by the native speaker to
redefine and negotiate the lexical world of any discourse. The first
step is an awareness in the learner of the significance of lexical choice
and of speaker options such as paraphrase, redefinition, matching,
contrasting and generalizing, and of respondent options such as challenging moves to force clarification, to introduce alternative terms,
and the respondent's own rights (where available, depending on
pragmatic features such as role and setting) to redefine, to paraphrase, to offer equivalents, summations, and so on. This can only
be done by a situated, discourse approach to vocabulary, ideally using
real data. Alternatively, encouraging learners to analyse their own
output, (in recorded role plays, simulations, etc.) and observing actual
vocabulary networks as they are realized, would also seem to be a
good idea. Benefits for motivation might be an added attraction, and
the resultant vocabulary lists and sets would be the learner's own.
At the same time, overt markers of discourse strategies could be
extracted and consciously taught and practised. The reassuring
feature of this whole discussion is that, if indeed the unequal
encounter is the norm, and if the meeting of world views is all-perva-

sive in lexical choice in written and spoken language, then data for discourse-based language teaching, especially vocabulary teaching, will positively leap out at us, and we should not fear the invasion of lexis into our teaching concerns at all levels, for it will be seen to be the fundamental thread of which interaction is woven and by which communication is realized.

Notes

1. We are grateful for example 10 to David Brazil, ELR, University of Birmingham.

Bibliography

Aborn, M, Rubenstein, H and Sterling, T D 1959 Sources of contextual constraint upon words in sentences. *Journal of Experimental Psychology* **57** (3): 171–80

Abramovici, S 1984 Lexical information in reading and memory. *Reading Research Quarterly* **19** (2): 173–87

Adams, M J and Huggins, A W F 1985 The growth of children's sight vocabulary: a quick test with educational and theoretical considerations. *Reading Research Quarterly* **20** (3): 262–81

Adams, S J 1982 Scripts and the recognition of unfamiliar vocabulary: enhancing second language reading skills. *Modern Language Journal* **66** (2): 155–9

Aisenstadt, E 1981 Restricted collocations in English lexicology and lexicography. *ITL Review of Applied Linguistics* **53**: 53–61

Albert, M and Obler, L K 1978 *The bilingual brain*. Academic Press, New York

Alderson, C and Alvarez, G 1979 The development of strategies for the assignment of semantic information to unknown lexemes in text. *Lenguas para Objectivos Especificos* **5**: 2–13

Alexander, R J 1978 Fixed expressions in English: a linguistic psycholinguistic and didactic study. *Anglistik und Englischunterricht* **6**: 171–88

Alexander, R J 1984 Idiomaticity and other related problems. (MS) English Language Research, University of Birmingham

Allen, V F 1983 *Techniques in teaching vocabulary*. Oxford University Press

Allerton, D J 1978 The notion of givenness and its relations to presupposition and theme. *Lingua* **44**: 133–68

Ames, W S 1966 The development of a classification scheme of contextual aids. *Reading Research Quarterly* **2** (1): 57–82

Anderson, R C and Shifrin, Z 1980 The meaning of words in context. In Spiro R J et al. (eds.) *Theoretical issues in reading comprehension*: 331–48. Lawrence Erlbaum, Hillsdale, New Jersey

Anthony, E M 1975 Lexicon and vocabulary: some theoretical and pedagogical aspects of word meaning. *RELC Journal* **6** (1): 21–30

Artley, A S 1943 Teaching word-meaning through context. *The Elementary English Review* **20** (1): 68–74

Asher, J 1969 The Total Physical Response approach to second language learning. *Modern Language Journal* **53**: 3–17

Asher, J, Kusodo, J and de la Torre, R 1974 Learning a second language through commands: the second field test. *Modern Language Journal* **58**: 24–32

Atkinson, R C 1975 Mnemotechnics in second-language learning. *American Psychologist* 30: 821–38

Atkinson, R C and Raugh, M R 1975 An application of the mnemonic keyword method to the acquisition of a Russian vocabulary. *Journal of Experimental Psychology* 96: 124–9

Ayto, J 1983 On specifying meaning. In Hartmann, R R K (ed.) *Lexicography: principles and practice*: 89–98. Academic Press

Bateson, M 1975 Linguistic models in study of joint performances. In Kinkade, M, Hale, K and Werner, D (eds.) *Linguistics and anthropology: in honor of C F Voegelin*. Peter de Ridder Press, Lisse

Bauer, L 1980 Longman Dictionary of Contemporary English: review article. *RELC Journal* 11 (1): 104–9

Baxter, J 1980 The dictionary and vocabulary behaviour: a single word or a handful. *TESOL Quarterly* 14 (3): 325–36

Beck, I L, Perfetti, C A and McKeown, M G 1982 The effects of long-term vocabulary instruction on lexical access and reading comprehension. *Journal of Educational Psychology* 74: 506–21

Béjoint, M 1979 The use of informants in dictionary making. In Hartmann, R R K (ed.) *Dictionaries and their users*. Exeter Linguistic Studies 1 (4): 25–30. University of Exeter

Béjoint, M 1981 The foreign student's use of monolingual dictionaries: a study of language needs and reference skills. *Applied Linguistics* 2 (3): 207–22

Benson, J D and Greaves, W S 1973 *The language people really use*. The Book Society of Canada, Agincourt, Canada

Benson, J D and Greaves, W S 1981 Field of discourse: theory and application. *Applied Linguistics* 2 (1): 45–55

Bensoussan, M and Laufer, B 1984 Lexical guessing in context in EFL reading comprehension. *Journal of Research in Reading* 7 (1): 15–32

Berlin, B and Kay, P 1969 *Basic color terms*. University of California Press, Berkeley

Bialystok, E and Frölich, M 1980 Oral communication strategies for lexical difficulties. *Interlanguage Studies Bulletin* 5 (1): 3–30

Blum, S and Levenston, E A 1978a Lexical simplification in second language acqusition. *Studies in Second Language Acquisition* 2 (2): 43–64

Blum, S and Levenston, E A 1978b Universals of lexical simplification. *Language Learning* 28 (2): 399–415

Blythe, R 1963 *The age of illusion*: 90–1. Hamish Hamilton, London

Bolinger, D 1965 The atomization of meaning. *Language* 41 (4): 555–73

Bolinger, D 1975 *Aspects of language* 2nd edn. Harcourt Brace Jovanovich, New York

Bolinger, D 1976 Meaning and memory. *Forum Linguisticum* 1 (1): 1–14

Bones, J 1986 *Some teaching strategies from text analysis with particular reference to cloze procedure*. Unpublished M. A. dissertation, Department of English Studies, University of Nottingham

Bongers, H 1947 *The history and principles of vocabulary control*. Woerden, Wocopi

Brazil, D 1985a *The communicative value of intonation in English*. English Language Research, University of Birmingham

Brazil, D 1985b Phonology: intonation in discourse. In van Dijk, T A (ed.) *Handbook of discourse analysis*, Volume 2: 57–75. Academic Press

Breen, M P and Candlin, C N 1980 The essentials of a communicative curriculum in language teaching. *Applied Linguistics* 1 (2): 89–112

Bright, J A and McGregor, G P 1970 *Teaching English as a second language*. Longman

Britton, J *et al.* 1975 *The development of writing abilities*. Heinemann, London

Broughton, G 1978 Native speaker insight. *English Language Teaching Journal* 32 (4): 253–6

Brown, D 1974 Advanced vocabulary teaching: the problem of collocation. *RELC Journal* 5 (2): 1–11

Brown, G and Yule, G 1983 *Teaching the spoken language*. Cambridge University Press

Brown, J 1979 Vocabulary: learning to be imprecise. *Modern English Teacher* 7 (1): 25–7

Brown, R and McNeill, D 1966 The tip of the tongue phenomenon. *Journal of Verbal Learning and Verbal Behaviour*: 325–37

Brumfit, C J 1985a Ideology, communication and learning to use English. In Brumfit, C J *Language and literature teaching: from practice to principle*: 14–17. Pergamon Press, Oxford

Brumfit, C J 1985b Creativity and constraint in the language classroom. In Quirk, R and Widdowson, H G (eds.) *English in the world*. Cambridge University Press

Brutten, S 1981 An analysis of student and teacher indications of vocabulary difficulty. *RELC Journal* 12 (1): 66–71

Bullard, N 1985 Word-based perception: a handicap in second language acquisition? *English Language Teaching Journal* 39 (1): 28–32

Burling, R 1982 *Sounding right*. Newbury House, Rowley, Massachusetts

Candlin, C N 1981 Discoursal patterning and the equalizing of interpretive opportunity. In Smith, L E (ed.) *English for cross-cultural communication*. Macmillan, London

Carlson, G N 1983 Marking constituents. In Heny, F (ed.) *Linguistic categories: auxiliaries and related puzzles*: 69–98. D. Reidel Publishing Co., Dordrecht

Carlson, G N and Tannenhaus M K 1984 Lexical meanings and concepts. In Testen, D, Mishra, V and Drogo, J (eds.) *Papers from the parasession on lexical semantics*. Chicago Linguistic Society

Carnine, D, Kameenui, E J and Coyle, G 1984 Utilization of contextual information in determining the meaning of unfamiliar words. *Reading Research Quarterly* 19 (2): 188–294

Carrell, P and Eisterhold, J 1983 Schema theory and E.S.L. reading pedagogy. *TESOL Quarterly* 17 (4): 553–73

Carter, R A 1982a Responses to language in poetry. In Carter, R A and Burton, D (eds.) *Literary text and language study*: 26–55. Edward Arnold

Carter, R A 1982b A note on core vocabulary. *Nottingham Linguistic Circular* 11 (2): 39–51

Carter, R A 1983 You look nice and weedy these days!: lexical associations, lexicography and the foreign language learner. *Journal of Applied Language Study* 1 (2): 172–89

Carter, R A 1985 Core vocabulary and discourse in the curriculum. In *XXth SEAMEO Regional Conference, Conference Proceedings*. RELC, Singapore

Carter, R A 1986 good word!: vocabulary, style and coherence in children's writing. In Harris, J and Wilkinson, J (eds.) *Reading children's writing*: 91–120. Allen and Unwin, London

Carter, R A 1987a *Vocabulary: applied linguistic perspectives*. Allen and Unwin, London

Carter, R A 1987b Is there a core vocabulary?: some implications for language teaching. *Applied Linguistics* 8 (2): 178–93

Carter, R A and Long, M N 1987 *The web of words: exploring literature through language*. Cambridge University Press

Cassells, J R T 1980 Language and learning: a chemist's view. *Teaching English* 14 (1): 24–7

Chall, J 1958 *Readability: an appraisal of research and application*. Ohio State Bureau of Education Research Monographs

Channell, J 1981 Applying semantic theory to vocabulary teaching. *English Language Teaching Journal* 35 (2): 115–22

Channell, J in preparation Vocabulary acquisition and the mental lexicon. *Theories of Meaning and Lexicography*. Benjamins, Amsterdam

Chapman, J 1983 *Reading development and cohesion* Heinemann, London

Clark, E and Berman, R 1974 Structure and use in the acquisition of word formation. *Language* 60: 542–90

Clarke, D and Nation I S P 1980 Guessing the meanings of words from context: strategy and techniques. *System* 8 (3): 211–20

Clarke, M and Silberstein, S 1977 Toward a realization of psycholinguistic principles in the ESL reading class. *Language Learning* 27: 135–54

Coady, J M 1979 A psycholinguistic model of the ESL reader. In Mackay, R *et al.* (eds.) *Reading in a second language*: 5–12. Newbury House, Rowley, Massachusetts

Cohen, A D and Aphek, E 1980 Retention of second language vocabulary over time: investigating the role of mnemonic association *System* 8 (3): 221–36

Cohen, A D and Hosenfeld, C 1981 Some uses of mentalistic data in second language research. *Language Learning* 31 (2): 285–313

Collinson, W E 1939 Comparative synonymics: some principles and illustrations. *Transactions of the Philological Society*: 54–77

Connolly, P G 1973 How to teach families of words by comparison. *English Language Teaching Journal* 27 (2): 171–6

Corder, S P 1973 *Introducing applied linguistics* Penguin Books, Inc. Baltimore

Coulmas, F 1979 On the sociolinguistic relevance of routine formulae. *Journal of Pragmatics* 3: 239–66

Coulmas, F 1981 *Conversational routine*. Mouton, The Hague

Coulthard, R M 1985 *An introduction to discourse analysis*. 2nd edn. Longman

Cowan, J R 1974 Lexical and syntactic research for the design of reading materials. *TESOL Quarterly* 8 (4): 389–99

Cowie, A P 1978 Vocabulary exercises within an individualized study programme. In *ELT Documents* 103: 37–44. The British Council, ETIC, London

Cowie, A P 1981 The treatment of collocations and idioms in learners' dictionaries. *Applied Linguistics* 2 (3): 223–35

Cowie, A P 1983a On specifying grammar. In Hartmann, R R K (ed.) *Lexicography: principles and practice*: 99–108. Academic Press, London

Cowie, A P 1983b English dictionaries for the foreign learner. In Hartmann, R R K (ed.) *Lexicography: principles and practice*: 135–43. Academic Press, London

Cowie, A P 1984 EFL dictionaries: past achievements and present needs. In Hartmann, R R K (ed.) *LEXeter '83 Proceedings*. Niemeyer, Tübingen

Cowie, A P 1985 Collocational dictionaries – a comparative view. Paper presented to the Anglo-Soviet Seminar on English Studies, University of Manchester, September 1985

Cowie, A P, Mackin, R and McCaig, I R 1975/1983 *Oxford Dictionary of Current Idiomatic English* (2 volumes). Oxford University Press

Craik, F I M and Lockhart, R S 1972 Levels of processing: a framework for memory record. *Journal of Verbal Learning and Verbal Behaviour* 11: 67–84

Crombie, W 1985 *Process and relation in discourse and language learning*. Oxford University Press

Crothers, E and Suppes, P 1967 *Experiments in second language learning*. Academic Press, New York

Crow, J T and Quigley, J R 1985 A semantic field approach to passive vocabulary acquisition for reading comprehension. *TESOL Quarterly* 19 (3): 497–513

Cruse, D A 1975 Hyponymy and lexical hierarchies. *Archivum Linguisticum* VI: 26–31

Cruse, D A 1977 The pragmatics of lexical specificity. *Journal of Linguistics* 13: 153–64

Cruse, D A 1986 *Lexical semantics*. Cambridge University Press

Crystal, D and Davy, D 1975 *Advanced conversational English*. Longman

Curran, C 1976 *Counselling-learning in second languages*. Apple River Press, Apple River, Illinois

Cutler, A and Fay, D 1982 One mental lexicon, phonologically arranged. *Linguistic Inquiry* 13(1): 107–13

Cuyckens, H 1982 Componential analysis in psycholinguistics. *ITL Review of Applied Linguistics* 57: 53–75

Cziko, G A 1978 Differences in first- and second-language reading: the use of syntactic, semantic and discourse constraints. *Canadian Modern Language Review* 34: 473–89

Davies, A, Criper, C and Howatt, A (eds.) 1984 *Interlanguage*. Edinburgh University Press

Davis, F B 1968 Research in comprehension in reading. *Reading Research Quarterly* 4: 499–545

Davis, F B 1972 Psychometric research on comprehension in reading. *Reading Research Quarterly* 7: 628–78

Deyes, A 1984 Toward an authentic discourse cloze. *Applied Linguistics* 5 (2): 128–37

Dirven, R and Oakeshott-Taylor, J 1985 State of the art: listening comprehension. *Language Teaching* 18 (1): 2–20

Donley, M 1974 The role of structural semantics in expanding and activating the vocabulary of the advanced learner: the example of the homophone. *Audio-Visual Language Journal* 12 (2): 81–9

Dooling, D J and Lachman, R 1971 Effects of comprehension on retention of prose. *Journal of Experimental Psychology* **88**: 216–22

Dulin, K L 1970 Using context clues in word recognition and comprehension. *Reading Teacher* **23** (5): 440–65

Ellis, J 1966 On contextual meaning. In Bazell, C E, Catford, J C, Halliday, M A K and Robins, R H (eds.) *In memory of J R Firth*: 79–95. Longman

Engels, L K 1968 The fallacy of word counts. *IRAL* **6** (3): 213–31

Fay, D and Cutler, A 1977 Malapropisms and the structure of the mental lexicon. *Linguist Inquiry* **8**(3): 505–20

Firth, J R (1935) 1957a The technique of semantics. In *Papers in Linguistics*: 7–33. Oxford University Press

Firth, J R (1951) 1957b Modes of meaning. In *Papers in Linguistics*. 190–215. Oxford University Press

Firth, J R 1968 Linguistic analysis as a study of meaning. In Palmer, F R (ed.) *Selected papers of J R Firth*: 12–26. Longman

Foley, J 1982 More questions on assumptions about cloze testing. *RELC Journal* **14** (1): 57–69

Fox, J and Mahood, J 1982 Lexicons and the ELT materials writer. *English Language Teaching Journal* **36** (2): 125–9

Francis, G 1986 *Anaphoric nouns*. Discourse analysis monographs 11. English Language Research, University of Birmingham

Francis, W N 1963 Word-making: some sources of new words. In *The English language: an introduction*. W. W. Norton and Company, Inc., New York

Fraser, B 1970 Idioms within a transformation grammar. *Foundations of Language* **4**: 109–27

Freebody, P and Anderson, R C 1983 Effects on text comprehension of differing propositions and locations of difficult vocabulary. *Journal of Reading Behavior* **15** (3): 19–39

Fries, C C 1945 *Teaching and learning English as a foreign language*. University of Michigan Press, Ann Arbor

Fries, P 1983 On the status of theme in English: arguments from discourse. In Petöfi, J S and Sozer, E (eds.) *Micro and macro connexity in texts*: 116–52. Buske Verlag, Hamburg

Fromkin, V 1973 *Speech errors as linguistic evidence*. Mouton, The Hague

Fromkin, V 1980 *Errors in linguistic performance*. Academic Press, New York

Gairns, R and Redman, S 1986 *Working with words: a guide to teaching and learning vocabulary*. Cambridge University Press

Gibbons, H 1940 The ability of college freshmen to construct the meaning of a strange word from the context in which it appears. *Journal of Experimental Education* **9** (1): 29–33

Gimson, A C 1981 Pronunciation in EFL dictionaries. *Applied Linguistics* **2** (3): 250–62

Gläser, R 1981 *Phraseologie der Englischen Sprache*. Pädagogische Hochschule, Potsdam

Goodman, K S 1976 Reading: a psycholinguistic guessing game. In Singer, H and Ruddell, R (eds.) *Theoretical models and processes of reading* (2nd edn.): 497–508. International Reading Association, Newark

Gougenheim, G, Michea, R, Rivenc, P and Sauvageot, A 1956 *L'élaboration du français élementaire. Etude sur l'établissement d'un vocabulaire et d'une grammaire de base.* Didier, Paris

Gouin, F 1880/1892 *L'art d'enseigner et d'étudier les langues.* Fischbacher G Paris. Translated as: *The are of teaching and studying languages* Swan, H and Betis, V (transl.) George Philip and Son, London

Greenbaum, S 1969 *Studies in English adverbial usage.* Longman

Greenbaum, S 1970 *Verb intensifiers in English: an experimental approach.* Mouton, The Hague

Greimas, A 1960 Idiotismes, proverbs, dictons. *Cahiers de Lexicologie* **2**: 41–61

Grice, H P 1975 Logic and conversation. In Cole, P and Morgan J L (eds.) *Syntax and semantics, Volume 3: Speech acts*: 41–58. Academic Press, New York

Hafner, L E 1965 A one-month experiment in teaching context aids in fifth grade. *The Journal of Educational Research* **58** (10): 472–4

Hafner, L E 1967 Using context to determine meanings in high school and college. *Journal of Reading* **10** (7): 491–8

Hakuta, K 1974 Prefabricated patterns and the emergence of structure in second language acquisition. *Language Learning* **24** (2): 287–98

Halliday, M A K 1966 Lexis as a linguistic level. In Bazell, C E, Catford, J C, Halliday, M A K and Robins, R H (eds.) *In memory of J R Firth*: 148–62. Longman

Halliday, M A K 1985 Dimensions of discourse analysis: grammar. In van Dijk, T A (ed.) *Handbook of discourse analysis*, Volume 2: 29–56. Academic Press, London

Halliday, M A K and Hasan, R 1976 *Cohesion in English.* Longman

Halliday, M A K and Hasan, R 1985 *Language, context and text: aspects of language in a social-semiotic perspective.* Deakin University Press, Victoria

Halliday, M A K, McIntosh, A and Strevens, P 1964 *The linguistic sciences and language teaching.* Longman

Hanks, P 1979 To what extent does a dictionary definition define? In Hartmann, R R K (ed.) *Dictionaries and their users.* Exeter Linguistic Studies 1 (4): 32–8. University of Exeter

Harper, D P L (ed.) 1986 *Task-based learning in the King Abdul Aziz University in Jeddah, 1975–84* (provisional title). Pergamon, Oxford

Hartmann, R R K 1981a Style values: linguistic approaches and lexicographical practice. *Applied Linguistics* **2** (3): 263–73

Hartmann, R R K 1981b Dictionaries, learners, users: some issues in lexicography: review article. *Applied Linguistics* **2** (3): 297–303

Hartmann, R R K (ed.) 1983 *Lexicography: principles and practice.* Academic Press, London

Harvey, P D 1983 Vocabulary learning: the use of grids. In *English Language Teaching Journal* **37** (3): 243–6

Hasan, R 1984 Coherence and cohesive harmony. In Flood, J (ed.) *Understanding reading comprehension*: 181–219. International Reading Association, Newark, Delaware

Hayes-Roth, B and Hayes-Roth, F 1977 The prominence of lexical information in memory representations of meaning. *Journal of Verbal Learning and Verbal Behaviour* **16**: 119–36

Haynes, M 1984 Patterns and perils of guessing in second language reading. In Handscombe, J, Orem, R A and Taylor, B P (eds.) *On TESOL '83: the question of control*: 163–76. TESOL

Higa, M 1965 The psycholinguistic concept of 'difficulty' in the teaching of foreign language vocabulary. *Language Learning* **XV** (3/4): 167–79

Hindmarsh, R 1980 *Cambridge English Lexicon*. Cambridge University Press

Hjelmslev, L 1938 Essai d'une théorie des morphèmes. In *Actes du Quatrième Congrès International de Linguistes, 1936*. Einar Munksgaard, Copenhagen

Hoey, M 1983 *On the surface of discourse*. Allen and Unwin, London

Holley, F M 1973 A study of vocabulary learning in context: the effect of new-word density in German reading materials. *Foreign Language Annals* **6**: 339–47

Horn, L 1985 Metalinguistic negation and pragmatic ambiguity. *Language* **61**: 121–74

Hornby, A S 1948/1974 *Oxford Advanced Learner's Dictionary of Current English* Oxford University Press

Howatt, A R P 1983 *A history of English language teaching*. Oxford University Press

Hurford, J R 1981 Malapropisms, left to right listing, and lexicalism. *Linguistic Inquiry* **12**: 419–23

Hutchinson, T and Waters, A 1981 Performance and competence in English for specific purposes. *Applied Linguistics* **2** (1): 56–69

Ilson, R 1983 Etymological information: can it help our students? *English Language Teaching Journal* **37** (1): 76–82

Ilson, R (ed.) 1985 *Dictionaries, lexicography and language learning*. Pergamon, Oxford

Ingle, S and Meara, P forthcoming The formal representation of words in an L2 speaker's lexicon. *Second Language Research*

Jain, M 1979 Longman Dictionary of Contemporary English: review article. *Indian Journal of Applied Linguistics* **4** (1): 86–104

Jain, M 1981 On meaning in the foreign learner's dictionary. *Applied Linguistics* **2** (3): 276–86

James, A R 1984 Syntagmatic segment errors in non-native speech. *Linguistics* **22**: 481–505

Jeffries, L and Willis, P 1982 Review of McArthur, T: Longman Lexicon of Contemporary English. *English Language Teaching Journal* **36** (4): 277–8

Jenkins, J R, Stein, N L and Wysocki, K 1984 Learning vocabulary through reading. *American Educational Research Journal* **21** (4): 767–87

Johns, T 1986 Micro-concord: a language learner's research tool. *System* **14** (2): 151–62

Johnson-Laird, P N and Wason, P C (eds.) 1977 *Thinking: readings in cognitive science*. Cambridge University Press

Jordens, P and Kellerman, E 1981 Investigations into 'transfer strategy' in second language learning. In Savard, J and Laforge, L (eds.) *Actes du 5e Congress de L'AILA*: 195–215. Les Presses de l'Universite de Laval, Quebec

Judd, E L 1978 Vocabulary teaching and TESOL: a need for reevaluation of existing assumptions. *TESOL Quarterly* **12** (1): 71–6

Kameenui, E J, Carnine, D W and Freschi, R 1982 Effects of text construction and instructional procedures for teaching word meanings on comprehension and recall. *Reading Research Quarterly* 17 (3): 367–88

Katz, J and Fodor, J 1963 The structure of a semantic theory. *Language* 39: 170–210

Keller, R 1979 Gambits: conversational strategy signals. *Journal of Pragmatics* 3: 219–37

Kellerman, E 1977 Towards a characterisation of the strategy of transfer in second language learning. *Interlanguage Studies Bulletin* 2 (1): 58–145

Kellerman, E 1983 Now you see it, now you don't. In Gass, S and Selinker, L (eds.) *Language transfer in language learning*: 112–34. Newbury House, Rowley, Massachusetts

Kellogg, G S and Howe, M J A 1971 Using words and pictures in foreign language learning. *Alberta Journal of Educational Research* 17: 89–94

Klappenbach, R 1968 Probleme der Phraseologie. *Wissenschaftliche Zeitschrift der Karl-Marx Universität, Leipzig* 17 (2/3): 221–7

Klare, G R 1963 *The measurement of readability*. Iowa State University Press, Ames

Klare, G R 1974 Assessing readability. *Reading Research Quarterly* 10: 62–102

Krashen, S 1981 *Second language acquisition and second language learning*. Pergamon Press, Oxford

Krashen, S and Scarcella, R 1978 On routines and patterns in language acquisition and performance. *Language Learning* 28 (2): 283–300

Kucera, H 1982 The mathematics of language. In *The American Heritage Dictionary* 2nd College edn.: 37–41. Houghton Mifflin, Boston

Lado, R 1955 Patterns of difficulty in vocabulary. *Language Learning* 6: 23–41

Lakoff, G and Johnson, M 1980 *Metaphors we live by*. University of Chicago Press, Chicago

Laufer, B and Sim, D D 1985 Taking the easy way out: non-use and misuse of clues in EFL reading. *ET Forum* 23 (2): 7–10, 20

Leech, G 1967 *Towards a semantic description of English*. Longman

Leech, G 1974/1981 *Semantics* 2nd edn. Penguin

Leech, G 1983 *Principles of pragmatics*. Longman

Leech, G and Svartvik, J 1975 *A communicative grammar of English*. Longman

Lehrer, A 1969 Semantic cuisine. *Journal of Linguistics* 5: 39–56

Lehrer, A 1974 *Semantic fields and lexical structure*. North Holland Publishing Company, Amsterdam/London

Lehrer, A 1978 Structures of the lexicon, and transfer of meaning. *Lingua* 45: 95–123

Liu, N and Nation, I S P 1985 Factors affecting guessing vocabulary in context. *RELC Journal* 16 (1): 33–42

Locke, J 1690/1975 *An essay concerning human understanding*. Oxford University Press

Longman Active Study Dictionary of English 1983 Longman

Longman Dictionary of Contemporary English 1978 (2nd edn. 1987) Longman

Looby, R 1939 Understandings children derive from their reading. *The Elementary English Review* 16: 58–62

Lord, R 1974 Learning vocabulary. *IRAL* 12: 239–47

Lozanov, G 1979 *Suggestology and outlines of suggestopedia*. Gordon and Breach Science Publishers, Inc., New York
Lyons, J 1977 *Semantics* (2 volumes) Cambridge University Press

MacFarquhar, P D and Richards, J C 1983 On dictionaries and definitions. *RELC Journal* 14: 111–24
Mackey, W F and Savard, J-G 1967 The indices of coverage. *IRAL* 5 (2–3): 71–121
Mackin, R 1978 On collocations: 'Words shall be known by the company they keep'. In Strevens, P (ed.) *In Honour of A S Hornby*: 149–65. Oxford University Press
Makkai, A 1972 *Idiom structure in English*. Mouton, The Hague
Makkai, A 1978 Idiomaticity as a language universal. In Greenberg, J H *et al.* (eds.) *Universals of human language, Volume 3: Word structure*: 401–48. Stanford University Press
Makkai, A 1980 Theoretical and practical aspects of an associative lexicon for twentieth century English. In Zgusta, L (ed.) *Theory and method in lexicography*: 125–46. Hornbeam Press, Columbia, S.C.
Malkiel, Y 1959 Studies in irreversible binomials. *Lingua* 8: 113–60
Mansouri, A N H 1985 Semantic field theory and the teaching of English vocabulary, with special reference to Iraqui secondary schools. Unpublished Ph.D. thesis University of Sheffield
Manzo, A V and Sherk, J K 1972 Some generalizations and strategies for guiding vocabulary learning. *Journal of Reading Behavior* 4 (1): 78–89
Marks, C B, Doctorow, M J and Wittrock, M C 1974 Word frequency and reading comprehension. *Journal of Educational Research* 67 (6): 259–62
Martin, A V 1976 Teaching academic vocabulary to foreign graduate students. *TESOL Quarterly* 10 (1): 91–7
Martin, M 1984 Advanced vocabulary teaching: the problem of synonyms. *Modern Language Journal* 68: 130–7
Martin, J R and Rothery, J 1981 Writing project reports: 1980 and 1981. *Working Papers in Linguistics*, Volumes 1 and 2. University of Sydney Press
McAlpin, J forthcoming *Longman Dictionary Skills Workbook*. Longman
McArthur, T 1978 The vocabulary control movement in the English language 1844–1953. *Indian Journal of Applied Linguistics* 4 (1): 47–68
McArthur, T 1981 *Longman Lexicon of Contemporary English*. Longman
McCarthy, M J 1984 A new look at vocabulary in EFL. *Applied Linguistics* 5 (1): 12–22
McCarthy, M J 1987 Interactive lexis: prominence and paradigms. In Coulthard, R M (ed.) *Discussing discourse*. English Language Research, University of Birmingham
McCarthy, M J, MacLean, A and O'Malley, P 1985 *Proficiency plus: grammar, lexis, discourse*. Basil Blackwell, Oxford
McCullough, C M 1943 Learning to use context clues. *The Elementary English Review* 20: 140–3
McCullough, C M 1945 The recognition of context clues in reading. *The Elementary English Review* 22 (1): 1–5, 38
McCullough, C M 1958 Context aids in reading. *The Reading Teacher* 11 (4): 225–9
McDonagh, S 1981 *Psychology in foreign language teaching*. Allen and Unwin

McIntosh, A 1961 Patterns and ranges. *Language* **37**: 325–37 Reprinted, with one additional footnote, in McIntosh, A and Halliday, M A K (eds.) 1966 *Patterns of language: papers in general descriptive and applied linguistics*: 183–99. Longman. Also reprinted, with some footnotes omitted, in Wilson, G (ed.) 1967 *A linguistics reader*: 309–26. Harper and Row, New York

McKay, S 1980a Developing vocabulary materials with a computer corpus. *RELC Journal* **11** (2): 77–87

McKay, S 1980b Teaching the syntactic, semantic and pragmatic dimensions of verbs. *TESOL Quarterly* **14** (1): 17–26

McKeown, M G, Beck, I L, Omanson, R C and Perfetti, C A 1983 The effects of long-term vocabulary instruction on reading comprehension: a replication. *Journal of Reading Behavior* **15** (1): 3–18

Meara, P M 1980 Vocabulary acquisition: a neglected aspect of language learning. *Language Teaching and Linguistics: Abstracts* **13**: 221–46

Meara, P M 1982 Word associations in a foreign language. *Nottingham Linguistic Circular* **11** (2): 29–38

Meara, P M (ed.) 1983 Vocabulary in a second language. CILT, London

Meara, P M 1984 the study of lexis. In Davies, A, Criper, C and Howatt, A (eds.) *Interlanguage*: 225–35. Edinburgh University Press

Merry, R 1980 The keyword method and children's vocabulary learning in the classroom. *British Journal of Educational Psychology* **50**: 123–36

Michea, R 1953 Mots frequents and mots disponibles. *Les Langues Modernes* **47**: 338–44

Miller, G 1956 The magical number seven, plus or minus two: some limits on our capacity for processing information. *Psychological Review* **63**: 81–97

Mitchell, T F 1971 Linguistic 'goings-on': collocations and other lexical matters arising on the linguistic record. *Archivum Linguisticum* **2**: 35–69

Mitchell, T F 1975 *Principles of Firthian linguistics*. Longman

Morgan, J L and Sellner, M A 1980 Discourse and linguistic theory. In Spiro, R J, Bertram, B C and Brewer, W F (eds.) *Theoretical issues in reading comprehension*: 165–200. Lawrence Erlbaum, Hillsdale, New Jersey

Morrow, K 1980 *Skills for reading*. Oxford University Press

Moon, R 1987 Monosemous words and the dictionary. In Cowie, A P (ed.) *The dictionary and the language learner*. Niemeyer, Tübingen

Nagy, W E and Anderson, R C 1984 How many words are there in printed school English? *Reading Research Quarterly* **19** (3): 304–30

Nagy, W E, Herman, P A and Anderson, R C 1985 Learning words from context. *Reading Research Quarterly* **20** (2): 233–53

Nation, I S P 1980 Strategies for receptive vocabulary learning. *Guidelines: RELC Supplement* **3**: 171–5

Nation, I S P 1982 Beginning to learn foreign language vocabulary: a review of the research. *RELC Journal* **13** (1): 14–36

Nation, I S P 1983a *Teaching and learning vocabulary*. English Language Institute, University of Wellington

Nation, I S P 1983b Testing and teaching vocabulary. *Guidelines, RELC Supplement* **5**: 12–25

Nation, I S P 1984 Understanding paragraphs. *Language Learning and Communication* **3** (1): 61–8

Nattinger, J 1980 A lexical phrase grammar for ESL. *TESOL Quarterly* **14** 337–44

Neisser, U 1976 *Cognition and reality*. W H Freeman and Company, San Francisco

Newmark, P P 1967 A note on the concept of correlativity in lexicology. *The Incorporated Linguist* **6** (4): 97–102

Nida, E 1975 *Componential analysis of meaning*. Mouton, The Hague

Nilsen, D L F 1976 Contrastive semantics in vocabulary instruction. *TESOL Quarterly* **10** (1): 99–103

Nolte, K F 1937 Simplification of vocabulary and comprehension in reading. *Elementary English Review* **14**: 119–24

Ogden, C K 1930 *Basic English: a general introduction*. Kegan Paul, Trench and Trubner, London

Ogden, C K 1968 *Basic English: international second language* (revised edn.) Harcourt Brace, New York

Oller, J W 1975 Cloze, discourse and approximations in English. In Burt, M K and Dulay, H (eds.) *On TESOL '75: new directions in second language learning, teaching and bilingual education*. TESOL

Omanson, R C, Beck I L, McKeown, M G and Perfetti, C A 1984 Comprehension of texts with unfamiliar versus recently taught words: assessment of alternative models. *Journal of Educational Psychology* **76** (7): 1253–68

Ostyn, P and Godin, P 1985 RALEX: an alternative approach to language teaching. *Modern Language Journal* **69** (4) 346–55

Pany, L, Jenkins, J R and Schreck, J 1982 Vocabulary instruction: effects on word knowledge and reading comprehension. *Learning Disability Quarterly* **5**: 202–15

Partridge, R 1937/1961 *A dictionary of slang and unconventional English*, 2 volumes (5th edn.) Routledge and Kegan Paul, London

Pawley, A and Syder, F H 1983 Two puzzles for linguistic theory: nativelike selection and nativelike fluency. In Richards, J C and Schmidt, R W (eds.) *Language and communication*: 191–227. Longman

Perera, K 1982 The language demands of school learning. In Carter, R A (ed.) *Linguistics and the teacher*: 114–36. Routledge and Kegan Paul

Perfetti, C A and Lesgold, A M 1977 Discourse comprehension and sources of individual differences. In Just, M and Carpenter, P (eds.) *Cognitive processes in comprehension*: 141–83. Lawrence Erlbaum, Hillsdale, New Jersey

Perfetti, C A and Lesgold, A M 1979 Coding and comprehension in skilled reading and implications for reading instruction. In Resnick, L B and Weaver, P (eds.) *Theory and practice of early reading*, Volume 1: 57–84. Lawrence Erlbaum, Hillsdale, New Jersey

Persson, G 1974 *Repetition in English: part I, sequential repetition*. Acta Universitatis Upsaliensi: Studia Anglistica Upsaliensia, 21, Uppsala

Peters, A 1983 *The units of language acquisition*. Cambridge University Press

Petöfi, J 1985 Lexicon. In Van Dijk, T A (ed.) *Handbook of discourse analysis*, Volume 2: 82–102. Academic Press, London

Pickering, M 1982 Context free and context dependent vocabulary learning. *System* **10** (1): 79–83

Postovsky, V 1974 Effects of delay in oral practice at the beginning of second language learning. *Modern Language Journal* **58**: 229–49

Prator, C N 1963 Adjectives of temperature. *English Language Teaching Journal* **17** (4): 158–64

Procter, P (ed.) 1978/1988 *Longman Dictionary of Contemporary English* 2nd edn. Longman

Quirk, R 1973 The social impact of dictionaries. *UK Annals of the New York Academy of Sciences* **211**: 76–88

Quirk, R 1982 International communication and the concept of nuclear English. *Style and Communication in the English Language.*: 37–53

Quirk, R and Greenbaum, S 1973 *A university grammar of English*. Longman

Quirk, R and Widdowson, H G (eds.) 1985 *English in the world*. Cambridge University Press

Ramsey, R M 1981 A technique for interlingual lexico-semantic comparison; the lexigram. *TESOL Quarterly* **15** (1): 15–24

Regional English Language Centre 1980 Guidelines for vocabulary teaching. *RELC Journal Supplement* 3. RELC, Singapore

Renouf, A J 1983 Corpus development at Birmingham University. In Aarts, J and Meijs, W (eds.) *Corpus linguistics: recent developments in the use of computer corpora in English language research*. Rodopi, Amsterdam

Richards, I A 1943 *Basic English and its uses*. Kegan Paul, London

Richards, I A 1970 A psycholinguistic measure of vocabulary selection. *IRAL* **8** (2): 87–102

Richards, J 1974 Word lists: problems and prospects. *RELC Journal* **5** (2): 69–84

Richards, J 1976 The role of vocabulary teaching. *TESOL Quarterly* **10** (1): 77–89

Rivers, W M 1968 *Teaching foreign language skills*. University of Chicago Press, Chicago

Rivers, W M 1972/1983 *Speaking in many tongues* (3rd edn.) Cambridge University Press

Rivers, W M 1972/1983 *Speaking in many tongues* 3rd edn. Cambridge University Press

Robinson, P 1986 Components and procedures in vocabulary learning: feature grids, prototypes and a procedural vocabulary. Unpublished MS. English Language Research, University of Birmingham

Rudzka, B, Channell, J, Ostyn, P and Putseys, Y 1981 *The words you need*. Macmillan

Rudzka, B, Channell, J, Ostyn, P and Putseys, Y 1985 *More words you need*. Macmillan

Ruhl, C 1979 Alleged idioms with HIT. In Wölck, W and Garvin, P L (eds.) *The fifth Lacus Forum*: 93–107. Hornbeam Press, Columbia, S.C.

Sampson, G 1979 The indivisibility of words. *Journal of Linguistics* **15**: 39–47

Scholfield, P J 1982 Using the English dictionary for comprehension. *TESOL Quarterly* **16** (2): 185–94

Schouten-van Parreren, M 1985 *Woorden leren in het vreemde-talenonderwijs* [*Vocabulary acquisition in foreign language instruction*]. Van Walraven b.v. Apeldoorn

Seibert, L C 1930 An experiment on the relative efficiency of studying French vocabulary in associated pairs versus studying French vocabulary in context. *Journal of Educational Psychology* 21: 297–314

Seibert, L C 1945 A study of the practice of guessing word meanings from a context. *Modern Language Journal* 29: 296–323

Simon, H 1974 How big is a chunk? *Science* 183: 482–8

Sinclair, J McH 1966 Beginning the study of lexis. In Bazell, C E, Catford, J C, Halliday, M A K and Robins, R H (eds.) *In memory of J R Firth*: 410–30. Longman

Sinclair, J McH 1983 Planes of discourse. In Rizvil, S N A (ed.) *The two-fold voice: essays in honour of Ramesh Mohan*. Salzburg Studies in English Literature, University of Salzburg

Sinclair, J McH 1985 Lexicographic evidence. In Ilson, R (ed.) *Dictionaries, lexicography and language learning*: 81–94. Pergamon, Oxford

Sinclair, J McH 1986 First throw away your evidence. In Leitner, G (ed.) *The English Reference Grammar: Linguistische Arbeiten* Volume 172. Niemeyer. Tübingen

Sinclair, J McH (ed.) 1987 *Collins COBUILD English Language Dictionary*. Williams Collins

Smith, F 1982 *Understanding reading*. Holt, Rinehart and Winston, New York

Soudek, M and Soudek, L I 1983 Cloze after thirty years: new uses in language teaching. *English Language Teaching Journal* 37 (4): 335–9

Spearitt, D 1972 Identification of subskills of reading comprehension by maximum likelihood factor analysis. *Reading Research Quarterly* 8: 92–111

Spiro, R J, Bertram, B C and Brewer, W F (eds.) 1980 *Theoretical issues in reading comprehension*. Lawrence Erlbaum, Hillsdale, New Jersey

Stahl, S 1983 Differential word knowledge and reading comprehension. *Journal of Reading Behavior* 15 (4): 33–50

Steffensen, M 1986 Register, cohesion, and reading comprehension. *Applied Linguistics* 7 (1): 71–85

Stein, G 1979 Nuclear English: reflections on the structure of its vocabulary. *Poetica* 10: 27–52

Sternberg, R J and Powell, J S 1983 Comprehending verbal comprehension. *American Psychologist* 38: 878–93

Stevick, E 1976 *Memory, meaning and method*. Newbury House, Rowley, Massachusetts

Stieglitz, E 1983 A practical approach to vocabulary reinforcement. *English Language Teaching Journal* 37 (1): 71–5.

Stock, P 1984 Polysemy. In Hartmann, R R K (ed.) *LEXeter '83 Proceedings*: 131–40. Niemeyer, Tübingen

Stubbs, M 1983 *Discourse analysis*. Basil Blackwell, Oxford

Stubbs, M 1986a 'A matter of prolonged fieldwork': notes towards a modal grammar of English. *Applied Linguistics* 7 (1): 1–25

Stubbs, M 1986b Language development, lexical competence and nuclear vocabulary. In *Educational linguistics*. Basil Blackwell, Oxford

Svartvik, J and Quirk, R 1980 *A corpus of English conversation*. Liberläromodel, Lund

Swan, M and Walter, C 1984 *The Cambridge English Course: Book I*. Cambridge University Press

Sweet, H 1899 *The practical study of languages*. Dent, London. (New edition, Oxford University Press, 1964)

Tadros, A 1984 Prediction as an aspect of the structure of didactic text and its implications for the teaching of reading and writing. In Swales, J (ed.) *English for Specific Purposes in the Arab World*: 52–67. Language Studies Unit, University of Aston, Birmingham

Tarone, E 1974 Speech perception in second language acquisition: a suggested model. *Language Learning* 24: 223–33

Taylor, L 1986 Vocabulary acquisition: a study of teacher and learner strategies. Unpublished M.A. dissertation. Department of English Language and Literature, University of Birmingham

Terrell, T D 1982 The natural approach to language teaching: an update. *Modern Language Journal* 66 (2): 121–32

Thomas, J 1983 Cross-cultural pragmatic failure. *Applied Linguistics* 4 (2): 91–112

Thomas, J 1984 Cross-cultural discourse as 'unequal encounter': towards a pragmatic analysis. *Applied Linguistics* 5 (3): 226–35

Thorndike, E L 1973 Reading as reasoning. *Reading Research Quarterly* 9: 135–47

Thorndike, E L and Lorge, I 1938 *A semantic count of English words*. Columbia University Press, New York

Thorndike, E L and Lorge, I 1944 *The teacher's word book of 30,000 words*. Columbia University Press, Columbia, S.C.

Tulving, E and Thomson D M 1973 Encoding specificity and retrieval processes in episodic memory. *Journal of Experimental Psychology* 80: 352–73

Twaddell, F 1972 Linguistics and the language teacher. In Croft, K (ed.) *Readings on English as a second language*: 268–76. Winthrop, Cambridge, Massachusetts

Twaddell, F 1973 Vocabulary expansion in the ESOL classroom. *TESOL Quarterly* 7: 61–78

Ullmann, S 1962 *Semantics*. Oxford University Press

van Dijk, T A 1985 Semantic discourse analysis. In van Dijk, T A (ed.) *Handbook of discourse analysis* Volume 2: 103–36. Academic Press

van Ek, J 1977 *The threshold level for modern language learning in schools*. Longman

Wallace, M J 1982 *Teaching vocabulary*. Heinemann

West, M P 1935a *New Method Dictionary*. Longman

West, M P 1935b Definition vocabulary. *Department of Educational Research Bulletin* 4. University of Toronto, Toronto

West, M P 1941 *Learning to read a foreign language*. Longman

West, M P 1953 *A General Service List of English Words*. Longman

West, M P 1960 *Minimum adequate vocabulary*. Longman

Whitcut, J 1979 *Learning with LDOCE*. Longman

Widdowson, H G 1978 *Teaching English as communication*. Oxford University Press

Widdowson, H G 1979 *Explorations in applied linguistics*. Oxford University Press

Widdowson, H G 1983 *Learning purpose and language use*. Oxford University Press

Widdowson, H G, and Moore, J (eds.) 1979–80 *Reading and thinking in English*. Oxford University Press

Wilkins, D A 1972 *Linguistics and language teaching*. Edward Arnold, London

Wilkins, D A 1976 *Notional syllabuses*. Oxford University Press

Willis, D and Willis, J forthcoming *The COBUILD English Course* (provisional title). Collins

Winter, E O 1977 A clause-relational approach to English texts: a study of some predictive lexical items in written discourse. *Instructional Science* **6** (1): 1–92

Winter, E O 1978 A look at the role of certain words in information structure. In Jones, K P and Horsnell, V (eds.) *Informatics* **3**: 1: 85–97. ASLIB, London

Wong-Fillmore, L 1979 Individual differences in second language acquisition. In Fillmore, C, Kempler, D and Wang, W (eds.) *Individual differences in language ability and language behaviour*. Academic Press, New York

Xue G-Y, and Nation, P 1984 A university word list. *Language Learning and Communication* **3** (2); 215–29

Yap, K O 1979 Vocabulary – building blocks of comprehension? *Journal of Reading Behavior* **1**: 49–59

Yorio, C 1980 Conventionalized language forms and the development of communicative competence. *TESOL Quarterly* **14**: 433–42

Zgusta, L 1971 *Manual of lexicography*. Mouton, The Hague

Index